THE
BOOK
OF JOSE

THE BOOK OF JOSE

A Memoir

FAT JOE
with SHAHEEM REID

ROC
-
LIT
101

NEW YORK

2023 Roc Lit 101 Trade Paperback Edition

Published in the United States by Roc Lit 101,
a joint venture between Roc Nation LLC and One World, an imprint of Random House,
a division of Penguin Random House LLC, New York.

ONE WORLD is a registered trademark of Penguin Random House LLC.

Roc Lit 101 is a trademark of Roc Nation LLC.

Originally published in hardcover in the United States by by Roc Lit 101,
a joint venture between Roc Nation LLC and One World, an imprint of Random House,
a division of Penguin Random House LLC, in 2022.

All photos from the author's collection

LIBRARY OF CONGRESS CATALOGING-IN-PUBLICATION DATA
Names: Fat Joe, author. | Reid, Shaheem, author.
Title: The book of Jose: a memoir / by Fat Joe, Shaheem Reid.
Description: First edition. | New York: Roc Lit 101, 2022. |
Identifiers: LCCN 2022025253 (print) | LCCN 2022025254 (ebook) |
ISBN 9780593230657 (paperback) | ISBN 9780593230664 (ebook)
Subjects: LCSH: Fat Joe. | Rap musicians—United States—Biography. |
LCGFT: Autobiographies.
Classification: LCC ML420.F2766 A3 2022 (print) | LCC ML420.F2766 (ebook) |
DDC 782.421649092 [B]—dc23/eng/20220602
LC record available at https://lccn.loc.gov/2022025253
LC ebook record available at https://lccn.loc.gov/2022025254

Title-page art and chapter-opener art: @anakin13-stock.adobe.com

Printed in the United States of America on acid-free paper

RocLit101.com
oneworldlit.com
randomhousebooks.com

9 8 7 6 5 4 3 2 1

Roc Lit 101 logo designed by Greg Mollica

Book design by Edwin A. Vazquez

CONTENTS

PART IV: SQUAD STORIES

PART V: OLD CYCLES, NEW BEGINNINGS

ACKNOWLEDGMENTS   287

PART I

BRONX TALES

THE BIRTH OF JOEY CRACK

THE STREETS CROWNED ME "The Realest Walking the Earth." I earned it! Muthafuckas have been trying to kill me my *entire* life in one way or another. I've been shot multiple times *in front of my mother*. When I was just ten, a grown man named Papi Loco wrongfully accused me of trying to kill his infant daughter by throwing batteries from the roof of Forest Houses projects in the Bronx, and then pummeled me until I was bloody and had a concussion. When I was a young teen, a street don tried to scare me to death by threatening to stick my entire arm in a meat grinder. The police have done their best to beat me into oblivion. When that didn't work, crooked cops tried to frame me for murder so I could do life in prison. Through it all, though, I never folded.

People said it was a suicide mission when I went head-to-head with a gangster known for butchering adults and setting infants on fire. I squared up with the Feds when they stepped to me, and just when I thought shit was sweet, some of my best friends and family died or went to jail or betrayed me.

My name is Fat Joe, aka "Joey Crack," aka "JoPrah," aka "The Don Cartagena." But on August 19, 1970, I was born Joseph Antonio Cartagena at Bronx-Lebanon Hospital. The South Bronx to be exact, an auspicious and ominous birthplace.

Life in the South Bronx could feel like a movie. What kind of movie? Here's an emblematic South Bronx tale: Sixteen years after I was born, right across the street from Lebanon Hospital in the Fulton Avenue tenement projects, a twenty-year-old named Larry

Davis got into a shoot-out with damn near the whole police force. Not only did Davis get out of there alive, he left six cops filled with lead.

He was like a hood superhero. Nobody could believe his story. He was eventually caught after a seventeen-day manhunt, but in court, his lawyers' defense was that corrupt police were trying to frame Larry for the murders of some drug dealers, and when they stormed his sister's apartment, they were trying to kill Larry, not apprehend him. The defense worked. Larry Davis was acquitted of all charges except illegal gun possession. God bless the dead, Davis was eventually killed in prison in 2008, where he was doing time for a case unrelated to his famous shoot-out.

Me? By the time Larry Davis made his mark, I'd already been earning my own stripes as a shorty. My history with violence started almost as soon as I got out of the womb.

I'm the youngest of four kids, the baby of the family. My mother, Ruby, had two sons and a daughter before me: Angel Jr., Raymond, and our sister, Lisa. Ruby got married to their father, Angel Cartagena Sr., when she was still very young.

Angel was a bad guy who intimidated everyone around him. He was in jail when my mother met my father. Ernesto Delgado had just moved to the U.S. from Cuba. Ernesto, or "Ernest," as he was called in this country, was a little guy; he had a big heart though. My father busted his ass to provide for us. He was a baker; he was a carpenter. In the summertime he would sell Icees and pastelillos in Crotona Park. He taught me what it meant to be relentless.

Ernesto always worked hard, but he went extra hard in pursuing Ruby. My mom is a beautiful Puerto Rican woman. Both her parents are from the island but her dad is Taino, one of the indigenous people of Puerto Rico. My grandparents migrated from PR to the BX when they were still teenagers and that's where they raised my mother. Whenever my grandfather's family would come from Puerto Rico and visit us in the Bronx—which would only be about every five or ten years—they'd come dressed in traditional garb. My great aunts and them wore moccasins and reminded me of images I'd seen of Native Americans. Ironically, my grandfather was nicknamed "Cowboy."

My mother and her family all lived in the same building as my father's sister Esther. Yes, I had a real life Aunt Esther before that name became famous via the classic sitcom *Sanford and Son*. My aunt was nothing like LaWanda Page's outrageous Bible-totin' character though. God bless them both.

Once, when my father was hanging out with Esther, he laid eyes on my mom and it was love at first sight for him. He would see my mother all the time and go try to rap to her. He didn't care that she had three kids already. Shit, he had *nine* himself. They were back in Cuba with *his wife*. Stay tuned for that story down the line.

Ruby and Ernest started spending time together and next thing you know, she became his girl. They moved in together with my mom's kids in the Bronx's Forest Houses projects on E 165th Street and Trinity Avenue—1000 Trinity Ave to be exact. They lived in apartment 5E, which had two very small bedrooms and one bathroom. Soon after, Ruby got pregnant with me. All this time, Angel Sr. was in jail. My mother had moved on, but she was still married to my brothers' and sister's father. When I was born, I was given the name Joseph *Cartagena* because mommy was still legally a Cartagena. She actually still is. My mom and Angel Sr. never officially got divorced.

Angel got out of jail damn near right after they cut my umbilical cord. Back on the streets he caught wind of my birth and made a beeline to the PJs. He started yelling in front of the building, threatening to kill my mom. Then he threatened to kill my dad. Finally, he declared he was going to "kill the baby." What the hell did I do? I wasn't even a full two months old yet and already in the mix.

As Angel was making his way into the building, my mother frantically ran out of the apartment with me in her arms and gave me to the neighbor down the hall. My mother's instructions were concise: "Don't open the door under any circumstances!"

Angel finally made it up to the fifth floor and started banging on my parents' door, yelling once again that he was gonna "kill the baby!" The men in the building heard the commotion and gathered together to confront Angel. They told him, "You can't be threatening her."

When Angel Sr. resisted, the men in the building busted his ass. They beat him to a pulp and dragged him out the building and told him to never come back.

Angel came to accept my mother and dad's union without any more threats of violence. My mom is such a loving and forgiving person, she let him see his children. Unfortunately for my brothers and sister, he wasn't a real father. He never even gave them as much as a lollipop. He helped to *make* them biologically. You got to be grateful for that. But the man wasn't a real factor in their lives.

And he wasn't nothin' to me. I didn't really know him like that. I might have seen him once or twice when I was real little. He would look at me and I would look at him like he was weird. I don't know why. I didn't know the story of how he vowed to kill me. I just knew I didn't like the man or anything that came with him.

Even his family, who I'd see whenever they came to visit my sister and my brothers, I didn't like them either. It was just in me. My mother would be like, "This is your sister's aunt." I felt like *Maaannn, if these people don't get the fuck out the house.* I was just a little kid but my intuition has always been on point, even as a tyke. Angel wound up repeating the cycle of getting incarcerated, being released, coming home, then going back in. Eventually, he died of cirrhosis of the liver. He was also drinking too much.

My father, Ernest, drank a lot, too. Not as much as Angel, but Dad loved that firewater. Almost as much as I loved to eat. My family, even though we were poor, we ate good. My grandmother Tati was the best chef in the family. The best chef in the world if you really want my opinion. She was phenomenal. And she loved to make sure the whole family enjoyed their meals at gatherings.

When I was little there were always a lot of grandkids around my grandmother's house. It was like fifty of us. Fifty grandkids running around, but I would be the only one under the table. My reputation as the family black sheep preceded me, so at the gatherings, my family didn't even give me a chance to get in trouble. They kept me on lockdown as a precaution.

One time, I started a fire at my grandmother's house. Other times, I broke our chairs. You know, I was always fat, so I would jump around on the furniture. The weight and pressure of me jumping on the chairs would break their legs. On a couple occasions, I'd break a chair and put the leg back on it. I wouldn't tell anyone I broke it. I was just a little badass kid running around and the older people in my family would be like *nah, this guy's too much.*

I'd literally be forced to sit *under* the dining room table at my grandmother's house while my brothers and sister and all my cousins ran around playing.

I was punished all the time as a kid. That's why I'm so close to my Aunt Barbara. Because even when the rest of the family was treating me crazy, she would give me cookies and take me to her house and treat me kindly. Out of all fifty grandchildren, the rest of the family thought I was the one least likely to succeed. I love my whole family so this ain't shots at them, but I was always treated like the black sheep and that's a fact.

I learned a lot from sitting in seclusion on the floor though. Besides hearing about all the inner scandals of the family, like who was getting cheated on, I learned what not to do. I learned from watching my mother puff through four packs of cigarettes a day that smoking was nasty. I knew I never wanted to be involved with cigarettes. My father too; he would sit there and smoke.

Grandpa Cowboy made me not want to drink. My grandfather always had a bottle of Bacardi sitting on the windowsill. He loved his Bacardi. Many years later, I did a commercial for Bacardi and they paid me like half a million dollars. I felt like I got them back for all the times they hit up my grandfather for that bottle.

Another thing I learned sitting under that table was not to

gamble. We'll get deep into that chamber later. But that's what this book is really about: You can learn from other people's mistakes. I learned from theirs and hopefully you'll learn from mine. And I've made a lot of mistakes, almost from the beginning.

I got into a lot of trouble growing up in Forest projects. Back then, the South Bronx looked like a war zone. The projects were surrounded by abandoned buildings, vacant lots, and broken sidewalks, like a megaton bomb had been dropped from a fighter jet and blown up the entire borough. Stray dogs roamed the streets. It was desolate. We didn't have functioning playgrounds—equipment was ripped up and broken. Us kids, to have fun, we'd be doing flips on bummy, piss-reeking mattresses people left out with the garbage. That's all we had. But we were still kids so we made it fun.

For elementary school I attended PS 146, right across the street from my house. Having two older brothers and a sister in the school made it easier on me. Everybody knew the Cartagenas at my elementary. They had these classes in my school called "IGC," which stood for "Intellectually Gifted Child." Yeah, I was a badass, but I was also an intellectual. Every year I was in that class, I was competing to get the most awards. I'd get close, but got beat every time.

Candace Stallings was the girl I would always lose out to. Of all the awards a kid could receive, she would always win ten out of ten and I'd win eight. I'd never get the full ten because of my behavior. I was very bright, I was outspoken, but I was also the class clown.

Once, the school had an essay writing contest on the topic "What Does the Bronx Mean to Me?" And I won! Well, actually Candace and I both won. We got to meet Bronx Borough President Stanley Simon on 161st Street. That was a big deal for us. I was on the road to becoming *a scholar*.

Until I graduated elementary school.

I went to Junior High School 120 in the Bronx. Everybody thinks my nickname Joey Crack came from selling narcotics, but I got my name before anybody was even calling rock cocaine "crack." At JHS 120, the teacher would ask me a question and call me up to the front of the classroom. Being that I was chubby, my pants would sag under my stomach and the crack of my ass was always showing when I walked up to the chalkboard. All the girls would be like, "Yo, Joey Crack! Joey Crack!"

That year at JHS 120, I also discovered my first passion: graffiti. My bro Gismo, one of the founders of The Terror Squad, taught me lettering and how to write. When I first saw graffiti I thought it was so beautiful. It was art, it had emotion. Then I discovered that if you're able to create that art with enough flair and originality, you could get hood famous from graffiti writing. It was a way to have your name everywhere. I found it so intriguing. I kept practicing until I had my own style. Soon I was taggin' crazily.

What's wild is that graffiti is so celebrated today. It's in exhibitions in museums, filmmakers do documentaries on it. What we now understand to be one of the five pillars of hip-hop culture, back then, our parents considered it criminal. And I can't lie, there were some elements to graffiti that were pretty nefarious.

Me and Giz, we'd write graffiti on building walls and trains, both of which are crimes, and my father didn't have a problem busting my ass legendary when he caught me doing that dirt. He was giving me pretty traumatizing beatings at a young age, so I did what I could to avoid getting caught. At night, I would sneak out the house to go bomb the trains with Giz. My sister would always be up late, so before we left I would ask her to listen for us when we got back home and open the door. Her bed was right by the front door. Not bedroom, her bed. She didn't have a bedroom. Although Lisa always helped me, she didn't condone me sneaking out. Every night I left, she'd give me that look like *you're gonna get in trouble.*

Because my parents woke up at like six, seven in the morning, I had to race back from a bombing run before the sun came up. One night, when we went down to a station to hit the trains, the cops jumped out on us. This was all the way by 233rd and White Plains Road. That was Jamaican territory. Jamaicans in the Bronx know what's up. The cops were swarming all over the place and the only way to escape was to hide underneath the train cars.

That was the type of life-and-death risk we would take. If the train had pulled out of that station, we'd have been dead. My crew did all types of dumb shit that nearly killed us. Like white people jumping off planes, we'd jump off the train while it was moving. We'd walk on the side of the tracks from train station to train station through the tunnels. Fuck the third rail or an oncoming train. Shit was crazy, but that's just how it was. We did it for the culture.

Graff came with other risks, too. It wasn't just that it was a crime in and of itself, it brought other crimes along with it. No way around it. Just like if you rap and you don't write your own rhymes, you're considered a fraud, back then, if you wrote graffiti and you didn't *steal* your paint, you were not authentic. I learned to steal at Giz's house. It was so diabolical. Giz had a rack of paint in his house he modeled after the display in a hardware store. I would go there and spend hours practicing stealing the spray cans. The technique was called "racking."

All day, we learned how to put the paint cans up sleeves in coats or shirts, in pants, and all around your waist. At that time, we didn't have money like that to buy paint, but even if we could've afforded the paint, we still would've stolen it. You wasn't real if you didn't steal the paint.

I was the best racker. I don't know if it was because when I was a little kid I looked innocent, but the store owners never expected me to be the one racking the cans. Eventually, the stores figured out what was going on. These days, spray cans are kept in locked cages or cases.

Graffiti became an addiction for me. At JHS 120, they caught me maybe like six, seven times writing on the walls. At school, we would make these markers with ink—pen ink or ink from a mimeograph machine—and we'd mix it with alcohol. The combination would make the illest purple graffiti ink. Me and my crew, we'd take erasers from around the school and combine them with the ink to make these big markers. We would use the erasers as the tip of the marker. Then we'd just bomb the whole place.

I couldn't stop. It's like everything else. I loved to eat, so I ate everything until I was over 400 pounds. I have an addictive personality. I love to rap, I want to be the best. I've made a million songs. When I hustled, I had to take over *everything*. Graffiti was the same. I didn't know how to stop.

Years later, I brought graffiti into street marketing. In 1998 when we were promoting my artist Big Pun's *Capital Punishment* LP and my own *Don Cartagena* project, we created these poster boards that had graffiti writing on them and plastered them across the city.

We were blowing up the entire New York City with these poster boards; "Big Pun: *Capital Punishment* coming out!" "Fat Joe: *The Don Cartagena* coming out!" We'd put them on walls, light poles, bridges, wherever we knew there would be heavy traffic jams every day. The Westside Highway, The Harlem River Bridge, the 59th Street Bridge in Queens, Atlantic Ave in Brooklyn, all through East New York in Brooklyn, wherever there was traffic, we were going up.

We were going hard with the promo until one morning I turned on the TV and was watching NY 1. The Mayor of New York at the time, Rudy Giuliani, was giving a press conference in front of a bunch of poster boards. *Our* poster boards! He was like "They are destroying our city. When we catch the people who are doing this . . ." That was the end of that. We stopped then and there.

I WASN'T AS WISE when I was younger. Nothing would stop me. Eventually my graffiti writing got me kicked out of JHS 120 after only about a year. Then I got kicked out of *six more* junior high schools across the Bronx. Schools kept saying, "We've got your name here, Joe. You got thrown out the last school for graffiti and it says you wrote 'Crack!' all over the walls. Now our school has 'Crack!' all over the walls. You gotta go."

I was leaving a hip-hop paper trail.

Getting kicked out of 120 was a major life turning point. I was suddenly pushed out of the nest of my neighborhood, my comfort zone. Forest projects, where I lived, was 85 percent Black and 15 percent Latino. I didn't really know Latino culture that well because I was born and grew up so deep into Black culture as it existed in the Bronx of that era. Since I'd been in Forest projects since I was a baby, everyone accepted me, even though I was in the minority as a Puerto Rican.

Junior High School 148 was my final stop for junior high, the place I was supposed to finally settle. Instead I was as unsettled as I've ever been. JHS 148 was on Third Avenue between 169th and 170th Street in the Bronx. It was a horrendous neighborhood, but my grandmother lived out there. We were able to use her address to help register me for school. Mr. Ness/Scorpio of Grandmaster Flash and the Furious Five lived around there too. He was in the building right next door to my grandmother's. He was the first rapper I'd ever seen in person. One day he was walking around a supermarket called Fetco. My big brother Angel Jr. saw him before I did and pointed him out. "Yo, you know who that is? That's Mr. Ness from the Furious Five." I turned and looked. He was just so fly. His Nikes matched the black, white, and silver beads in his cornrowed hair.

"Wow!" was all I could say to my brother, as I looked at Scorpio in awe. "This guy's, like, a superstar right?"

Up until that point, my brother dabbled in rap, but I'd never really thought about being a rapper myself. I didn't really know what I wanted to be when I grew up, except I knew I wanted to be rich. Seeing Scorpio up close planted a huge seed of inspiration in my heart. Not just to be a fan, but to be an MC. Shit, I even tried to show off my rap skills when the year kicked off at my new school.

JHS 148 was 99.9 percent Black. Latin people had nooooo juice there. On the first day of school I went over there wearing a bubble goose jacket with my hat backward. I saw some kids had formed a rap cypher and I jumped right into it, battling my class-mates. My style was raw. So there I was, this big Puerto Rican kid they'd never met before, standing in the cypher, cursing crazy. The kids there were looking at me like *Yo, we never seen nobody like this. What the fuck?*

They hadn't grown up with me like the Black kids in my own neighborhood, so they didn't know what to make of me. What they did know was that they didn't like what they saw. I had problems from day one.

Even though I wasn't looking for trouble, I would constantly get into conflicts. The students at my new school bullied me. I never backed down but that just meant I was getting jumped all the time. I never had a Christmas, Easter, or New Year's picture back then without a black eye or fat lip. It was almost a joke. The girls at school would be sitting in class, looking out the window at a grow-ing mob of kids in the street as the clock approached three and be like, "Oh, they're waiting out there for Joey again."

When the last period bell rang, I would walk out the front door of the school, drop my bag, and it'd be on. The whole school was waiting for it, gathered around for the show. A mob of twenty guys or so would surround me and I would punch the toughest one in the face. That would set it off. The rest of them would just pound me out till I got on the bus.

This happened for around two years. Bullied literally every day, getting beat up by two dozen guys. Sometimes they'd get extra petty and spit on me or put gum in my hair. It was hard going to school, but I knew I couldn't let my family down again after getting thrown out of practically every other school in the Bronx. I espe-cially didn't want to let my mother down.

I was able to register because of my grandmother's address, but the real reason I went to that school was because my mom worked down the block. She was running one of my grandfather's number spots. Back in the days before there was a legal state lottery, there was the illegal numbers game, the people's lottery. You bet a dollar on a number combination and, if you're extremely lucky, your numbers hit and you win something like $800. Every day at lunch, I would go to my mother's job. They had a small arcade in the storefront where I would play Space Invaders or Pac-Man. Mom would go to the bodega next door and buy me a quarter water and a spiced ham-and-cheese sandwich for 50 cents. The store owner would make it with slices from those big blocks of government cheese. Grocery store owners weren't supposed to be selling that kind of cheese in their stores; it was meant for the poor on welfare to have for free. But the owner of that bodega would collect the cheese when the government handed it out and sneak it into his store. No complaints from me or any of his other customers though, it tasted great. The fact that my mother helped hold down the neighborhood numbers spot meant she was probably cool with the parents of all these kids who were kicking my ass. They all played the numbers.

I did have a best friend in junior high. His name was Leonard. Leonard would come with me to my mother's job at lunch and she would feed him like she fed me and treat him like a son. One day, toward the end of the school year, the crew of kids that always jumped me swarmed me and Leonard after school. They asked Lenny, "Why are you with this guy?"

"This is my *best* friend," Leonard told them.

The kids were like, "Nah, but why are you hanging out with the *Spanish* kid?"

They gave him an ultimatum: "Listen, if you don't jump Joey *with* us, we're gonna fuck *you* up every day like we do him."

My best friend Leonard turned on me instantly. He didn't even contemplate. Leonard jumped right in with the kids stomping me out. He had been like a brother to me and he betrayed me with no problem.

That is still one of the most traumatizing memories in my life. At that point, for all my black sheep tendencies, I was still just a clever kid, just a year from being in the gifted class, obsessed with rapping and graffiti, who only fought when he had no choice, which was, unfortunately, practically every day of my young life. But that day put me on a new path.

I remember going back home after that bitter beatdown. I had on a black hoodie, black pants, and black chukkas. Those were Timberland boots, the chukkas. I sat in my bedroom and I couldn't even focus, I was so overwhelmed by emotion. I remember tying and untying my chukkas maybe one million times. I sat on my bed and cried oceans of tears. But eventually the tears dried up. That's when my heart turned hard as charcoal.

"I don't care about human life no more," I told myself. "I don't give a fuck. Anybody who ever fronts on me, I'm gonna give it to him. I'm going to rob them. I'm gonna beat up *whoever*. I'm gonna victimize anybody breathing."

That was the real birth of "Joey Crack." Welcome to the foulest nigga* in existence.

---

* People have recently started to ask me about the "N-word." "How come Fat Joe and other Latinos are allowed to say nigga?" Here's what you have to understand: In the New York City housing projects I grew up in, there are 145 different families living on top of each other in each building. And each project has got about ten to twenty different buildings like this. And everybody who's living stacked up like this is mostly Latino and Black.

Before I was born, my mother came from Puerto Rico to the Bronx, to Forest projects, which is mostly Black. When I was born and she brought me home from the hospital, she remembers that one of the first people to greet us was one of the guys she knew from our building. He was Black. He looked at me and said, "Oh shit, this little nigga got green eyes."

When I got a little older, my earliest memories are of going outside with my parents, and when we'd see the older guys in the neighborhood they'd come over like, "Look at this little nigga with green eyes and blond hair cut like The Beatles." But they weren't mocking me; they were genuinely surprised at my green eyes and blond hair. They always treated my mother and me with real affection.

"Look at little Joey," they'd say. "Joey, what's up nigga!!!"

So one of the first things I learned as a kid was to look back at them and say, with equal affection, "Yo, what's up nigga?" I've been saying it since kindergarten. Through elementary, everyone called me the same thing. Junior high school, same thing, high school, same thing. Out in the streets, same thing. They said it to me and I said it to them. No one ever looked at me like I was saying something wrong. Blacks and Latinos grew up together, literally right next door. We went to the same schools, faced the same challenges of growing up in poverty. We got abused by the same police. We loved the same music, the same fashion, the boys chased the same girls and vice versa.

We used that word as a term of endearment: "My nigga, what's up? I love you, my nigga." Through my rap career I've been using it since day one and it's never been a problem with my Black friends and artistic peers.

But today, they ask me about it on social media. The people asking usually didn't grow up how we grew up in the Bronx, Latinos and Blacks together. They don't understand how someone like me could say it. A lot of them don't even like Black people saying the word. I respect where they're coming from; I understand the deep racist history of the N-word. But you have to understand, I've been saying "nigga" since I could talk. Now that I'm older, I try to use the word more consciously, and not as much, mostly out of respect for my status as an OG. In this book, I use it sparingly, and mostly when I'm quoting back dialogue, but I'd be lying if I said it wasn't—and isn't still—a part of the language I've lived with my whole life.

CHAPTER 2

SOUTH, SOUTH BRONX

AT THE START OF PUBERTY FOR ME, I was way more concerned with getting revenge and levying brutality than the average boy, who might just be thinking about playing ball and going girl crazy. I endured two straight years of bullies ganging up on me and jumping me every day. On top of that, my best friend broke my heart by joining them in trying to break my face.

This was my Anakin Skywalker moment, my turn to the dark side. Outside of my immediate family and a few friends, I felt the whole world was against me. While my body would repair itself from the physical trauma in time, my mental scars were cut deeper and beyond repair. It was an inner turmoil no child should have to reconcile. As kids, we're not equipped. You see it all the time with youngsters who realize how much the deck is stacked against them and throw in the towel. A lot of them allow the world to keep pummeling them or they retreat to the shadows and never really flower. The others fight back, no matter how extreme the odds or the cost. This can be a path to long-term glory or to early death. For me, it was like my soul turned to ice. How did Biggie say it? "Cold as the pole in the winter."

That was the same amount of rage I had in me. I sat in my bedroom with hatred festering. My heart turned black. I no longer cared about anybody. I wanted to inflict as much violence and fear as I could on anyone who stood in my path. It didn't matter whether they were good or bad. I *terrorized* mostly bad people, but a lot of good people were collateral damage. I was ruthless.

After Leonard double-crossed me, I felt like *I'm giving it to everybody*. I turned the corner. People picked on me every day. I got beat up by twenty people every day. Now it was my turn. It went from me having a conscience and having a heart to just dreaming about inflicting pain. I felt like they did it to me, I'm going to do it to everybody.

I started linking up with some of my friends from around my way that were just as or even more ruthless than me. I put some of my friends from around my projects in my crew, The Terror Squad. That was a name that some of my OGs were running with and was handed down to me. We had started off as just a graffiti crew, but more and more we started to emphasize the "Terror" in "Terror Squad." That summer, just like every summer, there were a bunch of block parties and park jams in the neighborhood. These jams had been happening all over New York starting in the '70s and they were where the foundations of hip-hop were laid. DJs would bring the speakers, turntables, and mics and people would come from all over the city to party together under the open sky. The best MCs from the neighborhoods would get on the mic and rap, too. In the BX, there'd be jams on Courtlandt Ave, a jam on Jackson, a jam on Forest, a jam on Webster—every weekend, all summer.

I was in Courtlandt projects, right in the park outside of the buildings, when I saw KRS-One performing "South Bronx" for the first time. It was also the first time I ever laid eyes on him period. KRS, "Teacha," "The Blastmaster," my idol, and, later on in life, one of my mentors. KRS and Boogie Down Productions (BDP) are where I was first introduced to conscious rap—songs that wove together the style of battle raps with commentary on culture and politics. I could write another book just about how influential he is. But he resonated with me in a specific way: KRS took the art of battling on records to new heights and here I was, a kid who'd had to battle every day from the moment he was born. His anthem to our hometown, "South Bronx," ignited one of the culture's most legendary battles: KRS-One vs. MC Shan. I followed it like it was a presidential campaign.

In 1985, Shan, who was one of the dopest MCs working and from Queensbridge, repped his hood with a classic, "The Bridge," produced by his Queensbridge neighbor Marley Marl, one of the greatest producers ever. Marley produced for people like Rakim, Heavy D, BBD (Bell Biv DeVoe), TLC, and even me. Do yourself the biggest favor, go back and listen to some of the biggest albums he produced, like LL Cool J's *Mama Said Knock You Out* or Big Daddy Kane's *Long Live the Kane* or *Goin' Off* by Biz Markie.

The biggest hip-hop radio DJs in New York at the time were Red Alert on 98.7 Kiss and Mr. Magic on 107.5 WBLS (we gotta give it up to the Awesome Two on WBHI, too). Magic and Marley formed one of rap's first and most successful super cliques, The Juice Crew: Kane and Biz, Roxanne Shanté, Masta Ace, Kool G Rap, Craig G, Tragedy Khadafi, and of course MC Shan. Shan, Marley, and Magic were at the top of the Juice Crew hierarchy. By 1986, The Juice Crew were the hottest, most dominant collective in rap.

When KRS was trying to get in the game, he wanted to be down with them. KRS went up to WBLS to give Mr. Magic his demo. The demo included soon-to-be classics "Criminal Minded," "My Philosophy," and "Advance." As KRS told me recently when I interviewed him on my Instagram program, *The Big Big Show,* Mr. Magic dissed him. He said KRS's "conscious raps" didn't fit in with what The Juice Crew were doing.

This put a major battery in KRS's back. The Blastmaster was already big in the Bronx, but he was known more for graffiti-writing than rapping. KRS would tag up the six train, the two train, the five train. He'd bomb the buses in the Fordham Road bus yards. But for all his hood celebrity he was still broke—in fact, he was homeless. He saw rap as his way to make some money and get out the streets. So when one of the culture's premier tastemakers dissed him, it sent him into a rage. KRS went back to the place where he rested his head to game-plan. The place was an old armory that had been renovated and turned into a homeless shelter, and it was right across the street from my projects, on 166th and Boston Road. Fellow Bronx legend Just-Ice lived at the shelter, too.

A furious KRS sat in the midst of six hundred other homeless men and began to put his angst into his bars. Since Magic didn't rap, he took aim at Magic's number one MC, Shan. KRS wrote "The Bridge Is Over" first, but held on to it. Then he penned "South Bronx." KRS set it off on the whole Juice Crew, but threw the lion's share of disses in Shan's and Marley Marl's direction.

On "The Bridge," Shan makes Queensbridge the foundation stone of rap: "You love to hear the story, again and again / Of how it all got started way back when."

Anybody in hip-hop culture knows *it* started in the BX. Although Shan denied implying *hip-hop itself* originated in Queens, The Blastmaster originally said that lie was the reason he dissed The Juice Crew. He reasoned he was defending the integrity of hip-hop and the honor of the Bronx. A masterful strategy if you ask me. Dissing The Juice Crew because Mr. Magic dissed him, some may call it "petty." But dissing The Juice Crew because you are upholding the rightful historic storytelling in hip-hop, you're a hero. In 1986, when BDP released "South Bronx," NYC erupted.

When I saw him at the jam in the Courtlandt projects, KRS may have recorded the song just a few days prior. It wasn't even on the radio or nothing like that. It was way, way early. But the streets already knew. KRS was a real skinny kid. He had a Bob Marley T-shirt on. He and Boogie Down Productions performed "South Bronx" and everybody in the park went crazy.

KRS was going at Shan and them so hard lyrically: "So you think that hip-hop had its start out in Queensbridge? / If you pop that junk up in the Bronx, you might not live."

The park was packed and we were all hearing this record for the first time, losing our minds. The song resonated with all of us. Everybody was yelling, "Holy fuck! Yo!" By the second time KRS and BDP yelled the chorus of "South Bronx, the South, South Bronx," the entire park was chanting that shit like a war cry. *We* had *our* anthem now. Borough pride set to music. Brooklyn was ringing off heavy with acts like The Fat Boys and Whodini; Queens was super-cemented with acts like Run-DMC and LL Cool J. Now KRS put the Bronx back on the map.

And even though I didn't know *all* that backstory that night in the park, I could feel the urgency in KRS's words and the passion of his delivery. I could feel it in my soul. He mirrored me in the fact that he had a fury inside him that he needed to unleash. KRS wanted to right a wrong by annihilating his enemies, and he didn't care if an entire borough caught the collateral shrapnel.

Here was another Bronx boy who'd been fucked with one time too many, another angry kid unleashing his fury on the people who doubted him and tried to make him disappear. KRS was not going to disappear. Instead, he turned the tables. I felt that. That night, in the park, I knew I wasn't alone.

That's how I fell in love with KRS-One. He, LL, and Big Pun are the greatest MCs of all time to me. And although that day I was channeling my angst in a much more dangerous, negative manner, in the years to come I'd eventually come around to following KRS's path.

Shan answered "South Bronx" with "Kill That Noise." The Juice Crew, they were the first rap conglomerate. I thought they all were gonna team up and start battling KRS. I envisioned them lyrically jumping him. Even though I'm KRS's biggest fan, I didn't believe he could beat Shan because Shan didn't roll alone: He just had too much backup. But my perspective changed one evening when I was hanging outside behind my building. It was freezing and I was listening to Red Alert on my Walkman.

"I got the brand-new KRS-One talking back to MC Shan," he said. "I'm gonna drop it after this commercial."

"What?" I couldn't believe it. Then Red Alert played it.

The opening drums were bone-chilling. Then KRS's manic voice came in: "I say, The Bridge is o-vuh, The Bridge is o-vuh . . ." I had never in my life heard that type of flow. How he flipped Jamaican reggae and made it gangsta. I was so hyped. My adrenaline was so high, I was running around my projects, sprinting!

"Oh God! Oh God!" I was screaming at everybody. "He did it! He did it! He won!" I heard the song one time and I knew KRS-One had prevailed. This was bigger than just having a dope record. KRS's win showed revolution was possible. You can come from literally nothing, you can be outmatched, you can be outnumbered, but if your heart is big enough, *you can* win. KRS spoke to a generation of underdog kids who felt alone, attacked, on the verge of defeat. He showed the way.

I love that song so much, every year on my birthday, I post "The Bridge Is Over" on my Instagram page and big up KRS.

I still remember dancing my ass off at that park jam in 1986, being on that natural high after seeing KRS-One live, debuting one of the greatest dis records in history. The music gave words and rhythm to all the wild feelings stirring inside me. But it was those feelings that drove me in those days. When going to most of these functions, partying was the last thing on my mind. Instead, I would roll through the park with my band of thieves and rob as many people at those jams as we could. We'd yoke up people who were there to dance and fuck up the whole party. The DJs would see us wildin', stop the music, and we'd just go through the party a cappella, beating up anybody in our path. That was how The Terror Squad got our rep initially.

It was time to stop playing defense and get on a relentless offense. Unlike KRS, I didn't have a positive influence like he did in his DJ, the late, great Scott La Rock, to take me to the studio as an outlet to harness my anger. For many years, the streets was all I had. The streets was all I knew.

Getting beat up and bullied and jumped every day, I realized that you're either going to be prey or predator. It felt better being a predator. The girls thought you were cuter. A different type of attention was on you. You weren't the butt of jokes or at the epicenter of humiliation and grief. Everybody feared you.

"Joey Crack," that name became so legendary. In my age group of young teenagers, my name became one of the most notorious in the entire Bronx.

CHAPTER 3

THE BEAST OF MORRIS HIGH

THE TRUE CHAOS COMMENCED the summer I graduated junior high. As my crew grew we roamed the five boroughs, robbing people from hood to hood. Everybody was hearing about "Joey Crack and The Terror Squad." We were wildin' out and the streets were talking.

That fall, I started at Morris High School. Back in the day, Morris was pretty prestigious, nothing like the incubator for criminals that it became by the time I got there. Some of the school's successful graduates include a Nobel Peace Prize winner, a NY State assemblywoman, and a former Queens Borough president. The two most *famous* famous alumni are legendary comedian Milton Berle and former U.S. Secretary of State Colin Powell. The most *hood* famous alum is one of my favorite gangsters ever, Boy George. He was the youngest and best to ever do it. Now, the Boy George who became a legend in the Bronx and throughout NYC obviously isn't the same Boy George (born George Alan O'Dowd) who went multiplatinum with Culture Club. They do have similarities though.

Both rose to stardom in the mid-1980s, both were flamboyant and charismatic, and both came from the slums to become self-made multimillionaires.

George "Boy George" Rivera made a blizzard in the Bronx, chiefly with his "Obsession"-stamped heroin business. He was reported to have brought in about $250,000 a week, but anybody who saw how this guy was living and how big his organization was knew he was more likely making millions a day.

George was older than me and he was years removed from Morris by the time I got there. We crossed paths a few times in the streets when I was a kid. We got off to an unceremonious start: He wanted to rip my head off because he felt I was running around the hood being too rambunctious and disrespectful. One day I was on Courtlandt Avenue chasing this guy who owed me money, and it just so happened we ran by George. George yelled out, "Who the fuck is this kid?"

Not knowing who George was or his stature in the streets, I stopped and responded: "Who the fuck is you?"

"Yo, nigga! I'll kill your whole fuckin' family."

Now, at this time I was at an age where I hadn't yet heard people regularly threatening to kill other people's families. His words shocked me, stopped me in my tracks like, *This must be a serious dude.* Some of my friends who were standing around watching the confrontation came up to me to tell me who George was. I immediately pleaded with him. "Yo, I'm sorry, Boy George, please don't kill my family. I don't want no beef."

At first he wasn't try to hear me, then he let me off the hook with an admonishment. "Every time I see you, you're always in some shit. You think you're tough."

I eventually earned his respect when a Bronx vs. Brooklyn brawl broke out in a nightclub in Manhattan. Somehow, me and George wound up fighting back-to-back against the same faction. He appreciated how I handled myself. George even talked about putting me on with his crew just a week before he got arrested by the Feds. Obviously his arrest and subsequent jail time squashed that plan.

In the mid-'80s when I went to Morris, the kids that attended were generally considered to be "the least likely to succeed." Y'all know I was familiar with that. My own family prophesied that for me when I was a young buck. At Morris, Joey Crack was right at home.

Morris was full of kids like me: tough, wounded, and sometimes cruel. A lot of people who turned out to be big gangsters in the Bronx (or one degree removed from big gangsters), went to school with me. Morris was the last stop for a lot of them before they landed in New York's infamous Rikers Island.

Back then in New York, you'd usually be designated to your school based on where you lived. That's called "zoning." The most prestigious schools aren't zone schools—you have to pass a test to get into them and they drew kids from all over. The same was true with Morris, but on the opposite end of the spectrum. People from every section of the Bronx came there. There were bad kids from everywhere.

There were people in the school from the notorious Courtlandt Avenue area. People came from Brook Avenue, another tough neighborhood. People came from the west side of the Bronx, they came from Highbridge. You might find a Jamaican from 233rd, or a Latin kid from the South Bronx.

I grew up on the side of the Bronx that was majority Black, so the Latin people, we're over there thinking that's our culture, too. Then there's other parts of the South Bronx where it was the flip side. Majority Puerto Rican and Dominican. So the Black kids over there, they thought they were Latino. They would hang Puerto Rican flags in their windows, it was wild.

Morris was homecoming for me, not only because I was with the other last-chance kids, but the school was right across the street from my projects. Unlike junior high, where I had to travel to an area where nobody knew me, my high school was in my own backyard. I ran things like a ruthless dictator.

I've always been a leader—I never knew anything but leadership. You'd see me with ten other kids and I'd be the one calling the shots. Don't ask me why, that's how I was born and raised. It might be the Leo in me.

On the very first day of high school me and my squad met in front of my building in Forest and walked to school together. It was a beautiful, sunny day and everybody was dipped fresh. The first day of school was like Easter Sunday, everybody had to be fresh. Parents who didn't make much saved up all year just so their kids could look good on those two days. There are people in jail now from robberies gone bad in the '90s when they were just trying get up the money to have a fly outfit for Easter.

We walked up the one-way block to our school and I had at least one hundred and fifty guys from Forest walking behind me. No exaggeration. About a third of them were Latino and the rest were Black. It looked like I was leading a parade. This was all before first period. I started hearing a buzz of people whispering as we walked past. Some were asking, "Yo, who's that?" Others were explaining, "That's Joey Crack, TS."

As we were mobbin' through there, I saw the guys who used to beat me up in junior high standing outside. About twenty dudes all staring in disbelief. They were looking at me like *What the fuck is that guy doing walking with this big-ass wolf pack? Why is this guy acting like he's tough and y'all believing him? We've been fuckin' this guy up forever.*

When they used to jump me in my grandmother's neighborhood, I used to tell them, "I'm not pussy, bro. I'm not the one. I'm tellin' y'all." I was just so outnumbered, I couldn't fend them off. Now the numbers were with me.

I walked right up to them. They were standing next to a guy from my hood who was down with the Five-Percent Nation.

"Peace, God," he greeted me with a smile. "These are my niggas from—"

"Webster and Washington! Yeah, I know them niggas," I cut him off.

"We know him too," one of their crew said. "We used to fuck him up every day."

"Shit is different around *here*. I told you I wasn't pussy."

They were still looking at me in disbelief but I was done talking.

I punched one of them in the face and all hell broke loose. My crew started chasing them all over. The main guy, his name was Kenneth. He was their leader and he had taken pleasure in ordering his hooligans to trample me. My heart was on fire with revenge. I wanted to maim him. Kenneth started booking it up the block to Boston Road, which is the main artery in the neighborhood. If he got there, he'd have a good chance of getting away.

But as soon as Kenneth made it to Boston Road, this Latin kid came out of nowhere and slammed him into the trash. This was my opening. I finally had him. It was like the scene in *The Godfather* when Sonny Corleone whupped the hell out of his brother-in-law, Carlo, with the garbage can and the garbage can lid. I jumped over the gate and me and this Latin kid—who I had never met before in life—beat the brakes off of Kenneth.

I had fantasized for years about this moment and it was even sweeter in real life. I started walking back toward the school and the guy who'd helped me yelled out.

"What's up?" he said. "Who are you?"

"I'm Joey Crack, TS," I answered.

"I'm Raul from Melrose," he told me.

I looked at him and smiled.

"Can I be 'Raul, TS'?" he asked.

"You could be 'Raul, TS,'" I affirmed. "Come meet us tomorrow. We'll be back right over here."

"I'll see you tomorrow then, man," he promised.

That's how I met Raul, one of my best friends for life. He's still top five, dead or alive in my hand. That was the first day of high school, and it was the equivalent of me going viral today. Even though there were no camera phones or social media, my name traveled everywhere. Everybody went home to every section of the Bronx saying, "There's this crazy Spanish kid. His name is Joey Crack. He's got three hundred Black guys with him. They're all going crazy. They're wildin' over there in Morris."

CHAPTER 4

THE REAL-LIFE TONY MONTANA

YOU CAN BE THE BIGGEST PUNK or a steel-willed gangster. There is no difference between the two when you have a machine gun aimed at you and you're unarmed. You're not in control. I was a young kid, but an even younger kid had me in his crosshairs.

He came from out of nowhere, planted himself on the sidewalk, and pulled out an Uzi on me and my best friend, Tony Montana. I was sure in that moment that I didn't have a minute left on Earth, but then Tone jumped in front of the machine gun so he could take the bullet instead of me. That's when I knew I had a brother for life, however long I had left to live.

ANTHONY CRESPO, bka "Tony Montana" in the streets, is a legend in the Bronx and my best friend for life. Growing up, we lived in the same building in Forest projects. He lived on the seventh floor, I lived on the fifth floor. Tone was a little chubby kid like me, but I guess his metabolism was better than mine because he leaned out as we got older. Meanwhile, I became Fat Joe. I was always heavyset, but it never got in the way. When I was still a little kid, I would be out in the project courtyards playing ball all day. Dean Meminger, who's now a broadcast journalist for the cable channel NY 1, was another kid from my building who'd be out there playing too. For a few years, when we were all still shorties, it was me, Tone, *and* Dean Meminger like the Three Musketeers.

Dean was named after his dad, who used to play for the New York Knicks. Dean Sr. went to Marquette University in the late '60s and early '70s. The Knicks drafted him in 1971 and he was an important cog off the bench along with Phil Jackson. In the 1972–73 NBA season, Dean Sr. and the Knicks won the franchise's second championship, and last to date.

Dean Sr. was running with basketball royalty. The Memingers moved out of the projects when me and Dean were young kids. I didn't see my man Dean Jr. again until he interviewed me at Big Pun's funeral, almost thirty years later.

Back to my best friend, Tone. He wasn't really into sports like me and Dean, but me and Tone would race up and down the block. That was *our* competition. We actually met running around outside, playing a game of freeze tag, back when we were nice little kids who went to St. Augustine's Catholic school.

Back then, Tone's dad had a nine-to-five job, but on the side, he would sing salsa and play the congas in little neighborhood bars, on that Puerto Rican shit. Mr. Crespo had a great voice. Me and Tone would go see him perform; two kids sitting in these bars with adults. I envied Tone's relationship with his father because they didn't have a dysfunctional home. I never saw Tone argue with his father. It was always *pure* love.

Me and my dad, Ernest, were sometimes cool, but we weren't *tight*. I moved out of my family's house when I was fourteen and a major reason—besides wanting to sell drugs in peace (more on that later)—was I couldn't get along with my father. We'd butt heads.

My father would work hard all week. Sometimes he would go gamble, lose all his money in a poker game, and wouldn't come home till three, four in the morning. Then he'd start screaming at my mother to make him some food. My mom would have to get up and make him a steak. Sometimes if the steak tasted a little too salty to him, he'd throw the plate of food against the wall.

My father was the type of guy who, when his nieces got married, his sisters invited my mother and told her, "Ruby, please bring the kids, but don't tell Ernest about the wedding." He was a problem. He would have gotten up there and called his niece a "ho." He was a prah-blem.

He eventually beat his alcoholism, but even now, we get into it. I pay every bill in his and my mother's house, but when we get into an argument he goes for the throat. He tells me if it weren't for rap, I'd be a drug dealer. He tells me I wasn't shit.

But my father never beat my mother, never got addicted to drugs like so many adults I grew up around. He worked every day, he provided for us. I try to be fair when I look at my father in hindsight. He used to kick my ass but, as you can imagine, I was stubborn and independent. My mother had cancer, but he never left her. A lot of muthafuckas would have just run away, left a woman with a cancer that put a hole in her neck.

My son Joey was born with Down syndrome and he's autistic. His mother abandoned him the day he was born. It would have all been left on me but my mother and father stepped up. They're the ones who really raised Joey, so I could have a career. Of course, financially I provided and I was always in my son's life. I see him every couple of days. But if it wasn't for them, taking care of Joey would've consumed my life. I never would've had a career. So that's my father, too.

Little Joey to this day, sleeps in the same bed with my father. They get up together, spend the whole day together. For many years now, my wife and I have been asking my parents to give us Joey, but they won't. My father takes care of that boy and cooks and cleans for my mother. My father long ago crossed over from being a bad guy to a good one. So there's a redemption story for you.

But that's now. Back then, he was really, really hard to deal with.

Tone and his dad had a different dynamic. You know the emoji with the smiley face that has two hearts where the eyes would be? That was Tone when he looked at his father singing. He'd be filled with so much joy.

Tone could sing, too, almost like his dad. Before we started selling drugs, singing was how we would get girls in our high school. Tone and our guy Mike Pacheco would be in the school singing on some New Edition shit. Tone would be in the hallways and see a girl he liked in one of the classrooms and start singing to her through the classroom window. You couldn't tell him he wasn't the brown Bobby Brown. The girls loved that.

Tone always had the baddest chicks too. But there was this girl that really turned him out. I can't remember her name, but Tone adored her because she could blowww. The girl had heavenly pipes and would serenade us like an angel. She lived right on the first floor in the projects on Washington Ave. We would go see her and she'd croon all of Anita Baker's songs. Tone would be so happy.

"Joe, look at my baby, she sings Anita Baker to me," Tone would say as the girl sat on his lap.

"Sing for me, baby. Sing for papi," he'd tell her. And she'd hit all the notes.

Playing ball and singing in the halls and getting girls was the fun part of high school, but the truth is me and Tone weren't kids anymore. Whatever innocence we came in with—which wasn't a whole lot, given all the dirt we'd already gotten into—that shit disappeared altogether in the halls of Morris. It wasn't that we were breaking rules—we'd been doing that for years. The difference was that the tables turned and we became what I most hated: Now we were the bullies. I look back and can see how it happened, how all the hurt I had came pouring back out of me. But it still devastates me to recall this final transition from the kid I was.

LIKE ATTRACTS LIKE and now the guys I started to associate with were the future drug kingpins and inmates of our school. One guy who became very influential in my and Tone's lives was "C." I won't use his real name, so we'll just call him C for now, because I don't fuck with him no more.

Me and C actually met through beef. I was talking to some girl from my high school. It's crazy because she looked like me, she had blond hair and green eyes. All the guys liked her. She loved me because I was a troublemaker but she was way too advanced for me. She was mature, especially sexually. She would say, "What you do with them big lips?" I was grossed out. I was still a kid, around fourteen. That's when I met C. He was from her neighborhood, he liked her and he was jealous of me. He started talking about me, I started talking about him.

When I finally ran into him in the street, I had a hockey stick that I would keep hidden in my sweatpants. I swung on him and was trying to take his head off with the hockey stick. We started fighting. Strangely enough, after that, somehow we became friends.

Like I said, I was fourteen, Tone was the same age and C was older than us by maybe four or five years. He was more advanced in the street game. The muthafucka was immersed in the gutter and gave me and Tone first-class tickets to join him.

Me and Tone were running shit in school, robbin' classmates in the bathrooms, stairwells, and hallways. But our only real weapon was intimidation.

"Yo, run your shit!" we'd tell some kid we cornered in a stairwell. If he didn't comply, he knew we'd jump him. So he'd comply.

While we were strong-armin' schoolkids, C was pulling off armed heists in places like the neighborhood McDonald's. His cousins were already in jail for murders. C was way ahead of us. He was already selling drugs but me and Tone hadn't gotten into the game yet. That was all about to change.

C lived on E 146th Street and Brook Avenue, not too far from me and Tone (Tone had moved out of Forest by then but was living in nearby projects). Brook Avenue may have been close but it was also the complete opposite of where I lived. For one, it was 90 percent Latino.

Like I said, even though my mother's Puerto Rican and my father's Cuban, we lived in a mostly Black neighborhood so we thought of ourselves as Black-Spanish. It wasn't just the people outside our apartment who made us feel that way, it was in the way we lived, including the music we loved. My siblings and I would be cleaning the house and we'd hear Gloria Gaynor blaring out the speakers, declaring, "I will surviiiiive!" My mother loved those female empowerment anthems. "Ain't nothin' goin' on but the rent! / You gotta have a J.O.B. if you wanna be with meeee!" That's Gwen Guthrie.

Every Mother's Day, all you'd hear coming from my house was "I'll always love my mama, she's my favorite girl." The Intruders would be blasting! My parents would be listening to Stephanie Mills, Diana Ross, Luther Vandross. Heavy, heavy R&B. But C was the first to introduce me to a variety of Latin music. All I had heard prior to that was what Tony's father sang. When I started hanging out with C on Brook Avenue, that's when I really dove into salsa music and learned about my favorite, Héctor Lavoe.

Besides the music, going around C's neighborhood would fascinate me because his hood was churning out millionaires from the drug game the way the Kentucky Wildcats churn out NBA players. Historically, a lot of street legends from the Bronx were *made* over there. At one point, it was a big heroin neighborhood. People were making millions of dollars daily. Back then, kids on the corners seemed to be selling drugs with no fear of arrest. I don't know if the laws were more lenient, but they weren't just selling drugs in the open, they would solicit customers with noooo discretion.

Across a ten-block radius, kids would work the corners like Wall Street stockbrokers trading on the floor. That was the kind of energy over there. You know when you see the footage of the stock exchange with brokers holding up pads and yelling "buy" and "sell" into the air? That's how dealers would run up to potential customers and try to sell them drugs. We'd be standing out there and in five minutes, thirty different people might come past touting their product.

"You want coke? You want crack? You want dope?" they'd ask. "What you want: weed? What you want?"

Whatever you wanted, they had it. Brook Ave was where I first got to see big money. So I guess we could thank C for putting that battery in our backs. I started to bring Tone with me. Back in the day, we all felt like we were bound to our own twenty-block radius. We all mostly stuck to our own projects. You didn't know what was going on twenty blocks down. So moving with C opened our eyes to a lot of shit.

One summer day, C came to pick me up and he was in this brand-new Chrysler Fifth Avenue. The whip had the burgundy velour seats and everything. We picked up two girls and we hung out with them, just chillin' all day until the sun set. That's when we all snuck into the pool at Crotona Park. A beautiful day.

Long story short, I found out the hard way that C *stole* the car from one of the biggest drug dealers on Brook. We called him "Gerrrrrrralllllldo!" but his name was Gerard. He was powerful, feared, and loved. There's a mural of the man in the Bronx today—somebody killed him in the late '80s, early '90s. But while he was here, he had the game on lock and could be ruthless. We'd heard a million stories of how he got rid of people. C was daring enough to rob *that man*. C knew he stole *that man's* car and didn't even tell me. I didn't know shit. I was just joy riding, hanging out with some chicks and my so-called brother C.

Somebody must have seen me in the car with C and the girls because Gerard's guys grabbed me up a few days later when I was back in the neighborhood. In addition to being a kingpin, Geraldo owned a grocery store/butcher shop. In the back of the store, he had a meat grinder.

The back of the store was exactly where his goons brought me on some real mob shit. Geraldo took a huge piece of beef and stuck it into the machine. Carefully, he showed me how it ground the meat to make burgers. While his henchmen restrained me, the man grabbed my arm as if he were going to put it in the grinder and crush it up into patties.

I would rap about this in 2019 on a Westside Gunn song produced by Statik Selektah called "Kelly's Korner." "I stole a don's car, he put my hand in a meat grinder / Now when I see hamburger, it's just a reeee-minder."

I don't know what it was, maybe because I was so young, still a high school kid, but Geraldo had mercy on me. He let me go. No thanks to this muthafucka C. He was always into some extra crazy shit, man. He was just a bad guy. I probably should have stopped fuckin' with him after almost losing a limb, but it was too late: The allure of the life had already taken me captive. I wanted to get money like C and he was showing us the way.

This was in 1984, when the crack epidemic really started hitting. The number of addicts in our community exploded and there was money to be made. Tone and I already had respect in the projects. Now we wanted to turn that juice into money.

There was a strip in our projects where a bunch of kids our age used to hustle. These were kids we grew up with, that we'd known since kindergarten. Me and Tone decided we'd set up shop there, too. We were smalllll time. We would go to W 145th Street and Broadway and buy two grams of crack cooked up. Then we'd come back to our hood and cut them up smaller and sell them two for $5. At the end of the day, after we'd been out there for hours, we would have made a couple hundred dollars to buy sneakers and clothes. The rest of our Terror Squad crew were in the Summer Youth Employment Program back then, working legitimate summer jobs. So it was just me and Tone trying to hold down a hustling spot. Next thing I knew, dudes we'd known our whole lives approached us.

"You can't hustle out here."

We held our ground. "Fuck, you mean we can't work out here?" we would say when they came at us. "We got crack. This is our hood."

The competition in our neighborhood was steep and our competitors had established themselves before us. The guys threatening us, they were working for older dealers who had guns and who were obviously making money from other spots. The thing about

Forest projects, it was so poor, the fiends really couldn't support a whole bunch of hustlers. They could barely afford to buy drugs. Imagine that! You couldn't get rich selling dope, even if you were *running* the neighborhood. Forest was like a desert when it came to money. And we had to go to war just to get that little bit.

Me and Tone never buckled under the threats, and eventually the words escalated into violence. One day another crew jumped *us*. I never thought I'd get jumped in my own projects.

We were fighting them like crazy. It was just me and Tone against what seemed like a hundred other kids. I just looked at it as part of the drug game. You try to open up shop and, even if you grew up there, people treat you differently when you try to take money out of their pockets.

Eventually we made a run for it. It was one hundred muthafuckas chasing us. We had set up on the other side of the projects from where our actual apartments were, so when the chase was on, me and Tone tried running back to where we lived. When we got close to our houses, my man Jose Paeaten's mom looked out, saw us getting our asses kicked, and threw us two bats out of her window so we could better defend ourselves. We couldn't do much with a deficit that huge, just swing and hope to stay alive. We finally fought our way into our building and ran upstairs to my crib.

I looked out the window in *my crib*, in *my projects*, where I lived my whole life, and I saw a mob still roaming around, hunting me. There were so many guys outside. A swarm of one hundred looks likes two thousand when they're hunting for *you*. And they were talking *crazy* out there.

"You gotta move out the projects!"

I could hear the yells of the riotous horde outside, while I was inside my apartment, staring out the window.

"Fuck you, Tone! Fuck you, Joey!"

I wasn't scared, though. At all. In fact, I started eggin' them on.

"Fuck y'all! Suck my dick," I yelled back out the window. "My cousins are coming. Don't worry!"

I started calling up my cousins. I called up my uncle Dan. Nobody was picking up the phone. Remember, I was on my house phone calling their cribs. Wasn't no cellphones. So if people weren't home, there was no other way to get in touch with them. By this time, my mother was coming home from work. As she walked by the assemblage of thugs downstairs, I could hear the mob starting to disrespect my mom.

"You fuckin' bitch! Joey gotta move."

"Joey, who are all these guys downstairs?" she asked me in a panic when she finally burst into the apartment.

This was a defining moment in all our lives. I called C.

"Yo, C, I got about *two hundred* muthafuckas outside," I told him. Then Tone and I broke down the entire story for him.

"All right, I'm coming," he promised me.

About twenty minutes later, a station wagon pulled up. C got out, he had on shades and a trench coat. A *trench coat* in the middle of the summer. This muthafucka looked like the Terminator. C was only one deep, but his presence was so formidable, everybody was looking like *Yo! Who the fuck is* thiiiis? Time seemed to stop.

C walked right into the middle of this group of kids. Because for all their threats and actual violence, they were still kids.

They all looked at C.

Me and Tone came running downstairs and worked our way through the crowd outside until we were standing with C.

"Who's the leader?" C asked me.

"Big Nick!" I told him. Nick was a biiig muthafucka.

C opened his coat and pulled out a shotgun. They all damn near shit themselves. They never saw anything like that. You gotta understand, my age group—fourteen, fifteen—they really wasn't into gunplay at that time. They worked for dons with guns, but none of *them* had guns. Though C was just a few years older than us, that shotgun put him into a very different category of threat.

C pointed the shotgun at Big Nick. Nick had a 40-ounce bottle in his hand.

"Let me see that forty," he told Nick.

Nick gave C the 40. C took a sip of the 40 and then broke the bottle on Nick's head. *Bong!*

All the kids started running and we gave chase. Me and Tone might have fucked up all hundred guys, just running them down and beating them with the bats. Eventually they escaped back to the other side of the projects.

Later that day, we did a hood victory lap. We walked around the whole projects with a ill swag, just diddy boppin'. Me, C, and Tone, we had no fear of anyone stepping to us. We had no fear of the police, rivals, nothing. We just walked around. We were looking for anybody who wanted problems. Nobody wanted it. That night, me and Tone got our first pistol. C gave us a .22 to share.

"Y'all hold yourself down. Here's a gun," he advised.

This wasn't the first gun I held. I had some adopted uncles from Cuba my father helped bring to the U.S. with some of his other kids. When they arrived in this country as refugees, they didn't have anywhere to live, so my parents let them stay in the house with us for a while. Sometimes when my parents were at work, a couple of my "uncles" used to take me with them to do stickups. They'd give me a couple of dollars. I was sworn to secrecy, and my parents are finding out just now by reading this book. But I never had a gun that I could say was mine.

Just like that, we went from brawling and fighting or bullying dudes to now *we* got a gun. It changed the whole game for everybody. Especially Tone.

I'm going to use another movie analogy. The best way I can explain it is he had that Tupac from *Juice* syndrome. You remember Tupac's character, Bishop, in the film *Juice*? The minute C put that gun in his hand for the first time, he changed. Just like that, In an instant, he was inducted into the life. It became his addiction— addicted to the money and the drugs and the guns. He had been a really good little kid before that. He was still just a kid, but that innocent boy was gone after we met C.

Tone's is a sad story because it didn't have to be that way for him. His parents were honest, hardworking, churchgoing people. They always embraced him, they showed him love. Tone just fell in love with the streets. Just like me—just like everybody—he wanted money. We would talk about it with each other, strategize and execute, but always with the same goal: We had to get to the bag. Tone was just willing to go further than most to get it.

That night, eventually C went home and it was just me and Tone walking around. We headed toward the Chinese restaurant on 163rd. To get there we had to walk past a place that everybody called "The Hill." The Hill was a prime location to peddle drugs but mostly it was just a place the hood used to kick it.

On those summer nights, literally a hundred guys would be just hanging out. All the Five-Percenters used to be there—Forest projects had such a sizable population of Five-Percenters living and "building" with one another out there, the whole projects was nicknamed "Godsville." Later, I used to joke with the brothers all the time and call myself "The God 'CracKim." Girls would be sliding through, with guys trying to holler at them and get their phone numbers. We'd hang out on The Hill like The Fonz and Richie Cunningham would hang out at Arnold's on *Happy Days,* or like kids from uptown would hang out at Harlem's Willie's Burgers. The Hill was our Willie's Burgers but with no food.

While we were walking, Tone saw some guys we grew up with and angrily approached one of them.

"What up? You said somethin'?" he asked.

This guy had nothing to do with the beef we had earlier. And honestly, he didn't say shit to Tone. I knew it. *Tone* knew it. This is where it was a little bit different with me and Tone. I wouldn't just start shit with people I grew up with for no reason.

Tone goes: "Yo, my man, give me your rings!"

Tone winds up robbing him and about four other guys in the middle of The Hill that night on some ruthless shit. Tone's mentality was like *We got a gun, y'all don't. We are doing whatever the fuck we want.*

We were the only ones with the hammer at the time. That night began a real shift for us. Our reputations—already well-known—were going to start growing out of control. But it added to our strength.

Needless to say, the day after C helped us with that beef, me and Tone went out to the strip and started hustling with noooo problems. We had our little corner, nobody came by beefin'. Everybody knew what it was. We'd met the first challenge you have as a young hustler in the projects during the crack epidemic: You have to carve out your own space to operate or you'll be running forever.

We used to hear the rumors that the young boys in our peer group were going to get some of their big homies to come to the block to fuck us up, but they never came. We held down our corner like legends.

Me and Tone spent literally every day together. Every fuckin' day was adrenaline and excitement. I never knew what I'd wind up getting into with him. Would we have beef today? Would we just kick it with some sexy-ass chicks? There was no tellin'.

Tone was equally charming and menacing, and we eventually got more guns. Tone couldn't fight much with his hands, but let's just say a lot of people were scared of him anyway. He got a reputation because he never backed down from a beef. And Tone had beef with everybody. One week he'd have beef with the Jamaicans, then he'd be beefing with the Dominicans. Tony was crazy, but he was smart and enterprising too. Our crew started to grow and he became our leader.

Our hustling on the corner in the projects expanded. We started to get bread and soon our friends saw how we were coming up and forgot all about the youth job programs. They joined us in the streets. Now we had our crew working under us. When bread started coming in, we splurged. You think I can dress? Tone was the flyest, most handsome dude ever. Every single day, he was rocking Dapper Dan Gucci or some type of name-brand expensive shit. Sometimes we'd wear matching Dapper Dan suits.

Even though we were best friends, I treated Tone like the don and made sure he was good all the time. We'd go to Tad's Steaks in Harlem on double dates and I'd actually frisk the girls we were with to make sure they didn't present a threat. It was the stupidest shit.

"Okay, put your hands in the air, I gotta search you. I gotta make sure *he's* aiiight," I would tell the chicks. We were too much. It was a movie. "Okay, she's all right, boss. They ain't got no guns on them."

Tone loved the ladies like he loved the streets. Sometimes the two loves intertwined, which caused so many problems for us. A lot of his beef stemmed from his constant pursuit of women. It complicated the work. We were trying to get rich but had to keep switching connects because Tone would ruin our relationships.

Our situation with the connects was simple: They'd give us the drugs and we needed to get them paid. Every new connect we'd meet, we knew these guys would have armies with machine guns behind them. And Tone would wind up fuckin' the connect's girlfriend—or even worse, his wife—behind his back. I'd only find out when Tone would come pick me up to make a run somewhere and he'd have the connect's girl sitting on the passenger side. I'd be like, "Tone! He is going to killlll us. Whyyyyy?"

The ladies loved Tone and he couldn't keep his dick in his pants. He was so far gone that he couldn't see the ramifications of it. But I wonder, was it really his fault? He was like me, thirteen, fourteen years old. The problem was that whether it was guns, drugs, or sex, the world didn't care that we were just kids. And we didn't know better. How could we?

When you're young, thuggin' and chasin' paper, just about every day is filled with adrenaline. One day you're cruisin' in your man's drop-top in Times Square, two fly chicks in the back, Al B. Sure!'s

"Off on Your Own" blastin', and it feels like you're at life's zenith. The next day, you're duckin' a hailstorm of bullets from rivals in the streets. Me and Tone were out in the streets but we hadn't started making that big, big money. We were doing pretty good though. I told you how hard it was for us just to get that one little corner on the block where we grew up. Even once we got our own little spot, the competition was still fierce. Too many sellers, not enough bread. We had to venture out.

THINKING BACK ON IT NOW, it was kind of crazy to try to open up spots in hoods that weren't ours. A spot is usually set up and run by somebody from the neighborhood who gets drugs fed to them by a connect. But Tone and I, we opened our next spot up in Harlem, all the way across the river from the Bronx. I didn't have a problem with opening up wherever and then going to war with whoever felt like I was infringing on their territory.

In our travels, me and Tone met a lot of characters. There were a lot of colorful dudes who ran the streets before they got killed or the RICO law put everybody in jail for a thousand years. One character was a cat named Howie from the South Bronx. Howie was Dominican but he looked like LL Cool J with that caramel complexion. He was very handsome and always, astronomically, dipped fresh. Very flamboyant. Howie was the type of dude to pull up during a snowstorm in a fuckin' convertible with the top down. Of course he'd be wearing the flyest mink and he'd always be icy no matter what season.

Howie could also be extremely violent. His whole family got down too.

Howie's big brother, Johnny Airborne, was murdered. His other brother, Rob, did a bunch of years in the Feds—he's out now and still my man. These three brothers had a lot of respect in the streets, their mother too. Howie was the wildest in the family and the one who really made bread. He had two BMWs, a white one and a red one with the wide body kit. They were the biggest two-seaters with the loudest sound system you ever heard in your life. From two blocks away, you knew he was coming. It sounded like Studio 54 on wheels.

Me and Tone liked Howie a lot but we never got money with him, he was just our friend. We used to bug out with one another. He had an army down with him; we had an army down with us, and sometimes we'd all clique up. Ironically, even with all that backup, Howie used to get shot every other week. All in all he got shot thirteen different times. Not thirteen different bullet wounds; he got shot on thirteen different oh-cay-sions.

But he seemed invincible. I don't know about what he was up to—if he was robbing, extorting, whatever—but obviously people wanted to kill this guy. It never stopped us hanging out with him, going to his block and chilling.

On this one night, we took a cab to his block. It was like 9:00 P.M.

As we get out the car, some kid jumps out at us and he says, "Yo, you Joey Crack?" He was an Ecuadorian kid about our age with funny spiky hair. He looked like a real nice guy.

"Yeah, nigga, what's up?" I answered.

The innocuous-looking shorty pulled out a MAC-11 on us, right in the middle of the sidewalk. Me and Tone weren't strapped, but Tone had a bulletproof vest on. So he pushed me behind him in the hope that if the Ecuadorian kid started shooting, *he'd* get shot and the vest could absorb the bullets.

"Joey go, Joey go!" Tone started yelling to me as he acted as my human shield.

I started hauling ass. I just kept runnin', runnin', runnin' down the block. I'm not the fastest in the world, but it looked I was doing the 40-yard dash. Even with the head start, Tone caught up to me. Fortunately for us, the kid didn't shoot and he didn't chase us on foot. The kid went to get his car.

So as me and Tone were running, all we heard was a car engine gunning and tires screeching behind us: *Urrrr! Urrrrr! Urrrrrr!* This dude was trying to chase us down. We ran into a projects playground. I don't know if y'all remember the old projects playgrounds, with the iron monkey bars and the splintered seesaw. They also had a concrete turtle. People used to sit on the turtle. We ran into one of those playgrounds trying to save our lives.

Mind you, I'm doing all this scrambling but I was really Fat Joe at the time. I was crazy-overweight. I can't believe I didn't catch a heart attack. I was gasping for air, breathing like Darth Fuckin' Vader. Me and Tone, we hid under the turtle. All we heard was the car tires screeching. I don't know what it was about those days, but the cops were never there when you needed them!

We were hopin' the cops would catch this fool. Not snitchin' but Jeeeee-zus! With no help in sight, we waited it out. The Ecuadorian kid left and we eventually crawled out from under the turtle and made it back to our projects. We always had beef in the streets. Shit like that happened to us all the time, but we didn't know *why* this kid just pulled out on us.

The very next day, me and Tone came out of our building in the Forest projects. We were standing in front of the building when a car pulled up—I want to say it was a Delta 88. This guy, the same Ecuadorian kid, came out the passenger side of the car and lit up the front of the building with the MAC. He missed and me and Tone ran into the building. My homegirl Sonia—she was my man Jose Paeaten's sister—was out there too and she almost got shot.

"Oh my God, they almost killed Sonia! Joey and Tone are always bringing trouble."

That was the talk of the projects. Everybody in the building was mad at us for a while.

We'd escaped again, but it was clear this Ecuadorian kid was acting like a hitman. We were sure he'd try again. I felt we needed backup. I called my guy Ron, who I went to Morris High with, and whose brother was the biggest kingpin in the Bronx. That kid was the richest guy in the world to us.

Ron picked us up in his ride two or three hours later. He had long hair in a ponytail. He was eager to hear what was going on with us.

"This nigga tried to shoot us last night and the same nigga shot at us earlier today," I told him. "Yo, man, you got to tell your brother or something. I don't know, we need help with this one. This kid is different."

As soon as I said that, the Delta 88 pulls up and there's the kid again, now he's hanging out of the passenger side window, and before we know it, he's shooting at us again. Ronny hits reverse, but he's so calm. I'm duckin', Tone is duckin', the kid is shooting at us in broad daylight and Ronny is so cool and collected, it was uncanny.

"Gimme a light, gimme a light," he says to me casually. Ron starts trying to light a cigarette while we're in a high-speed chase cutting through the projects.

"Oh my fucking God," I started yellin'. I guess Ron was so calm because he and his brother used to race cars. Thank God he had that expertise behind the wheel, because we got away.

We had Ron drop us off a ways from our building, on Fordham Road. We were away from the South Bronx, so we were safe.

"My brother ain't never gonna help y'all, man. Y'all niggas got a problem? *Y'all* gotta figure this one out," Ron offered before peeling off.

Me and Tone were kinda left out there hangin'. So in desperation we called another friend of ours who came through in a big way. He brought us a rental car and guns. By nightfall, we were ready for our restitution. We drove back to Howie's block and before long we found him: The Ecuadorian kid was just standing on the corner like it was nothing. We start creeping up toward him in our car. We were absolutely going to shoot him. The Ecuadorian kid calmly walked right into *the middle of the street*, holding the biggest gun we'd ever seen.

This dude looked like Heath Ledger in *The Dark Knight*. He

was like the Joker standing in traffic with a machine gun, antagonizing Batman to hit him with his motorcycle.

The kid started lettin' off at us and we hit reverse. We spun around the block and then tried to double back to get him, but he was gone. We just couldn't get this guy.

The next day, we were sitting in the rental car, parked outside our building, and we were strapped. Out of nowhere, the Delta 88 pulls up.

I don't know where the police were. I don't know how the police weren't around to stop this, but the Ecuadorian started lickin' shots at us crazily in broad daylight *again*. Our rental car was so riddled with bullets, it looked like Swiss cheese. If you had looked at the car, you would've thought we were *outta here*. I literally heard people talking later about "the death of Fat Joe and Tony Montana." The whole projects were like, "They killed Joey. They killed Tony!"

The kid aired that rental car out. Fortunately for us, he was a terrible shot. We ducked and he shot the seats, he shot the windows out, but not one bullet hit us. He was firing at us so rapidly, we didn't get a chance to let nothin' off back at him. We sat there in our bullet-scarred car after he left and were like, "Holy shit! This guy's like Steven Seagal in *Out for Justice.*" He kept coming. Wasn't nothin' we could do.

After the drive-by, I don't know why, but the kid's onslaught paused. Every day, me and Tone were strapped. We hid firearms under every trash can, every bush. We were crew deep, waiting for him. We had to stay on point. But the Ecuadorian never came back. If he had come back, it would have been over for him. Thank God he never returned.

Me and Tone and our guys were outside the next week and all we heard coming up the block was "You may be young but you're rea-daaayyy! Ready to learrrrrn."

Howie was coming up the block in his red BMW with the top off. The system was on ignorance level 10, blasting Keith Sweat's "Right and Wrong Way." He always blasted Keith Sweat. He pulled up right in front of us. Me and Tone loved Howie, but we were looking at him with the ice grill because the kid shooting at us was from *his* block.

As he pulled up, Howie made a spectacle as usual. Everything with him was so exaggerated. He took like five minutes to go through the motions of turning down the radio. He looked at us with a grin but we kept grillin' him.

"What? You ain't got love for Howwwwwwwwwww-eeee?" he asked. "Y'all ain't got love for Howwwwwwwwww-eeeee?"

"Fuck you, Howie," we blurted back. The timbre in our "fuck you" wasn't as strident as it could have been. He was still our friend. But he warranted a "fuck you" nonetheless. We almost said it hesitantly, because we really loved him.

"Oh, it's 'Fuuuuuck Howwwwwwwww-eeee'?" he replied indignantly.

He stepped out the car; he was too fly. It looked like he was going to shoot a music video. He had his left arm in a sling because he had recently been shot. *Again.*

"Tone Montana, Joe Crack. Y'all ain't got love for Howwwwww-eeee?" he asked again.

Even though we had crew all over, Howie walked up to us. He wasn't scared of nothin'.

"What's up, man?" he asked.

"You tell *me* what's up, nigga," I responded. My tone got more belligerent. "Yo, man, we went to your block and this little Ecuadorian nigga shot at us like eight times."

Howie just fell on the ground, dying laughing. He was crying real tears. He couldn't believe it. He grew up on that block with the shooter. He knew the Ecuadorian kid.

"Ohhhhh nooooooo! Not Cha-guito, the Ecua-dorrrrrian," he roared with glee. "*He's* got Tone Montana and Joe Crack shook? Oh! Myyyy! Gawwwddd!"

It was just so ridiculous to him; he found the situation hilarious. He knew me and Tone got busy and the Ecuadorian kid was known for being a punk. After about ten minutes, Howie convinced us to get in the car and come with him. We made it back to Howie's block in 2.2 seconds. He was the fastest driver in the world.

The Ecuadorian kid was outside, standing in front of this empty lot in front of an abandoned building. He saw us in the car with Howie and had a look on his face like *What the fuck is this?*

Me and Tone stayed in the car while Howie got out to talk to him.

"Yo! Yo! Yo! Yo! Give me the gun!" Howie demanded as the kid protested. "Give me the gun. Give me . . . Give me . . . Muthafucka! Give me the gun!"

The kid pulled out the rustiest .357 Magnum, but it was still some big-ass Dirty Harry shit. The Ecuadorian kid always had these oversized guns. Howie was the kingpin of the neighborhood, so the kid did as he was told.

"Ay yo, my man! Do you know who the fuck this is?" Howie asked the Ecuadorian kid. "This is Tony Montana. This is Joey Crack. These are my brothers."

"But Howwww-eeee," the kid responded in a whimper, almost in tears. "They told me it was Joey Crack who shot you."

Howie had recently gotten shot for like the eleventh time and he'd been in the hospital the whole time this Ecuadorian kid was trying to kill us. The kid had got some false info in the hood that I was the one who tried to kill Howie. He was trying to earn stripes by avenging the shooting.

"Howie, I have to fuck this kid up," I told him. "You must let me jump out this car and beat the shit out of this kid."

Howie didn't stand in my way. I had been terrified. I thought I was being hunted by an unstoppable, mysterious force, something more powerful than just another kid my age, another dumb kid caught up in a game with guns. I was seeing this kid's face in my nightmares. And when I was awake this same kid had looked me in the eye and pulled the trigger. He was ready to kill me and Tone just for the rep.

Howie was right, we were shook. I have no trouble admitting it: I was a kid and I was scared for my life. Again.

I was shaking when I got out the car. I beat him up. We never saw the Ecuadorian kid again.

To take you back all the way full circle, me and C remained good friends for a number of years. He wound up getting locked up for murder. I pawned all my jewelry to pay for a lawyer for the case. He said the cops were wrong about him, there's no witness. When we show to court after they picked the jury, a lady comes to court and she's a witness. She said she saw him. It turns out they had multiple witnesses. There was a bus driver, who drove the city bus, that said he saw the murder too.

I knew C was done. His lawyer conferred with us and said, "This guy is gonna lose this. I could get him a ten- to twenty-year sentence. He'll be home in fifteen years. What do y'all wanna do?" C asked me what I thought.

"Bro, I'm gonna be with you through this whole shit," I told him. "My brother, I got your back."

Tone told him he had his back too. So C took the time. This was way before I even started rappin'. I went to visit this guy for all the seventeen years he was locked up. I would go see him in snowstorms, I'd bring Big Pun with me, I'd take the bus up to the jail when I got off the road and go straight to see him. I kept it real with him, also made sure his family was straight. When C came out of jail, he immediately was one of the top dawgs of the Terror Squad family. Most of the Terror Squad would go with me to see him in jail, those that didn't heard a million stories about him.

Everybody showed the man love. I bought him a brand-new Hummer, got him an apartment, jewelry, I was taking care of him. Then, unfortunately, C wanted to start hustling again. Now in the past few years, there have been several rappers that have been arrested on R.I.C.O. charges, most notably Young Thug and Gunna. Back then, I knew about how the Feds could jam you up. I was legit and I didn't want any part of criminal activity.

I told C I came too far and went through so much to be legit to be caught up in crime. He started talking about the streets loved him and he's the man. So I had to fall back from him. That's how we fell out. He's the king of the traitors. *You come home and go bad on a nigga that kept it real with you for your entire prison bid? I paid your commissary, made sure your family—your mother and daughter—was taken care of and you go bad on me? You would try to kill me of all people? The one guy who really loved you like a brother?*

The last time I saw him was about eight years ago. I had just did the Hot 97 morning show. I came out of the building and he was there outside waiting for me. He looked demented. I knew what it was. I honestly feel he came there to kill me. It had to be out of jealousy, because I never did anything wrong to this man. I was with one of my guys and he had a hammer on him. When I saw C, I told my guy, "Do not play. If he pulls out, you gotta let that fire ring because this nigga is a murderer."

Most guys, when they are going to do something really bad, they don't look in the eye of the person they are going to do it to. They look away. C couldn't look at me. He kept looking to the side. I walked up to him.

"C, what up?" I said, in a huff. "Look at me, bro."

He kept looking to the side, because it's easier to hurt someone and I guess kill someone if you are not looking directly eye-to-eye. Especially if you know you're wrong. You look away.

My only defense was to talk to him.

"Yo, look at me," I told him. "If you gonna do something, look at me."

He looked at me for a split second, then smacked his teeth and just said, "Fuck it!" He walked away and I have never seen him again in my life.

PART II
FAMILY BUSINESS

CHAPTER 5

SUICIDAL THOUGHTS

SOME REAL SHIT I never told anybody before: I've actually thought about taking my own life. I guess now is the time to let it out. You only get one *first* book right? It's a bit of a relief to say it out loud.

It happened during the holidays when I was maybe seventeen, eighteen.

As you know by now, if you're keeping up, I have a different father from my older brothers and sister. My dad raised my siblings as if they were his own, but they didn't always reciprocate. On holidays, sometimes, they would tell him, "You ain't my father." Foul shit like that.

At that time, my money was flowing like a faucet. Our crew had gone from just me and Tone holding down the block to a growing organization. My oldest brother, Angel Jr., was now number one in our organization, I was number two. We called Angel "June" or "Junior" in the house, but in the streets, he was known as "Money Man." I trusted Angel. Truth is, even with all this money we were making, I wasn't getting paid what I was supposed to get paid, but I knew my brother would always take care of me. I knew he would always have my back.

My brother Raymond, he's the middle brother. He was supposed to be the clean-cut one. Raymond never ever used drugs, he was never around the drug game, and he never did anything illegal. To this day, a lot of people who know all of us still don't even know

Raymond is my brother. At the time, he was going to John Jay College; he was going to be a lawyer.

But he was full of shit. I don't even like saying his name.

One year, my brothers, my sister, Lisa, and I were doing Thanksgiving at my parents' house. Our family was really big on holidays, especially Thanksgiving and Christmas. At some point in the night, Angel, Raymond, and I started talking about money. Angel had saved a lot of money, well over a million bucks, and he wanted to talk about putting the bread away. No chance he could deposit street money in the bank, so we had to come up with a safe place to stash it. Angel wanted to leave it with Raymond.

I wasn't so sure. I told him, "Yo, you shouldn't leave all your money in one place."

Don't get me wrong, me and Angel trusted Raymond with our lives at that time, plus he lived legit. So if Junior was going to leave the money with any one person, it would have been Raymond. Still, I was stressing him not to leave all his eggs in one basket. We have an uncle named Fello who got caught out there like that. He lost it all, millions, in one swoop.

An idea came to me: our aunt who lived down in Orlando.

"Yo, bro, you could go visit our aunt, take some money down there, and throw that shit in her attic," I advised Junior. "She won't even know it's there. And if she did, who cares?"

I was convinced that Angel should split the money up. If we ever got knocked or whatever, he wouldn't have all his money in one spot where the Feds or the police could take it like they did Uncle Fello's. As I'm explaining it, Raymond gets up and says to Angel, "Why are you even listening to this nigga? He ain't really our real brother. He ain't a hundred percent our brother."

When I tell you that those words *devastated me* . . . Even though we had different fathers, my siblings and I were raised as one family. Never did the words "stepbrother" or "half-brother" ever come up. It was "The Cartagenas," all of us together.

So when he turned around and said, "This nigga ain't even *really* our brother," oh my God. It ravaged me.

Angel had my back like he always did. He started flipping on Raymond.

"Fuck you, nigga," Angel yelled. "Don't ever talk like that about Joey. Joey's my brother!"

The damage was done though. I got up and started crying so much I could barely see straight. I couldn't believe what Raymond had said.

"Man, fuck you, nigga," I said to Ray. I pulled out all the theatrics. "You bitch-ass nigga."

I got up and headed for the door, just weeping. My family tried to stop me. This is going to sound crazy, but I was so upset I actually threw the Thanksgiving turkey on the floor. My mother, my father, my sister, Lisa, everybody was upset and mad at me. I left the house and jumped into my 5.0 Mustang. We had two of them. Angel had a gray one and I had a white one. That 5.0 Mustang, them joints would get to 90 miles per hour in less than ten seconds. You could go from one end of the block to the other in a blink. Fastest car in the hood.

I drove off, crying more than I ever had in my life. I kept driving faster, pushin' the Mustang hard. Nobody was really on the streets because it was Thanksgiving. Most people were home with their families, but I'm sure they could hear my car speeding through. It sounded like the Batmobile was coming. I found myself racing all the way from Forest projects to City Island. City Island is a small enclave in the Bronx with a bunch of restaurants that serve giant plates of seafood: lobster, shrimp, crab. There's only one way onto or off of the island: two lanes over a bridge. I drove over that bridge at maybe 100 miles per hour and right through City Island.

At the end of the island, there is a restaurant named Tony's Pier, which was my favorite. You could eat good for affordable prices. Anybody from the hood knows Tony's. They'd sell you fried shrimp with fries, clams, lobsters. I loved all of that. But as I was whizzing down the streets, food was the last thing on my mind. See, I wasn't headed to Tony's, I was driving toward a landmark next to it.

The anger in my heart, the tears sliding down my face all intensified. I felt alone. I started to think I didn't want to be here. Right by Tony's there was this huge concrete barricade to stop you from driving into the Long Island Sound. That's where I was going. I contemplated ramming my Mustang right into the barricade at top speed. My car was traveling so fast that I only had a few seconds to choose between life and death as the barricade came into view. My eyes, almost blinded by tears, finally connected with the barricade.

Fuck this, I thought as the choice to kill myself overtook me and seemed to be the only decision. I felt like I didn't belong.

How could my own family betray me? I thought. My blood was boiling.

Let me freeze the frame there. My brother pushed me right back to that place: the kid who got beat up every day, the kid betrayed by his best friend, the kid hunted in the streets by a wild Ecuadorian, the kid a hundred other kids tried to beat to death because he was dealing on the block. The kid the cops abuse. I guess I had repressed those feelings, but in fact, emotionally, I was a ticking time bomb. Home was supposed to be my sanctuary. But now I was feeling like I had so many times in the streets: alone, vulnerable, attacked.

All of a sudden, as much as the thought of death consumed me in those would-be final moments, I knew I didn't want to die. I had more living to do. The feeling of wanting to live returned and overwhelmed me. I hit the brakes and slowed up in time.

Then I made a U-turn and ended up going to White Plains Road by the Soundview projects—Big Pun grew up in Soundview. There used to be this steakhouse around there called Seville's Steakhouse. It's closed down now. I wound up eating Thanksgiving dinner by myself at Seville's. It was, even after everything, the best steak I ever had in my life. I can still taste it right now. A New York strip and the way they caramelized the onions—it was a movie.

I never had a suicidal thought again through all the obstacles. I've gone through making money, then going broke, trying to make money again. Going to jail, getting robbed by one best friend, and watching another die. Through all the pressure, I never thought about killing myself again. I eventually understood the reason I was scared to die: I love life too much. Even if it's only eating a strip steak alone in the Bronx on Thanksgiving. I loved it all.

But I also know that suicidal thoughts are more complicated than a question of loving life or fearing it. You never know who might be having suicidal feelings. It's so difficult to wrap my head around, even when it came close to home.

FAST FORWARD: August 30, 2012, a day that shattered me and so many others. That's the day I got the call that my friend and mentor Chris Lighty had committed suicide. It bugged me out. Chris discovered me and signed me to my first record deal at Relativity Records. He was one of hip-hop's most successful executives ever, especially as a manager. His company, Violator, oversaw the careers of the likes of 50 Cent *and* Ja Rule (not at the same time, thank God), LL Cool J, Missy Elliott, Busta Rhymes, Q-Tip, N.O.R.E., Mobb Deep, and Foxy Brown.

It bugged me out. I met him as "Baby Chris," a strong guy from the Bronx. I would have never put Chris and suicide together. He was beautiful. He was spirited, he was all about family and so passionate when it came to music and the music business.

From the outside it's tough to fathom that somebody would be in such a dark place that they would take their own life. But I hear about suicide more and more these days, especially with Black and Latino people.

I get real melancholy when I think of Shakir Stewart, a former executive vice president at Def Jam, who had signed Young Jeezy and Rick Ross to their first deals, taking his life; or this young lady I knew named Jas Waters, who had become a great Hollywood film and TV writer. I can never know what was on their minds at that last moment. I know at that moment back on Thanksgiving when I felt betrayed by the people I trusted the most, the people I loved the most, I had that momentary urge. But so many of us came up on the same streets, whether we were the predator or prey. Even when we survived physically we carry so much inside of us, so many scars and traumas, old fears, nightmares, regrets. You just don't know what anyone is carrying. But man, God bless everybody who's going through it. Life is a gift.

CHAPTER 6

PARENTS ON LOCKDOWN

I GREW UP IN A FAMILY of degenerate gamblers and cigarette smokers. They were hustlers too. My grandfather Cowboy ran numbers spots, the lottery of the ghetto. The spots were also places you could go to socialize while you gambled. They weren't fancy casinos but they were right in the neighborhoods.

The government realized that there was so much money in that business that they shut down all the illegal numbers spots after a while. The hood didn't eat anymore from gambling. So many lives were affected, because these spots had kept economic power in the ghetto. But that's exactly why they got shut down, so the government could run their own lottery and powerball, selling tickets in bodegas. They took that blueprint from the gambling spots.

I feel like I got my demeanor from my grandfather. I was young when he passed, but from what I remember of him, he was a no-nonsense guy and was always respected for it. He took care of his family, he loaned people money, and nobody fucked with him. Nobody tried to rob his numbers spots.

My mother, all my aunts and uncles, worked in his numbers spot. It was the family business. When you sell drugs, one of the rules is "never get high on your own supply." But my family, I watched them pretty much work just to get money to play numbers. All the time with all them it was "give me $10 on this," or "give me $20 on the nine." These were broke people and they were gambling every day! My entire family! And they, of all people, should've known better.

For the most part, you lose at the numbers spot. Then one good time, maybe once every five, six months, after you'd spent like $1,200 trying to win, you hit a number for like $800. Then you would have to tip the person you gave the bet to. Then comes your family: They all know you won $800, so they're on you, hands out. So you lend or give them money. By then, you done gave out $250, $300 of it. You got $500 now, which means you $700 in the hole. And you won! Doesn't matter. You lose regardless.

I was a little kid doing the math and watching these grown-ups like *Yo, these people are dumb. They really play this shit?* I was really, really turned off by them gambling. They never got ahead even when they thought they'd *won*. They were broke.

My family was also hamstrung by cigarettes. My whole family used to smoke. When I was eighteen, my mother was diagnosed with cancer from smoking cigarettes. On one of her chemotherapy visits, I caught her taking a puff outside the hospital after her treatment. She was a chain smoker. Both my parents went through four packs of Marlboros a day. As a little kid, I'd be like, "Yo, that shit is nasty. I'll never smoke cigarettes." To this day, I've never smoked a cigarette.

I smoked weed once. That was a disaster. I always stayed away from drugs because I saw how they fucked up the lives of my family members and so many other people in the hood. I learned through their mistakes. But one time, I had a girl over my apartment when I lived in Throgs Neck in the Bronx. A beautiful girl. And she partook of that Mary Jane. She wanted me to smoke with her.

"You don't understand, it's gonna be nice. The sex is going to be so good," she explained, coaxing me to indulge. "We gonna go for hours."

I finally went for it. I took a few pulls of the weed and I had what they call "a bad trip." I did research on this later. Too late. It was just my luck the weed made me paranoid. I ran out the house at 4:00 A.M., in my birthday suit. I must have had an anxiety attack.

"I'm gonna catch a heart attack," I yelled running down my block, ass out. "I'm gonna die!"

Thank god the girl jumped into my car to come get me. I had a white Lexus at the time.

"Joey, get in the car," she told me, riding alongside me as I'm hotfooting it around my neighborhood, naked as Baby New Year.

"No, I'm gonna die. I gotta go to the hospital," I countered.

"Joey get in the car. I'll take you. I'll take you," she promised.

Instead of taking me to the hospital, she drove back to my place. I went inside and took seven showers. The girl took care of me. I laughed so much when I came down off my high and she told me what happened. I never smoked weed again. Even though I'm in the studio every night and other rappers and producers are smoking mountains of green, and probably good shit, I don't think I'll ever smoke again. You definitely don't want to see the 2022 version of Fat Joe running down the block butt-ass naked. TMZ would have a field day.

You can't make a move today with everything going viral. Thank goodness they didn't have camera-phones back in the day when the numbers spots were prevalent.

My aunt Barbara, that's my favorite aunt, she's my mother's younger sister. Aunt Barbara met my Uncle Fello at the numbers spot. Uncle Fello was a *man's man*. He's one of the main men I looked up to my entire life. Uncle Fello had a wife and my aunt was more like the young, bad mistress. He eventually left his wife for Aunt Barbara though. Smart move.

Fello was industrious like my grandfather. He owned *three hundred* numbers spots throughout the city. This is how I know all of New York. I know Washington Heights because he owned numbers spots in Washington Heights. I know all of Brooklyn because he had spots in different parts of Brooklyn. He had spots in Harlem, Queens, the Bronx. Everywhere! This is how I became familiar with the ins and outs of the Big Apple. Wherever there were Black and Latin people, Fello owned a numbers spot.

When the Feds eventually put out a task force to close down all the numbers spots in New York, they came for Fello. He had all types of offices and houses. This guy would sleep in a different house every night on some El Chapo shit. He'd spend Monday night in Castle Hill, Tuesday night in Washington Heights, Wednesday in Brooklyn. He had apartments all over. I guess he wanted to stay mobile in case stickup kids tried to rob him.

In one of his apartments, he had a television with a secret compartment. That's where he had six million dollars stashed. Six million dollars in the late '70s, early '80s, that would be like $24 million today. Unfortunately, the Feds raided that apartment and found the money.

"Yo, this is yours?" they asked him when they brought him in to ask about the cash.

"Nah," he said.

He didn't take responsibility for the money because he couldn't show them how he legally made it. That would have opened a Pandora's box of tax evasion, which is how the Feds took down many an underworld Goliath, including Al Capone. Can you imagine losing your fortune in one shot? Overnight, he went from being a super-rich dude with a successful hustle, to the Feds stopping the whole numbers game and him going back to a regular life. The thing I respect most about Fello is he never complained once. He never said, "Yo, I used to have money. That's fucked up."

He took his loss on the chin, which is why my uncle Fello is my hero for life. He and my aunt Barbara stayed together until he recently passed away. Fello lived to be ninety-six and played numbers until he died. His funeral was beautiful. It was held in the Bronx at the Ortiz Funeral Home, the same place Big Pun had his homegoing. Hundreds of people came out to pay their last respects to Fello, which amazed me, because usually when someone who's that advanced in age passes, the turnout for their funeral is smaller. But Fello affected so many lives, people came out from all different generations. I caught Covid-19 around that time, so I was saddened not to be able to make it out to the service. But Fello knows I loved him and still do. He showed me early on what it meant not to fold even when facing the worst adversity.

A little while before Fello's operation got taken down, my grandfather's number spot got raided. The good thing was numbers weren't like drugs. Even if you went to jail for numbers running back then, you would be in and out the precinct. At most, you'd stay locked up overnight and then they'd let you go with a ticket. One day, when I was maybe eight years old, I came home from school and they told me that my mother got arrested at her job. She was working for my grandfather, of course.

My mother was taken to the 42nd Precinct in the Bronx. I didn't know what to do, but I wanted to cheer her up. It hurts when you see family members going through trials and tribulations and nobody's around to help them through their struggle. You have to be there in good times and bad. Just like a marriage—in sickness and in health.

I went around our block and I got everybody to chip in money. I ended up with $2.50. I went to the Chinese restaurant and I bought my mother's favorite dish: pork fried rice and shrimp and lobster sauce.

I walked from 170th Street and Third Avenue to the 42nd Precinct. It was about a mile away. I was only eight. I went to the precinct and I begged to see my mother and they wouldn't let me in.

"*Please* I need to feed my mother," I implored the officers at the front desk.

The police gave me five minutes to see her. They escorted me back to the cell, I kissed her and I brought her the food. I was overcome with relief after seeing her smile. She didn't stay in the precinct but a few hours. But that was all she needed to learn her lesson. My mother never took numbers again. She went back to school and got a legitimate job.

I wish I could say that was the last time I had to see one of my parents behind bars at the 42nd Precinct, but it wasn't. My father got jammed up too.

The biggest thing we would do as a family was once a month, my father would take us to see kung fu flicks at the Prospect Theatre. Inside that theater, the air had the foulest aroma. There were rats running down the aisles; it was a dump. But we still went and thought it was *big time*. My family was poor, man.

Around the corner from there was this restaurant. It was a typical ghetto Chinese restaurant but the owners were Chinese from Cuba and spoke Spanish. My father loved taking us there. I guess it reminded him of his childhood in Cuba. So we would go once a month. One evening after we'd eaten dinner there, I remember us going outside and getting into the car to go home. The police pulled us over. My father, he never did anything wrong. He's never been a gangster, he's never been a troublemaker or nothin'. So when they stopped him, he showed them the registration for the car, he showed them his license. The two officers who detained us were white and one of them kept telling him, "Yo, speak English."

"No speaky English. I'm from Cuuubah. I'm from Cuuubah," my dad tried to explain.

The cops were insisting that he reply in English but he wasn't lying; my father didn't really know English. He still doesn't know English that much to this day. It was raining and they made him stand outside. Then I watched the police rough my father up. They didn't beat him to the ground or nothing like that, but they roughed him up, pushed him around, threw him on the car. They put handcuffs on him and took him away in the squad car. They locked him up because he didn't speak English.

From that day on, I've hated the 42nd Precinct, because that's where I saw my mother in jail then my father in the cage with his hands locked behind his back. They left him cuffed in his cell. He looked so hopeless; that shit killed me. They let him go a couple of hours later, but that was traumatizing.

A few years later though, the boys in blue would focus their attention on me. You better believe they wanted me in jail for more than just a few hours. They wanted to put me away for life, by any means necessary. Even if it meant breaking the law themselves. I would be embroiled in a bitter feud with the NYPD for decades to come. A family tradition.

FAST FORWARD: I'm on the run. A close friend of the family went to the police and told them they saw me roughing somebody up in my building. What that friend of the family didn't know was that the person I allegedly "put hands on" was part of a scheme where Tony Montana had been set up to get robbed and killed. We were in the height of our drug-running days as older teenagers now. The money was pouring in, we weren't shy about showing off, especially with cars and jewelry. No one loved that spotlight more than Tony, which made him a target.

And while we stayed on point for the most part, there was one night when we almost got caught slippin'. They hit us up where we least expected: home. I was walking with Tony into his building late one night. The lobby in the projects at night would be either eerily quiet or bustling with some kind of illegal action. That night, we ran into some guys who announced they were there to take Tone's shines and cash. Stickup kids. They stood about six feet away from us, guns out. Our casual stroll to the elevator turned into a full-on Mexican standoff.

When we told them to fuck off, they started firing. I wasn't strapped, so I took cover behind a big concrete wall. Tone always had the burner on him and sent shots back their way. We were literally just a few feet away from each other and nobody got shot, even with all those bullets flying. The stickup kids then ran out of the building after a few rounds were let off. It was one of those kids that the friend of the family saw me putting hands on.

A short time later, I heard from a confidant that the cops were looking for me. They didn't have a warrant for my arrest or anything, but they wanted to bring me in for questioning. I didn't want to talk to the cops. I must have hid out at about ten of our neighbors' houses in the projects, trying to shake the jakes.

One day, I was staying right across the hall from the apartment where I lived. I watched through the neighbor's peephole as the cops busted into my home looking for me. My mother was the only one there. They left the door open and stood in the living room castigating my mom.

"Where the fuck is Joey?" they asked.

When my mother wouldn't tell them my whereabouts, one of the officers mushed her hard. Her head and neck snapped back. I was helpless. My neighbors held me back. I wanted to kill that cop so bad. *He mushed my mother? Nah. He's gotta go.*

The cops eventually let that one go, but they never stopped harassing me.

Most of my life I've dealt with police harassment. *Insane* police harassment. Was I a bad guy? Obviously. If you're reading this book, you know I was bad as fuck. But man, some of the levels and lengths the police went to to put me in jail were crazy. My real indictment of the cops is that it didn't really matter how bad I was. I was guilty just on the strength of being a young Puerto Rican kid in those projects. They were looking for a reason from the day I was born.

If we're going to talk truth, the only white people we would come in contact with in the Bronx were either school teachers or police. And now that I'm older, I realize that so much of the conflict between us and the cops came from a racial divide. These were mostly young, inexperienced white men who grew up in another part of town. The NYPD had them patrolling the projects with these underprivileged, outspoken, and sometimes hot-tempered Black and Latin people. Those cops were never going to truly understand where we were coming from and our point of view. They were like an occupying army and they abused us kids.

Somehow it's worse with a lot of Latino and Black cops. You

know the story, they want to prove to the white cops that they're part of the "boys in blue," so they go above and beyond the call of duty to dis their own communities.

I'll take you back to when I was fourteen, fifteen years old, in Morris High. I'd garnered the attention of this cop, his name was Officer Messer. He hated me. Admittedly, I was causing chaos. Their radios were always buzzing: "Fat guy with a red hoodie on, shots fired. Fat guy running away." I was into all types of shit. So he hated me.

He wanted to catch me so bad. One time, I remember I was sitting with my crew in the back of "Cheeky" Tina's building. Tina ran "the party house" in the projects. Me and my friends, we were out there joking and laughing. I was telling a joke about Officer Messer. Little did I know Messer was standing behind me. He was on one of his foot patrols, saw me and stopped. He was obsessed.

"Fuck Messer!" I said, and everybody was dying laughing. Nobody told me, "Yo, he's standing right *there*, Joe." I finally saw him.

"*Ohhhh shit . . . Messer*, what's up?" I was shocked, but trying to play it off.

When I stood up he grabbed me with one arm and hit me on my legs with his baton. After a couple of painful blows he let me go. He didn't lock me up, but he *fucked me up*.

Mainly I'd run into him in front of Morris High School. After junior high, I thought my days of getting bullied were over. Five-0 had different ideas. On any given day you'd see the squad car pull up with that quick siren call, *eeerrrrrr*. The car doors would fly open and out would come Messer. He'd come up to me, make me "spread 'em," and kick my legs apart. He'd smack my head and roust me. I wouldn't have nothing on me—no guns, no drugs—so he had to let me go. This guy was so frustrated that he didn't make a collar, but he would just keep brutalizing me.

There was a morning I was going to school, maybe like 7:00 A.M. I came out my apartment. The second I closed my door, Messer came out of nowhere and jumped on me. He tackled me to the ground. He was possessed. After he dove on me, he searched me. He thought I had a gun or a knife, something. That's when I realized *Yo, this guy's really* thinking *about me.* I knew I had to be very, very careful.

The police used to roll into my projects early in the morning with this big-ass light like the Bat-Signal. At 3:00 A.M. they would shine it up to my house on the fifth floor.

"Jooooeeeeey," they would taunt me, yelling into their megaphones. "You fat muthafucka, you piece of shit. Come down. We're gonna catch you, you piece of shit. We're gonna get you, Joey." For an hour straight, the brightest light in the world would be beaming and the cops would be screaming while people were trying to sleep.

On this one morning in particular, it was the same drill: three in the morning. Bat-Signal shining through my window, Messer yelling on the megaphone, waking up my entire family and all my neighbors. But this time the message was a little different from the usual harassment.

"Joey come down to move your car. It's double-parked," Messer shouted.

I came downstairs to move the car, afraid they'd tow it. And that's when they locked me up. I didn't have a driver's license; I was only fourteen. I had managed to get myself a car, but wasn't old enough for a license. At that time, you would get seventy-two hours in the bullpen—a large holding cell for short-term stays—for driving with no license.

On another day, I got stopped by Messer and I was sure he had me. I was driving without a license *and* I had a gun on me. When the cops pull you over, they ask, "Yo, you have a license?" If you say no they take you out the car, they lock you up. But this time I had this beautiful girl with me. Anytime the cops saw me with a female, they made sure to go out their way disrespecting me and trying to humiliate me in front of my date.

"Oh shit! I'm gonna get locked up. I got a gun on me," I told her.

"Joey, give *me* the gun," she insisted.

I was like, "I can't give you the gun. That's not my style, to have you go to jail because of me."

Meanwhile, Messer comes to the driver's side window.

"You fat muthafucka! You piece of shit!"

Then he starts talking to the girl. "What are you doing with this fat muthafucka? Joey ain't shit!" Mind you, I'm in a brand-new car, I'm icy. I'm fifteen, getting money.

Messer was going so bad on me verbally, he forgot to search me.

"Muthafucka, get the fuck out of here!" he screamed. The *one time* Messer had me dead to rights, he forgot to search me because he was so focused on dissing me in front of the girl!

Messer tried to jam me up for years. And his ill will against me spread in the NYPD. One day, a young Latino officer who had worked under Messer decided he wanted to level the playing field. I walked into the lobby of my building in my projects and saw six cops in there. They're wearing their uniforms and were like, "Yo, Joe? What the fuck is up?"

The young cop steps up, he's like, "Yo, muthafucka, this is your lucky day." He has this real sinister grin on his face.

"So what's up?" I ask with reservation.

"I'm going to take off my badge, take off my gun," the young cop says. "I'm gonna fight you one-on-one. So it's not like I'm a cop. It's *me and you*."

I was *delighted*.

"Let's go, muthafucka! I've been waiting to bust your ass," I said. "But you're telling me I can fight you one-on-one and I ain't going to get locked up when it's done?"

I was in disbelief. Under normal circumstances, you know damn well a civilian cannot fight a cop. You're at least going to jail, but more likely, you're gonna get shot and killed. And mind you, in addition to this being a cop challenging a civilian, this was a grown man challenging a minor.

"He wants to fuck you up, Joey," another cop said, answering me. All the cops knew my name.

"Fuck *me* up?" I said defiantly. "I'll fuck *him up!*" I fell for it.

The other five cops backed up. The young cop took off his gun and badge as promised. I rushed him and grabbed him. I had the upper hand. I picked him up in the air to body slam him. All of a sudden, all the other cops jumped in. *Boom! Boom! Boom!* They started punching me in my face and kicking me. They beat the shit out of me in front of everybody in the lobby.

"You think you're fighting one-on-one, muthafucka?" the young cop howled. "You ain't getting no one-on-ones."

They beat the shit outta me. In the aftermath, the cops left laughing. I got on the elevator with a bloody lip and black eye. When I got into the house, I sat there thinking, *I just caught an ass-whupping for no fuckin' reason!*

This torment from the cops would go on for all my teenage years, and if anything it got even worse when I became an adult and started rappin' professionally.

FAST FORWARD: When I was around twenty-two years old, I opened up a sneaker store: Fat Joe's Halftime. I was always into being an entrepreneur and after I made some money from my debut single, "Flow Joe," I could try to do it legit. I took a few grand and opened up a store. I was just trying to make money so I would never have to go back to hustling. My store was right on E 149th Street and Third Avenue in the BX. One day a detective car pulled up in front of the store while I was standing inside.

"Who the fuck is that?" I said to the employees around me.

A Black cop comes out the car and walks into the store. He approached me.

"Fat Joe?" he asked.

"Yeah," I reluctantly responded.

"Somebody wants to see you," he continued.

I come outside the store, and who do I see sitting there in the squad car? Officer Messer.

Oh shit.

I hadn't seen this man in about a half a decade. Now he wasn't dressed like a patrolman. He had a white uniform on like one of them captains. He looked older, old as fuck actually, and he wouldn't look at me. Instead, he kept staring out the window past me as I stood on the pavement.

"Yo, Joe," he said, still gazing aimlessly. His tone initially had no emotion in it. "I hear you did good for yourself."

"Yeah, Messer," I responded.

"I heard you're a rapper now," he added.

Before I could say anything else, he started spazzin' like back in the day. He went on a tirade.

"Fuck you, you a piece of shit!" he started screaming. Now he was looking at me, aiming his words in my direction. "Fuck you! You need to go to jail, you piece of shit."

And then the guy who had been driving the car, the Black cop, ran back into the vehicle and peeled off.

That was the last time I saw Officer Messer. He lost his cool. He still hated me all those years later.

Although that would be the end of my and Messer's feud, the NYPD was still out to get me. Eventually, I would have to fight two separate murder cases that would have given me life in prison.

CHAPTER 7

MY BROTHER'S KEEPER

ANGEL CARTAGENA JR. My big brother. My first idol. Angel is the one who introduced me to hip-hop.

Angel would go to all the block parties and the park jams—Zulu Nation, Grandmaster Flash, DJ Kool Herc—and he would bring me back cassette recordings of the live parties. Angel used to MC too. I wanted to be like him. So that's really why I started to rap.

Angel always looked like he was in control, like he mastered whatever he wanted to do. He made everything he did in life look effortless, until I saw firsthand a struggle that would shatter everything for him and change our family's lives forever.

One night, it was about one in the morning and I was maybe ten years old. I was awakened by the sound of people outside yelling up to our window for my mother. "Ruby! Ruby! Ruby!" The voices were coming from the front of our building.

My mother looked down out the window to see what was going on.

"Angel!" they were yelling. "You've got to get Angel!"

My parents hurried downstairs and I got out of bed to see what was going on. Soon they came back into the apartment with a cluster of neighbors. My brother was with them. He was bugging. This was the first time I'd ever seen him or anybody on drugs. My parents put him in a bathtub and my moms gave him a bath. My mother had never dealt with this before either, but the neighbors were coaching her on what to do. Apparently, that was the first time Angel ever smoked *angel dust* aka PCP aka elephant tranquilizer. The water in the tub was freezing and they were giving him milk to drink. That night changed all of our lives. He would have issues with drugs for a long time, especially with that dust.

In addition to making me worry about my brother's health and well-being, his addiction embarrassed me. Kids, even when they are your friends, tease one another. In the hood, that usually meant getting teased for every visible tragedy in your life: deep poverty, missing parents, and, most of all, family members who were on drugs. I'm sure I used to tease other kids about all of that stuff, but it killed me when the homies got on me about my brother always being high.

We lived maybe twenty blocks from Yankee Stadium. At night you could see its lights; they illuminated the entire sky. One night me and my little crew were going to a game and we decided to take a back road. We were on foot. Our path took us down these back-alley stairs and at the bottom we could see someone holding on to a light pole, right there in the middle of nowhere. It was my brother. He wouldn't let go. None of us expected to see him there and my friends started laughing at him and snappin'. That shit really hurt my feelings and I ain't go to the game. Instead, I helped bring my brother back home.

Angel dust was genocidal poison before crack cocaine. It was fuckin' up the hood mentally. It gave the users a sense of invincibility. You had young teens high off that dust jumping off roofs. Angel dust is different from pure cocaine or crack or heroin. Unlike with crack or heroin, where the addicts chase that high daily, dust was so potent I never saw somebody get dusted every single day and survive it.

Every now and then, my brother would come home still high off dust. My mother would break down in tears. She was beyond stressed out.

I kept hearing my mother complaining about my brother using drugs until I couldn't take it no more.

I walked up to Boston Road where the adults who were selling my brother this junk were at. I'm talking they were twenty-eight, thirty years old. I couldn't have been no older than twelve. I had borrowed this .22 from a friend—it actually belonged to my friend's big brother and he loaned it to me on the low. I went up to Boston Road in front of Morris High School where the roundabout was. I was crying the whole way over there. When I saw the junk dealers I pulled out the gun on them with tears in my eyes.

"Everybody on the floor! I will kill y'all niggas," I said. I was such a little boy, my voice hadn't even changed with puberty yet. "If y'all ever sell my brother drugs again, I'm killing y'all niggas!"

They didn't even know me as "Joey," they knew me as "Lil Angel."

"Nah, nah, nah, Lil Angel. We won't never do it again," they insisted.

"I'm telling you. I'm gonna kill one of y'all niggas," I threatened again. "My moms crying, my moms suffering. Fuck that. I'm gonna kill one of y'all niggas."

Then I just left.

After that day, they told my brother, "We're not treating your little brother like a kid no more. He pulled a gun out on us. He might as well be a fuckin' adult. We will hurt that nigga."

I'm sure they kept selling to him. Angel would battle addiction for several more years. Miraculously though, he got the monkey off his back and shook drugs cold turkey when he was in his late teens. Angel cleaned up and started working on Wall Street after he graduated high school. He was so smart, and without the drugs to hamper him, my brother was shinin'. Angel was now wearing a suit every day. We were proud of him. He was working hard.

HIS TIME ON WALL STREET was very short though. Angel was best friends with this guy Danny from around the way who was getting a lot of money in the dope game. Danny was managing one of the biggest spots in the neighborhood. One day Danny asked Angel a very profound question about his Wall Street earnings.

"Why are you working downtown for $300 a week when you

can make $500 *a day* working with me?" Danny asked Angel. "All you have to do for me is stand out here and be a lookout."

Good question! The offer was too sweet for Angel to turn down. It just made great financial sense for him. Angel immediately came into the organization making really keen suggestions to better the business. The first thing he did was show Danny how to restructure customer traffic outside of the drug spot so the fiends lining up didn't attract as much attention.

Angel kept giving them these brilliant ideas and putting them on to how to get more and more money. He basically turned the corner block corporate. He had it moving like a fucking Target. The main bosses noticed how astute Angel was and promoted him to having his own spot in a different neighborhood. Angel went from getting a couple of dollars a day to pulling 40 percent of all profit. Angel recruited me as his number two. My main job was to hold him down. I was sixteen. Angel recognized that I had the muscle he needed to back him. By this time me and Tone Montana had branched off into doing our own thing. Me and Tone were still close as brothers, but we grew so large, he had his own crew and I had mine. My crew later merged with Angel's. I was second-in-command.

It got real sweet, real fast. For a while, we were *getting it*. Angel had the game—money, a fleet with every fly car you could think of, jewelry—and I was right there with him. We were getting money in a spot people had been getting money since the '60s. Nicky Barnes and Guy Fisher were oooooooone million percent getting money out there. It was a cesspool of smack.

We were working a ten-block radius and every block had a bunch of different dope spots. Dealers were getting their dope from a variety of plugs so even though everybody was pushing dope, the dope was all different. Dope was like any other product: It had to be marketed and promoted. It's like if muthafuckas were selling soda. On the block it was like some guys pushing Pepsi, some pushing Coke, some pushing Fanta, some pushing Malta.

I don't want to say the exact name of our brand—frankly, this shit is kinda terrifying for me to talk about. I've never talked about this shit before in my life. But let's say the drug was nicknamed "Cupid." There would be a heart stamp on the dope so the dope fiend would know the brand. He'd be like, "Who has the Cupid?" Or if the dope was named "Strong Arm," it would come with a stamp of a man with muscles. Throughout the area, there could be ten different stamps sold on one block. And the next block would have ten new stamps, and the next block would have ten more. That's how saturated it was out there.

But we were so strong, our block was the only block with one stamp. This is not me trying to convince you that we were tougher than everybody else. There's no argument. Nobody can debate this fact. No OG reading this book right now can say, "He's lyin'." Nobody else could come on our block and try to hustle. We owned it. Let your imagination run on what we did to hold it down. The point is: We were heavily respected.

We had a unique way of setting up shop. We took over an abandoned building and closed all the windows with concrete. All the doorways were closed with concrete. Every day we would break this one concrete wall to get in. It would take like thirty, forty minutes. Then we'd send in one of our crew. He'd have enough food and drink to last him the entire day.

Then we would lock our guy in with cement, except for a tiny hole we'd leave. He would sell through the peephole. "What do you want? Two bags? Okay. I got you. You want five bags? You want a bundle?"

Our spot was like Fort Knox. Nine times out of ten, the biggest risk for the guy going into the building was going hand-to-hand with a drug addict, but we'd eliminated that problem. Sometimes cops would try to bag us up, but it would take them the same thirty, forty minutes to break down the wall. By that time, our worker would have flushed the drugs and cleaned everything up. We had a fortress.

We kept our supply of drugs at the houses of friends of our

family. One of my father's best friends let us use his apartment as a stash house. He was a Cuban guy, a real civilian. He was never in the street life, never did any crimes. He lived two blocks away from our narcotics citadel and we'd pay him $5,000 a week to store our merchandise and some of the earnings. The real stash.

When our workers sold ten bundles, they ran out of work. So they'd take the $1,000 they earned from the ten bundles, go to my father's friend's house and re-up with him. My father had no idea this was going on. We had another stash spot at my friend's mother's house. We did the same thing with her for five grand a week. The hood never knew these people, never knew where our stash spots were.

A guy named George Calderón had his own territory in that same general zone. As much as we were respected, this guy was feared even more. People were terrified of Calderón. He was an old-school Puerto Rican gangster, in his thirties but he looked like he was close to fifty. He had this thick mustache that looked like Hitler's. Along with older cousin Angel "Cuson" Padillia, Calderón ran the C&C drug gang in the Bronx, one of the top organizations in the five boroughs. There were all these elaborate tales floating around town that Calderón was killing everyone—old people, babies, whoever. The first time I saw him, he was on the block like Don Corleone. It was broad daylight, he had like four soldiers with him, and they all had machine guns in their hands like a hit squad. They had no fear of police intervention.

Calderón used to charge hustlers rent for them to hustle on *their own* blocks, like he was the landlord. All the drug dealers in the neighborhood who were supposed to be real and all that, they were getting extorted. Ten thousand a week per dealer. Calderón never approached us. Again, I'm not saying we were tougher than everybody else, but he never approached us for money. We were coexisting for years without interacting.

One day though, in 1992, Calderón got into it with our guy Danny. Danny wasn't technically part of the crew but he was my brother's friend. He and Calderón had some type of dispute that ended up with Calderón taking Danny's Porsche. Calderón told him if he wanted his ride back, he had to bring $10,000 to Calderón's building.

Calderón operated out of a building where it was rumored he killed people and chopped up the bodies. It was like a slaughterhouse. Some people said he had a torture chamber in the basement. Crazy, scary stories used to come out that muthafucka. Danny was in trouble. So he came to us asking for help.

Angel wasn't really inclined to get violent. He was more cerebral. I was the one in charge of the muscle. And muscle was important. We were dealing with money and when people are making a lot of money, other people want it. They see a weakness and try to take advantage. I was in charge of preventing all of that.

I tried to explain to Angel that if we gave Calderón $10,000 for the Porsche, next thing you know he would be stepping to us to give him $10,000 a week for rent.

"I'm telling you, this is what it is," I tried to reason with Angel. "They set up homeboy to get to us. If we don't respond, next thing you know they're gonna try to make moves over here."

We had all the respect in the world, but in truth, nobody had really tested us before, especially not a villain like Calderón. Every Latin street guy was terrified of him because of the legendary horror stories I told you about earlier. My Spanish brothers didn't want to go at him because to them he was the boogeyman. So I recruited some Black guys from my projects to help us out. The Black guys from my hood wasn't aware of Calderón rep, so they didn't give a fuck. But I told them he didn't play around and to be prepared for an all-out battle. We were strapped, forty of us assembled looking like we were ready for war.

We go to Calderón's building to see him. As soon as I catch sight of him outside the building I'm in his face like, "Yo, where the fuck is the car?"

"Who is you?" he asked me.

"It don't matter who the fuck I am! Give me the Fuck-INNN' car!"

Calderón looked at my brother Angel, who was standing next to me. Calderón smiled at Angel and said, "We family."

My brother jumped between us and said, "Joe, calm down. Calm down. Please chill."

I didn't like that, but the situation relaxed a little. Calderón told us he didn't want no problems, he gave the car back and we left. I wanted to hurt him so bad that when he thought of us, the fear of God would always be in his heart. Letting him off so easy, I felt it was a mistake because I knew Calderón would retaliate. I felt he would try to kill us. I would bet any amount of money he was going to kill me. I got word he was looking for us, asking around "where these guys live?"

As fate would have it though, we never came across Calderón or his C&C gang after that. A few days after we stepped to him, he got killed in the Bronx, right by Yankee Stadium, in front of the parole building.

The only way to get to Calderón, when he didn't have his goons or wasn't packing a gun himself, was when he was coming out of court or the parole building. And that's just what happened: Somebody ran up on him coming out of the parole building and shot him dead. I had nothing to do with that. In 1994 when the Feds took down the remaining members of C&C, prosecutors said it was Cuson who put out the hit because Calderón was too brazen and making things hot for their organization. They killed his sister too. I always wondered what would have happened if Calderón did retaliate against us. I guess we were lucky. I'm sure it would have turned into something really big between his army and ours. It would have been a war where a lot of people would have gotten hurt.

Don't get me wrong, I was always with the shits, I never backed down from no one. I never even understood being scared of anybody. But as the saying goes: No one wins in a war. We avoided a war with Calderón, but what would happen the next time with someone else? What would happen if we had to battle with the police? The thing that stayed on my mind after Calderón's murder was this: It really didn't matter if Angel was right to de-escalate or if I was right that we should've hurt Calderón. Either way it would've meant war, and war meant more of everything that had haunted every day of my life: more looking over my shoulder, more hurting people and getting hurt, more cops, more jail, more death. I started to realize that at a certain point in the game, every path leads to the same place. I was getting a little older, I wasn't a kid anymore. In my late teenage years, my attention started to wane from hustlin'. I was fatiguing from the streets. I was disgusted by all the violence. I didn't want my people to get hurt; I didn't want to get hurt. And the truth is, I started to witness the possibilities of another, better life.

I had another set of childhood friends I was hangin' out with more and more. These friends were heavy in the streets too, not with drugs and guns, but music. They slowly started chippin' away at me, tryin' to get me to see that a life of being a dealer would only end with me in jail or dead. Then my guys started to blow up off rap. They showed me better than they could tell me that it was really possible.

Music started stealing my heart. Like I said, my brother Angel had introduced me to rap. I had dabbled in writing rhymes since I was around ten. I started getting better through the years but wasn't really serious. By the time I was around seventeen, eighteen, though, I got more serious. But I knew that life would mean a pay cut. I'll get to that story later, but suffice it to say, the transition from the streets to really going all in on music was bumpy.

EVEN AS I DRIFTED from the game, my brother and my friends were still in it, ballllllin'. Angel in particular always had plenty of money. *A lot* of money. I'm talking about a mill plus! One of the worst mistakes of Angel's life was not listening to me in regard to stashing his money with our aunt. Instead, he chose to trust a close childhood friend we knew all our lives to store his paper with. Around the time my first record came out, the cops initiated a sweep and wound up locking up the entire crew. They took everybody down. The cops and Feds confiscated all forty-seven of Angel's cars. I'm talking about Benzes, Corvettes, trucks. Angel owned literally *forty-seven* cars at one time.

The only person in the crew who didn't get knocked was big bro. Junior just so happened to be on vacation in Santo Domingo, and he stayed there while things in NY were hot. Eventually though, Angel needed bread. He had only taken enough cash with him for what was supposed to be a short trip. Angel started calling our friend like, "Yo, send me ten grand. Send me twenty grand."

Our so-called friend did send the money once or twice. But then he stopped responding.

Angel called me from Santo Domingo flustered. This was back in the day, before social media and smartphones. It was before 9/11 so, even though I didn't fly at that time, I can tell you: It was much easier to fly back then. You could get on a flight with fake paperwork. No computer databases or facial recognition or nothing like that. My brother was on the run, but he told me he was going to fly home to see what was up with his million plus.

"The nigga is ignoring me, Joey," he explained. "He's not sending that money."

Angel flew in and I picked him up at LaGuardia Airport. We went right to our friend's house in Queens, not too far from the airport. Our former homie was shocked to see both of us, but especially Angel. It was like he'd seen a ghost.

"Yo, what's up?" I asked our friend, angrily.

"Yo, nigga, I've been calling you. I was in Santo Domingo," Angel jumped in. "I ain't got no money. I'm starving."

Angel's first son, my nephew Junito, had just been born. Angel needed his money more than ever. Sure enough, our friend finally broke it down and came clean: He spent all the cash. This was biiiiiig money.

"What?!!!" Angel screamed.

"Yo, I ain't got the money," our former friend kept insisting. "I spent the money."

"You're fuckin' lying," Angel answered back, refusing to believe the truth. I didn't blame him. We would have never thought that somebody who grew up so close to us would steal everything. Not just skimming from the top, but the entire mother lode.

Angel's cars and jewelry had all been confiscated by the authorities. Now his money was gone. He had nothing. Me and Junior were so enraged, almost to the point of being homicidal. The fact that we did have a history with this guy and we knew his mother would be inconsolable saved him from death. We didn't kill him. We *had* to fuck him up though. A friend is supposed to be someone we could trust. We never forgave him for his treason. Never, never spoke to or saw him again.

That treachery took an irreversible toll on Angel. It shattered him. Junior was broke. You couple that with the pressure of being on the run from the police, and Angel spiraled into a deep depression. He started using drugs again. I can't tell you if it was heroin or crack, but it was definitely one of the two. My mother went back to that familiar suffering, sitting up every night looking out the window for him when he was out getting high. He fucked up his whole life. And, of course, the police caught up to him. He did five years in the pen. It broke my heart.

FAST FORWARD: When Angel came out five years later, he was great at first. He was sober; he was cock diesel, extremely fit. His attitude was refreshed. My career had skyrocketed and I had gone from being a struggling artist to becoming an executive, breaking my first artist, Big Pun. When he got home, I set Angel up with a fully furnished apartment and a brand-new Cadillac. A couple of months later though, he started using drugs again. He sold the car and all the furniture. He probably would have sold the apartment too if he could have.

In the back of my mind, I always thought maybe, just a little bit, he was having a tough time dealing with the reversal of roles, so to speak. Maybe it was difficult to come to terms with it, because he had always been the boss. He was the big brother, and now his little brother was shining brighter because he's a rapper. Angel'd had hip-hop dreams, too, when we were kids.

When you have family on drugs like that, it's perplexing. What do you do? Do you support them or cut them loose? Let them go out on their own, even if it means they'll live in the streets and be homeless? At first it seems obvious that the right thing to do is to support them, but after some time you start to wonder. I've got friends who have brothers who are addicts still living in their mother's house. The addicts stay getting high and the people around them try their best to ignore it, to let it go. Some people say that's the realest love. But after my experiences with Angel, I became a believer in tough love. Either you change or I can't fuck with you. I might still love you. But I can't fuck with you.

I tried everything in my power to help my brother. Just like I did when I was a kid, I found out where my brother was getting drugs from. I went to the spot and warned them not to sell to Angel anymore. I've cried with my brother for hours, begging him to change his life. I went to rehabilitation programs with him.

My brother has been arrested 10,000 times. The only reason my brother isn't in jail for 10,000 years is because every time he got arrested, even at times when I wasn't fuckin' with him, I would pay for his lawyer. There's a big difference between having a public defender and an actual paid attorney who can say to the judge, "This guy is *on* drugs. He's not *selling* drugs. He's an addict. Put him in rehab. Put him in a program."

Angel did a couple more bids, but he didn't do as much time as he could have given his rap sheet. A guy who has been arrested as much as him is supposed to be *under* the jail right now. He struggled with drugs and addiction for almost all of my career. But to this day, even with all our ups and downs, me and Angel are tight.

IN THE SUMMER OF 2016, one of my dreams came true. The City of New York finally let me perform a major show in the Bronx. I was living in Miami by now, but the Bronx is always home for me. I got booked for a concert at Crotona Park, right in the neighborhood where I grew up. It was right after the Fourth of July and my record with Remy Ma, "All the Way Up," was *scorching*. Literally one of the biggest records on the planet, my first Top 40 hit in almost ten years, and I was on top of the world. I had just landed in NY from Miami to do the show and was getting ready to leave the airport when my mother called. Angel was in Columbia Presbyterian hospital up in Washington Heights, she said. And he was "blind."

"Blind?" I asked her.

I was confused and to be honest, I didn't believe it, because my family exaggerates a lot. But I went straight to the hospital and up to the ward he was on. I walked into the room and got confused again. Instead of Junior, I saw a stranger sitting at the edge of the bed. He looked maaad skinny.

Oh shit, I thought after a beat passed. *That is Junior.*

He was half his normal size.

"Junior. What's up, man?"

His answer was sobering and surreal.

"Joey, where you at?" he said meekly.

He really was blind. That shit sucked the life out of me. I was there looking at my hero, the smartest guy in the game, who taught me everything. He was there, *broken.* I sat with him and I practically begged him to get out of New York, get away from the temptations and spots he knew. Get back with people who cared for him.

"June. Listen, you need to come down to Miami, you can stay in

Mommy's house," I began to plead. I had moved my mother down to Miami already. "You would be chillin' in a house, you could jump in the pool every day. They'll cook for you every day, they'll take care of you. Move to Miami and act like you're retired. Just come."

"Nah, Joe, I'ma just press my luck in the Bronx," he answered without even considering my offer.

It felt like he chose drugs over everything else. Drugs are addictive and addiction is a disease. I know this. But it's hard to shake the feeling that the addict in your life is being selfish, sacrificing family for the drug. It hurts. My brother broke my heart again that day. That shit destroyed me.

But the truth is that Angel and me made money *selling* drugs to addicts just like Angel—people who'd been turned upside down by their circumstances and disease and needed to escape. Just like Angel. This heartbreak I felt: It wasn't unique. It was all around us even when we were in the clubs popping bottles, the bills we tossed into the air came to us crumpled up in the fists of drug fiends who were breaking the hearts of everyone they loved. This is what it means to come from a place where people are both under tremendous stress *and* have easy access to cheap, crazily potent, and addictive drugs. We looked at that equation as kids and saw a chance to make money and take care of ourselves and the people we loved. We had impossible choices and were too young to know better but we jumped in with both feet. We thought we could be the ones who made the game work for us. But it destroyed my brother. And a million other brothers. And sisters. And mothers and fathers and sons and daughters and on and on and on. The disease, the violence, the incarceration: We didn't invent any of it. But it ripped us apart.

Back then, I didn't understand drug addiction being an "illness" or "disease." I thought it was a choice. I could've gotten high too, but I didn't. I could only see it as being selfish. You're hurting your mother, you're hurting your kids. And it was dumb, too. If you're trying to escape your problems through the drugs, so you get high, the truth is when you wake up, your problem is even worse. You're smoking crack and shooting heroin, now you lose your job, you lose your family, you ruin your health, you blow your money. I always looked at it as a losing situation.

So with Angel and me, it was always tough love. I knew I had a mission in life, I didn't know what it was. I didn't have time to be hands-on every day getting my brother off drugs. To help somebody who's addicted to drugs to get clean takes emotion, time, pain. And I have to admit I was mad, too. My brother is the one guy I looked up to as my hero in this world and I felt he let me down. To this day, when something goes wrong with my parents, all the pressure to make things right comes back to me. I feel like if my brother would have never done drugs, he would have been right by my side. He would have really been here with me, helping me run this music and entertainment business. To be honest, my brother is 100 times smarter than me. When he wasn't on drugs, Angel had all the traits of a great boss: business acumen, he was honest, generous, the connects loved him.

I believe in karma. Sometimes I ask myself if the misfortunes that have fallen to me, to my own son, to my family, if these are because of all the destruction I took a hand in? The pain I caused? My brother sold millions of dollars of drugs. I don't think it's a coincidence that he fell to the drugs. You see that constantly in the drug game. I don't think that if you made your empire off of selling drugs that you're gonna live the rest of your life being happy. That trauma, one way or another, is going to follow you. It's sad. All the guys I knew that made money off of drugs, even if they didn't go to jail, they had real tragic lives. You made your money off of people's pain. There's a price to that.

My mother was in the window almost twenty-four hours a day looking out, waiting for my brother to come home. That's a lot of pain. I know drugs can seem like a quick fix to get money: You can walk out your door and sell and be successful to a certain extent. But you don't think about the parents who stay up at night worried about their children. You don't think about parents who have two jobs, work all day and then again all night, and in the few hours they have left, they're sick with worry over their sons risking their lives in the street or their daughters selling themselves for drugs.

I didn't really start to analyze the drug game like this until about five years ago. I never looked at it from the standpoint of the families we drug dealers destroyed, even with my brother battling addiction. I looked at it like *yo, get your money. It's the weak or it's the strong.* Then one day I started thinking about people I knew—my brother and others—that were fucking geniuses, that fell to the drugs. I was like *yo, sometimes the strongest and best of us can be overpowered by addiction. The drugs are the problem, not the people.*

Think about the addiction DMX had. DMX was somebody the culture needed and loved. He was a fucking genius. He was charismatic, he had great heart, he was dedicated to the people and his art. But how many times did we see him fall to drugs, fight to get back, fall and fight to come back before he ultimately died? The cause of his death was an overdose. Sometimes that addiction is just way too strong.

Angel is fortunate he didn't meet his demise through narcotics. But he did lose his sight. My brother's blindness could have been the result of decades of abusing drugs, it could have been from diabetes. If Angel had not used drugs, on both ends of the transaction, he would have had an amazing life. And I probably would've had a better life, too. He was my mentor; he guided me.

At that point, I took over caring for Angel's son, Junito.

Junito, he's a special kid and I make sure he knows who his father was before Angel was on drugs. Angel was one of the illest. Junito takes a lot of pride in Angel being his father. He doesn't look at the flaws of my brother. He looks at him like a hero.

My brother is still in the Bronx. He gets major love when he walks the streets because he was really good to the neighborhood when he was on top. He used to really take care of people. When people from the old neighborhood come around Junito, they're like, "Yo, Money Man had shit on lock. Money Man was that nigga!"

Just like my brother thirty-plus years ago, Junito likes to rap too. He rhymes, but a couple of years ago, he asked me to get into *the other* family business. He wanted a job in one of my sneaker/clothing franchises, UP NYC. I have a few locations in New York and I'm actually moving from Miami to New Jersey so I can expand, open more stores in NYC, and become an empire. I want at least ten more franchises in the next couple of years.

"Unc, can I work in the store?" Junito asked me one day. It was a welcome surprise, because Junito's the type that don't bother you for nothin'.

"Sure, no problem," I told him. "Come on! Let's go." And I've been teaching him the business ever since.

I've been waiting his whole life to give my nephew a shot at something he wants to do. *I owe* my brother. But I can't give Angel any more shots. I would love to just give my brother some major bread. But every time I gave him anything, Angel would use it on drugs.

Junito works at the store, he does his thing, but I tell him I want him to be a boss and an owner. I want him to own franchises like I do.

"Learn everything," I insist to him. "I don't want to come see you in the Bronx. I want to see you in a fuckin' mansion in Jersey. I want to see you living good. You're not going to have no other situation like this. Your uncle's telling you, if you learn everything in this business, he's going to make you an owner."

My brother Angel is drug free now. He lives a very simple life in the Bronx. He's got a friend named Thor who takes care of him and has never asked me for a dollar. Angel and Thor's relationship makes me a true believer that there can actually be brotherhood and real friendship that isn't based on money, just love.

But that's today. Before I got to the music and the stores, and before my brother got to a place of peace, I needed to survive the game. And escape it.

CHAPTER 8

WHO SHOT YA?

"WE RUN THIS SHIT!" I felt like that every morning waking up. Me and my brother Angel *were* running shit, but it was more than that. It's one thing when you're out there hustling and making bread, but it's a whole next level of ecstasy when your *entire crew* is getting it. We had Beamers, Benzes, all types of sports cars and trucks. Angel drove an all-white convertible Mercedes. He had a white McLaren, piped out.

There was not one person on Earth who could tell me I was not untouchable. My rep was too strong, my team was legendary. But I would soon get a sobering reality check from the unlikeliest of muthafuckas.

There was a kid from my block named S. He was known as a punk. Major key, don't sleep on the little guy.

One time S asked me to borrow $10. Cool. I had *$10,000* in my pocket on any given day. We were in the heyday of getting big drug money. So I *lent* it to him. But my whole thing back then was: If you borrow money, no matter how little it is, you pay it back. That's the respectful thing to do.

So when I would see S, maybe every couple of weeks walking through the projects, I'd ask for the money. He'd never have it. He was taking a long time to pay me back that $10. Every time I saw him, it was almost like in the movie *A Bronx Tale*, where Calogero would chase the guy who owed him a couple of dollars. When the guy didn't pay Calogero back, Sonny told him, "Look at it this way, you got rid of him for $2," or whatever it was. That was a big jewel.

But I didn't realize that at the time. I wouldn't leave S alone about that $10.

"Yo, my nigga, where's my $10, B?" I would ask S as soon as we crossed paths.

S would always say he was going to get it to me and he didn't have it. I would give him a hard time. He was clearly humiliated by my constantly punking him over the debt but I didn't notice or care.

Months went by, and me and my team went to a park we called "184." It was by Junior High School 184 in the Bronx (coincidentally the neighborhood where Swizz Beatz grew up. Swizz is eight years younger than me, so he wasn't outside yet). It was the Fourth of July, all of my guys were out there, playing softball and barbecuing. Kids were running around, everyone was enjoying the day.

I drove my Beamer that day and stashed two guns under the passenger seat, so I could play ball comfortably. Plus I knew all my boys were holdin'.

Another lesson I learned that day was you can be untouchable anywhere with thirty or forty people with you. But if you dip off by yourself, no matter how strong your rep is, you're *alone*. At some point in the day I went around the corner to get a Diet Pepsi from the bodega. I walked in, bought the soda, and I came back out onto the sidewalk, a little glass bottle in hand. That's when I saw S. How did he know I was gonna be there? I don't know. Maybe he caught wind we were gonna play softball around there and was lying in wait. Anyway, S is in front of the store and wearing a black leather trench coat. It was *July 4th*, hot as fuck, at least 96 degrees, and S had on more leather than Kool Moe Dee. Immediate red flag, right? Arrogant Fat Joe just ignored it.

I looked at him, and he had a demented expression on his face, like the devil had his soul. Red flag numero dos. With all these signs staring me in the face, you would think my Spidey-Sense would have been ringing off crazily. But no, my bold ass approached him.

"Yo, my man, what the fuck you doing out here?" I said as I walked toward him. "Don't you owe me that $10, nigga? What you doing around here? You owe me that $10."

If I knew then what I know now, I would have been smarter. I would have seen the trench coat, I would have put two and two together and I would have gotten up out of there. But at the time, I'm thinking that I'm the toughest guy *in the world*.

S pulled a gun out, but even armed, he was still the softest guy I ever met in my life. I didn't even flinch. I wasn't scared. I was insulted. *How dare he?*

"Yo, nigga, what the fuck you gonna do with that, you bitch-ass nigga?" I scolded. "You crazy, nigga? You pull a gun out on *me?*"

I was talking reckless to him and I meant every word. Before he knew it, I took the bottle of Diet Pepsi and cracked him over his head. Hard. His forehead cracked open and blood was trickling. At that point, I would have had my way with him if I could have dived on him. But he had stumbled several steps back and was tooooo far away for me to make a quick move. The blood started flowing more intensely down his face, but he just looked at me with a real ominous smile.

It seemed like me hitting him gave him the fuel, the energy to do what he came to do. He cocked the gun, aimed at me, and shot. That's one of the two times in my life where shit actually turned into *The Matrix*. The world really slowed up. All I'm seeing is the gun going *Pow! Pow! Pow!* He was letting it go! I saw the shells dropping to the concrete in slow motion like it was a John Woo movie. That's when I finally took off running.

I'm a big muthafucka, but when it's time to haul ass, I can haul ass. I was always athletic. I was running straight and I came to a fork in the road. My car with the two guns in it and all my guys in the park were both to the left. So if I'd cut left and turned that corner, S wouldn't have been able to get me. I could've gotten to safety. But when I looked to the left, I saw a bunch of little kids playing skelly on the ground directly in the path of my escape.

Fuck! I thought.

I made the choice to keep running straight so the children wouldn't be in jeopardy.

Boom!

A bullet hit me in my back and came out my stomach. Maybe it was the adrenaline, but I didn't even break stride. Then *boom!* I got hit again, this time in my arm. I still managed to keep running. I could sense that S wanted to finish the job—he must have known he *had* to—and I didn't want to let him.

As I'm trying to get away from S, I got to a main street. I actually ran by my mother, who was in the middle of the street. Remember, this was Fourth of July and everybody was out enjoying the day. My mom was there with my oldest son, Joey, who was just a baby. My white tee had turned dark red, covered in blood. My mother and I made eye contact as I ran past her and my child. She looked scared to death. I was more hurt from her being in pain than I was from my gunshot wounds—I just kept running.

I finally got to my car. I opened the passenger side door. I was thinking S was gonna jump on top of the hood or something, air me out, and finish me. But he never got to me. I took the two guns from the seat and I got out.

"Yeah, nigga!" I started screaming, covered in red. I looked like DMX on the cover of his *Flesh of My Flesh, Blood of My Blood* album cover. I started getting woozy from losing blood. My legs were turning into spaghetti. My uncle Will had seen me running in the street at some point and followed me. He jumped into my car.

"Joey, give me the keys," he told me. I was reluctant because it was a brand-new car and I was bleeding so much. I told him I couldn't mess up my seats.

Uncle Willie finally convinced me to get in. He saved my life by driving me to Lincoln Hospital. I walked in on my own, no wheelchair, no EMTs. The nurses rushed up to me and they cut my clothes off right in front of everybody. I was stripped down. They put me on a gurney and wheeled me into a room and then gave me—I don't know the name of it. I think it was a "catheter." They put it up your dick. I was like, "What the fuck?" They put it *in your dick.* And then they put this thing up my nostril that felt like it cracked my nose bone. It felt one hundred times worse than a Covid-19 test. It went into my nose, down to the back of my throat. That was to check for internal bleeding.

I didn't think I was gonna *make it,* and as I'm fighting for my life, the police came up in there. The cops told me I was on borrowed time.

"Joey, you're dying," they tried to convince me as I lay in my hospital bed, almost fading into unconsciousness. "Do you know who shot you?"

"Nah, I ain't see him," I insisted, lying with a game face. Snitching was never in my DNA, even if they were right and I was about to die.

"Joey, once again. You're gonna die. Do you know who shot you?"

Next thing you know, they bring *the guy* in. They brought S into my room to be identified. Of course I knew who he was, but he was barely recognizable. He looked like the "Elephant Man."

Later on, I got the story. It wasn't my crew that lumped him up. He ran out of bullets and the *parents of the kids playing in the street* were so mad that he was out there shooting by the children that they beat him to a bloody pulp. This was on top of my having already hit him over the head. We didn't know at that time, but some undercover cops were watching us. So two undercover cops jumped on him by the time my boys showed up. The police ultimately saved him. But before the cops got to him, the moms and dads had beat the brakes off of him.

"I don't know him" was my only response when the cops brought him in front of me.

S folded though. He took a long pause and started crying, then he shouted his confession.

"I was the one. I did it! I did it!" he admitted. Then he started implicating me. "They're going to kill my mother! They're gonna kill my mother! Joey's gonna kill my mother!"

He went to jail for shooting me, but I never testified. I never even went to court.

My homie Tony Montana arrived at the hospital when they were rushing me to the operating room. I heard him screaming and weeping.

"Ahhhhh! Joeeeeeeyyyyyyy!" he was screeching and banging on the walls. I got goosebumps while they were taking me to surgery. I already knew Tone was going to tear shit up legendary in the streets behind this.

That's exactly what happened. Tone and our crew tore up the whole hood. They didn't let nobody sell not one piece of crack around the way in the hood. Anybody who ever hadn't liked me, they pounded them out. They robbed them, they extorted them. It was like my shooting gave them a free pass to go crazy in the Bronx.

As bad as it looked for me, I left the hospital that night. By the grace of God, I wasn't bleeding internally. I hadn't sustained life-threatening injuries. It was important for me to get out the hospital as soon as possible because there were already rumors going around that "Fat Joe is dead."

I was discharged, my arm was in a sling, almost like Scarface in the movie. The next day, I was in slippers and I was in the car, driving. I was cruising all around the Bronx pumping that Keith Sweat, "There's a right and a wrong way to loooooove sommmmmeboddaaaaayyyyy!"

I had to touch the hood and prove the talk of my demise was premature. I pulled up, jumped out the car with brazenness. I had sandals on, that's a big no-no. Walking with slides, that's never been big in my hood, because you never know when you've got to run because you've got beef.

People were dashing up to me like, "Yo, Joe!"

Drug dealers from different neighborhoods were showing me love. Regular neighbors were happy to see I was still here. What's unique about me is that people love me from different crews. And always the craziest ones from each crew. I don't know why they were attracted to me. I was out of the hospital just a day after getting shot multiple times. I was showing the whole Bronx I couldn't be killed.

FAST FORWARD: Just a few years later, I didn't feel nowhere near Superman. My brother Tone Montana was killed outside his house. I kept thinking, if Tony, the livest, the realest that God ever created, could die, then *anybody* could die out here. I was really contemplating my own mortality.

This was around the time a lot of our crew and a lot of dealers from different neighborhoods started getting locked up.

I had also just signed a record deal with Relativity for two albums and I really had things in perspective. I needed to get out of the life. I was focused on music. But I had one last loose end to tie up.

I chose to do so the day before my very first music video shoot, for the song "Flow Joe." Now usually the day before a video shoot, especially *your first ever video shoot* that's gonna change your life, you're picking out outfits. You should be going over last-minute preparation with the director, doing everything in your power to make sure the production is flawless. Me? I was going back to the trenches to settle the score.

Somebody told me that S was out of jail and was working at a twenty-four-hour crack spot in Hunts Point. And this is why God is so great and I believe in divine intervention. I went over there at midnight to retaliate. I drove the "stash car." A stash car, it's like a hooptie. It looks like your regular soccer mom car. It is very inconspicuous. But in the car, you can press buttons and compartments will open up like you're James Bond, 007. There were secret compartments in the air conditioner or in the radio. There were different places to hide guns and money and drugs. I was in the stash car and I was gonna shoot the person who shot me.

I waited all night outside like I was on a stakeout. I watched the building until about 4:30, 5:00 A.M. S never came out. Nobody came out. It was false information. I was so tired, I couldn't drive home. I lived in the Throgs Neck section of the Bronx, which was considered the nicest part of the borough. It was too far to drive. So for the first time in maybe eight years, I went to my mother's house to sleep because it was close by. I always kept my key. I wanted to get a little sleep before my big day, the video shoot.

I must have closed my eyes for about fifteen minutes before the police and Federal agents kicked in my mother's door around 6:00 A.M.

"We got him! We got him," they said as they put handcuffs on me.

The cops sat my mother and my sister on the couch. They were crying. As I was sitting in the living room with the cops berating me, I was just looking out the window. I could see the mural we put up for Tone Montana on the wall over on the handball court. It read, "In Memory of Tony."

Damn! I was thinking. *This is how it's gonna go down?* I was supposed to shoot "Flow Joe" at 9:00 A.M. The whole hood was waiting for the shoot. The Feds waited till the morning of my video to lock me up.

I didn't even know what I was in trouble for.

Then one of the officers came in with a photo in his hand and said, "Oh. It ain't him."

They were looking for my brother Angel. They had locked up a bunch of guys that morning, like twenty, thirty of my crew, including my uncle Dan, who books all my shows now. They confiscated the cars from my brother. They even tried to grab my chain, the one with the medallion that I would wear in the "Flow Joe" video.

One of the DTs came up to me and said, "Yo, what was you doing at Hunts Point all night long?"

I looked at him like *What???*

"Yeah. I was behind you. I followed you," he revealed. "We were watching you all night long."

I quickly fabricated a reason.

"The truth is, I was looking for my girlfriend. I heard she was cheating on me with a guy who lives there. But thank God it wasn't true," I explained. "Nothing happened. I came to my mom's crib."

God protected me. I was thinking I was going to go to jail instead of shooting "Flow Joe." I would have never become Fat Joe the rapper. To add to that, if S had walked out of the building, I would have shot him with the Feds watching me.

After they let me go, I went to Greenpoint, Brooklyn to shoot the video.

There's a scene in my video where you can see this infamous jacket my brother had that said "Money Man" on the back of it in graffiti. My brother couldn't be in the video because he was on the run. But my man Semi—God bless the dead, he's no longer with us—wore it instead. We put the jacket on Semi and covered his face with a hoodie so he, for a moment, looked liked Angel. But Angel was gone.

PART III

YOU GOTTA FLOW

CHAPTER 9

D.I.T.C. PART I

WHEN IT COMES TO THE STREETS, me and my brothers who are down with me in The Terror Squad did it all, from sticking up Mister Softee to warring with heroin battalions. Our syndicate's concrete accreditation is beyond reproach. But there's another part of my life that I haven't really mentioned yet. And when it comes to rap, my musical crew have reps that are just as impregnable in their fields of expertise as my boys in the streets.

Diggin' in the Crates got our name because that's exactly what we used to do. The founders were DJs and producers before they were rappers and our exploits in the studio became legendary. Lord Finesse, Diamond D, Showbiz & A.G., O.C., Buckwild, the late, great Big L. *And* Fat Joe. We're a clique of icons who made number-one hits, took dominion of the underground, and influenced generations of hip-hop.

It all starts with Robert Hall, better known as Lord Finesse. Finesse was from my projects, where he was the man you needed to know. When we were growing up, there was no Instagram, there was no social media. We actually got our news from *the newspaper*. Finesse was a ghetto entrepreneur who'd go to all the neighborhood stores and buy a bunch of newspapers for fifty cents each. He'd then go around the buildings and sell the same papers for a dollar to the people who didn't want to go to the store. He had the buildings on lock. He would go through the hallways and lobbies yelling out, "Paaayyy-purrr. Paaayyy-purrr." And my nosy mother would always be like, "Yo, buy the paper." My family would buy the *Daily News* every day like a lot of the families in the projects. And Finesse picked up the profit.

Finesse was a real nice guy. Everybody loved him, even my mom. Our drug crew loved him so much, we treated his paper route the same way we treated a block where we were pushing dope: No competition allowed. One time, somebody else tried to come into our building and sell papers and we ran the guy out. That was Finesse's turf.

Me and Lord became cool and we started hanging out. I'd go with him to his grandmother's house—she was a beautiful person but we didn't go there to hang out with Big Mama. We went because that's where he had his DJ setup. He would spin and he would rap and I'd watch and learn.

We were both mad young, like fourteen, fifteen, but I was in the streets already, getting money and wildin'. Finesse was my friend, but he wasn't in the streets like that. He was the paper guy. He always talked about wanting to become known as an MC, though.

We would spin records and he would tell me, "Yo, I'm gonna be a big rapper."

"Yeah riiight," I'd dismiss. I knew a lot of kids who loved to rap, but outside of my brush with Scorpio in the supermarket, I really didn't know anybody who started from our hood and became successful as a rapper.

As we got older, Finesse got deeper into rapping, DJing, and producing. Four or so years later, on February 6, 1990, Lord Finesse and DJ Mike Smooth released their first album, *Funky Technician,* on Wild Pitch/EMI Records. I remember being in my first apartment on Tinton Ave, listening to the radio one night, 98.7 Kiss, and DJ Red Alert starts playing mad Finesse joints. He played damn near all the songs off the album, and Red was the biggest hip-hop DJ in the world in 1990.

"Oh shit," I yelled out to no one. "This nigga made it."

Not just "made it," Finesse turned out to be theee best young rapper/producer in the game. The album was heralded a classic immediately and even hit the Billboard charts. Less than a decade after it came out, *The Source* magazine listed it as one of the top one hundred rap albums ever. Finesse and Jadakiss are the same type of MCs, punch line kings, but Finesse was Jadakiss before Jadakiss; top five dead or alive.

Sometimes you gotta see somebody else become successful before you can believe it could happen for you. Watching Finesse made me think for the first time that a career in music was actually possible. Even for me.

I was still in the streets while Finesse was blowing up, but around that same time I also reconnected with Diamond D, who produced the bulk of *Funky Technician*. Diamond was from our projects, too, and we had been friends since our graffiti days. We used to go bombing together. His tag name was "ZRock," mine was "Crack." Our connection was always deep. His name is even Joe— Joseph Kirkland. Diamond D changed my life for real.

Even before Finesse got on, Diamond and a guy named Master Rob formed a duo with the moniker "Ultimate Force." They were signed by pioneering DJ/producer Jazzy Jay. Jay is a Hall of Fame DJ. He was down with Zulu Nation so he came up under Afrika Bambaataa. He had a popular show on 98.7 Kiss in New York in the '80s and is one of the first DJs to really be a hip-hop ambassador, spreading the culture through the airwaves and on the ground. When anyone asks me who were the first big DJs in the culture, I say: Kool Herc, Afrika Bambaataa, Grandmaster Flash, Grandwizard Theodore, and Jazzy Jay. Jay's spot in hip-hop history is assured if only because he's the one who introduced Rick Rubin to Russell Simmons. Rick and Russ went on to build the Def Jam empire. T La Rock and Jay's "It's Yours" is the first release to ever have the Def Jam logo on it.

Ultimate Force recorded their album, *I'm Not Playin'*, for Jay between 1988 and 1989. They featured me on two songs, "Oh, Shit" and "C'mon." It was my first time rapping on a real album, but I didn't get too excited because the project never came out. They did release the title track to the underground and it remains one of the most amazing beats I have ever heard in my life.

Even though Ultimate Force didn't take off, Diamond kept active. He got rocking underground then got a deal with a major label, Mercury/PolyGram. He wanted to bring me with him.

"Yo, Joe man, you gotta change your life," Diamond told me. This was in 1991, right before he started recording his classic album *Stunts, Blunts & Hip Hop.*

Finesse and Diamond weren't into hustling. They would see me coming through with big chains on, custom-made Dapper Dan suits, fly whips, and instead of giving me props they told me I was in danger. It wasn't just that they thought I had real talent. As friends, they genuinely feared for my life.

"Joe, you're gonna go to jail or die," Diamond would tell me.

I'll never forget: I was standing in the same park in my projects under the same light pole where years later DJ Premier would meet up with me to drop off the remix for my song "Shit Is Real." Diamond found me there and offered to pay for studio time for me to go in and record some music.

"I know you love hip-hop," he began. "Come to the studio. Use the music to tell your story. I'll do the beats. You're gonna die out here, Joe. I'm telling you. Just tell your story *in the music.*"

We went to Jazzy Jay's studio in the Bronx to record a demo. My style was built around everything Diamond encouraged me to rap about, my own authentic street narratives. I was raw and unapologetically Joe, a hallmark—for better or for worse—that I would keep my entire career. I didn't know how to be anything but me. I still don't. Me and Diamond did three songs for a demo. Then we recorded a fourth: "Flow Joe." We had made the beat together in Diamond's kitchen at 1020 Trinity Ave, right across the street from my parents' place. When we finished the track, I yelled out, "Oh my God." I couldn't wait to rhyme on it. The horns, right from the start, gave me goosebumps. The energy was sinister but regal. It was the perfect soundtrack for my theme, which was my life.

Diamond's got his own swag. He was in the studio diddy boppin' to the beat while I laid down the rhymes. Jay wasn't in the studio that day—it was just me, Diamond, and his man Wiz One. The original version of "Flow Joe" has no punches on it. Punches are edits you can do on a song while you're rapping so you can take a breath. When you're rapping on a track, sometimes you need to stop to catch your breath, especially if you're delivering an intricate flow. So you record a few lines, then stop to collect yourself. Sometimes you breathe, sometimes if you're rapping and composing the song in your head, you stop and think of the next line or lines. Then the recording starts again: a few more lines, then stop. That's called "punching in" your lines.

It's the engineer's job to edit it all together so it sounds seamless on the finished product. When we did "Flow Joe," I didn't know shit about punches. I rapped my verse all the way through to the chorus. And the chorus was just me and four or five guys chanting the hook: "You gotta flow, Joe / You gotta flow, Joe!"

One of those guys in the studio with us, Armageddon, signed to Terror Squad—the label, not the street crew—as an artist years later. Arme was just a kid at the time. I met him because he lived right on Gun Hill Road around the corner from the studio.

As depleted as our hood was of most resources, it was really bountiful with talent. I was surrounded by hungry, creative artists everywhere I looked. They all wanted an outlet. Armageddon was younger than me by a few years, but he loved music and was determined to get on too. He'd be hangin' out by the lab.

Jay's studio was the foundation in the early '90s. Me, Diamond, and Finesse all recorded there as well as people like Grand Puba and A Tribe Called Quest. When you walked into the studio, there was a huge wall of signatures or tags from everybody who worked there. Everybody you could think of had their name up there.

With "Flow Joe" finished, Diamond shopped my demo but didn't have any success getting me a record deal. Everybody turned him down. Labels couldn't see the vision. There really weren't Latino rappers yet. Cypress Hill wouldn't be debuting for another year or two. Kid Frost was out, he had love in the hood, but little mainstream success. Here I was, a Latino kid in his early twenties, kicking gangsta shit. Labels didn't know what to do with me. But Diamond never stopped trying to help me out.

At the same time he was trying to get me my situation, Diamond was crafting *Stunts, Blunts & Hip Hop* with his crew, The Psychotic Neurotics. I'm on every single ad-lib on the project. Throughout the album you may hear a guy go, "What the fuck you talking about?" or "Yo, that's that shit." That's me! Diamond shouted me out on the very first single, "Best Kept Secret," and he let me close out the album.

The very last track on the album is an interlude called "A View from the Underground." I got on there and talked my shit.

"Ah yeah. This is Joe the fat gangsta," I said. "And I'm tired of these muthafuckin' bullshit rappers gettin' dope deals and all that. Well, they can just suck my dick, you know what I'm sayin'? Huh. To hell with them."

I was excited that one of my great friends was putting out a project, I was excited to have my voice on wax that was hitting the marketplace. At the same time, I was eager to let the world hear my rhymes on my own album. I was frustrated that a lot of those cookie-dough-soft rappers pretending to be gangsters were getting deals by lying in their raps. I thought most of them kickin' that street lore were frontin'. I was spittin' the real and I was getting fronted on by the labels. Diamond was grooming me and transitioning me though, trying to let people know: "Fat Joe is coming."

D.I.T.C. were friends of mine who showed me an alternative to street hustling. I think because we were so cool and because I'm from the neighborhood, I became an honorary member. "Joey's a

real nigga, he's from our hood. Fuck that, we're puttin' him down."
But I was still just a drug dealer running with a bunch of MCs.

When you went to a Lord Finesse show, I was the Puerto Rican cat with them with the Dapper Dan shit on and gold Cuban links around my neck. I'd go to a Diamond D show and make a movie. I'd pull up in a convertible Benz outside and start fights. People in the industry would see me and think that I was just a drug dealer from the block who rolled with Diamond. They looked at me like I was his muscle holding him down, similar to how Eric B. & Rakim rolled. When Eric B. & Rakim were blowing up as the biggest rap group in the country, they had a strong street figure named Puerto Rican Supreme Magnetic rolling with them. Supreme Magnetic had a very heavy name in New York. Him and his Puerto Rican guys was out there from Fort Greene with big rope chains and fly shit on. You knew they were the ones who held Eric and Ra down. You needed muscle in the rap game, too.

As I was getting deeper into the rap's underground, I found myself comparing it to the dope game. In the game, I was mentally exhausted from waking up every day worrying about going to jail or getting killed, having to be on edge. D.I.T.C. didn't have to live like that—and one by one they were taking on the industry. Finesse got put on, Diamond got put on, then Show & A.G. had gotten on. They were making hits and living good. I was happy for all my brothers, but I was in the streets still hustling. It really was clear as day: My friends in the streets began to go down, my friends in the industry began to prosper. I wanted to explore this music thing. I knew I could do it.

I knew I had to shoot my shot, and not with a firearm—it was one thing to be known in the hood as a nice rapper, but I needed more people to know me as an MC, beyond the BX. I found my first big exposure outside of my own hood in New York at the world-famous Apollo theater. They were starting a new season of their amateur night and were gearing that classic showcase more toward hip-hop.

Before the early '90s, traditionally, *Amateur Night at the Apollo* was more like an R&B and jazz type of thing. *Amateur Night* was launched back in 1934; Ella Fitzgerald was a winner that year. Over the decades, artists like Sarah Vaughan, Marvin Gaye, James Brown, D'Angelo, and Lauryn Hill were all discovered at the Apollo's *Amateur Night*. Michael Jackson used to hire Hollywood makeup and special FX people to make disguises for him, just so he could go and enjoy *Amateur Night* anonymously, as one of the crowd.

If you've never been to the Apollo in person when they do *Amateur Night,* or seen it on television, here's how it goes: You come out to perform your song or talent and will get your ass booed off the stage if you don't win the audience over immediately. I knew this because *I* used to go to the Apollo *Amateur Night* and boo people off the stage. Other times I would throw money at people on the stage while they were performing to show my appreciation.

Back then, I went to the shows as a fan. I was coming into my own as a big boy so I would roll up in a Beamer or a fly truck or a Benz. Everybody knew me as a money-getter, not as an aspiring artist. But this time I would be attending in a much humbler position: a first-time amateur performer. And let's be real, the elephant in the room was that Fat Joe was a Latino kid in *Black* Harlem. There really weren't no Latinos going up to the Apollo rappin' at the time. I told my hood delegates I was going up the Apollo to try out and they were lookin' at me like a crazy. I'm talking from Harlem to the Bronx—the feedback was unanimous.

"Yo, bro, you're making money. You're clickin'. The fuck you talkin' about 'rappin'?" everybody asked.

The talk didn't get me off my square though. Once I decided, I never second-guessed myself. I committed to music. I was determined to go to the Apollo and wreck the stage. I went to the tryouts and there were like 150 people there, groups and solo artists. I walked in and looked at everybody like *I don't even know why y'all are here. I'm gonna win.*

Now, this is a major key. Anybody you study historically, whether it's in business, in entertainment or sports or whatever, the big winners have that killer mentality. I believed in myself at the Apollo. Realistically you would never have thought that a fat Puerto Rican kid could look at everyone in the Apollo that day and think, *None of the competition stands a chance.* I wasn't even that good at that time; I was still developing as an MC, learning my wordplay and how to make hit songs. But still, truthfully speaking, they had no chance. I killed it at the tryout and got my chance to compete on *Amateur Night*.

My brother Angel bought a bunch of tickets so our whole hood could come out. The entire D.I.T.C. crew was in the crowd, even Kid Capri, who became the biggest DJ in hip-hop through his mixtapes and by spinning at all the clubs, was in there.

I wore a yellow-and-white Dapper Dan suit. I had three female background singers from my projects. They were there to sing my song's refrain: "He's a big shot. Fat Joe is a biiiig shot." When I think about it, it's weird, because I don't think the people in the crowd even heard a lyric of mine. When I stepped out onstage, the people just started screaming. The roar of the crowd drowned me out. They loved it. I won that night and went back and won first place four weeks in a row.

After the fourth time, they retired me. This was like 1991 going into '92. Red Alert came up to me my last time at the Apollo and that's when I met him for the first time. He asked me if I could make a promo jingle for his radio show. I went to the studio and recorded a specialized version of "Flow Joe" for Red—but my demo of the song still hadn't been picked up by a label.

Around the same time, I was at the Fever, a hot night club, one night and ran into Ralph McDaniels, the co-creator and one of the hosts of *Video Music Box,* a legendary show on New York public television. *Video Music Box* was the Holy Grail of hip-hop culture music video shows. It started in 1983 and was the very first show dedicated to the rap and R&B music videos in New York. This show set the blueprint for programs that would become television staples several years later, such as *Video Soul, Yo! MTV Raps, Rap City, Total Request Live,* and *106 & Park.*

Ralph and his partner, Lionel C. Martin, gave an outlet to our culture when no one else would. Before the mainstream even had a grasp of how important hip-hop was, "Uncle Ralph" was in the trenches bringing our stories to the forefront. He'd go wherever the artists were—the projects, the park, a club—and interview your favorite rapper. He brought R&B singers on too. He'd play all the new videos for our culture. I'd be writing a whole new book if I took time to talk about all the artists they broke.

The show used to come on around 3:30 P.M. in New York City and air on a UHF channel. This is before everybody had digital cable. We all had antennas on our television sets. UHF was like bootleg station, it wasn't on as high a frequency as the main stations in New York: ABC, NBC, and CBS. So if you had the fucked-up antenna, you would put aluminum foil around it or stick a wire hanger in it to get better reception while watching UHF. You made sure that muthafucka was working and crisp when *Video Music Box* came on.

Wasn't no "On Demand" back then. So after school, you'd rush home to see *Video Music Box* because you didn't want to be the corny one who missed the new Big Daddy Kane or Heavy D video.

Everybody who loved hip-hop loved *Video Music Box.*

Ralph and Lionel also parlayed the popularity of their outlet into producing and directing videos for artists themselves. Lionel became a legendary director, shooting joints for Bell Biv DeVoe, Boyz II Men, New Edition, TLC, Whitney Houston, Usher, and on and on.

When I ran into Ralph at the Fever, he already knew me from the streets but now he had heard that I was startin' to rap. So he asked to hear some rhymes right there in the club. I kicked a few of the bars from "Flow Joe" on the spot, rapping directly into his ear (damn, I really got the most out of that song, right?). I don't think even Ralph, who had seen it all, had ever seen a fly, young, fat Latino kid who had money and rapped.

Ralph took a liking to me, thank God, and invited me to come on the show, as a host. I was just five minutes out the drug game, so I was sitting on paper and of course my wardrobe was immaculate. I'd be hosting on-air dipped fresh with Dapper Dan on, sporting Cuban linx and medallions. I would get outfits from this store called Vamps on the east side of Harlem. They had these sets with the ill colorways. I'd have on Vamp suits with an orange suede shirt with purple sleeves. I'd be on UHF television just stuntin'.

The whole world was tuned in to *Video Music Box* and people would be like, "Who is that Spanish kid hosting with Uncle Ralph? They got *a drug dealer* doing the fuckin' hostin'?"

Viewers may have seen me as a drug dealer, but when I was on there introducing videos and interviewing rappers like Big L, I felt like I was among my peers. The show played a big part early on in building my rep as a personality, and allowed people beyond hustlers and underground rappers to know who I was—around the whole tri-state area. It's ironic that my first consistent foray into the music business was as a TV show host. But that's what I did until my music career started taking off.

A couple of months after giving Red the promo jingle, I was lying on my mother's couch suffering from the flu. I'm like a baby when I get sick so I'd gone to my mom's house so she could take care of me. As I was lying there, listening to the radio, suddenly I heard my jingle on Red Alert's show. It was the first time I'd thought about the song since all those weeks ago at the Fever. But now it was on the radio! I jumped so high, I might have hit the ceiling.

I put my speaker on the windowsill so the entire Forest projects could hear the song.

"Yo! This is my shit! This is my shit! They're playing it on the radio," I screamed out.

Everybody started losing it in front of the building. The jingle was so popular, Red played it every Friday and Saturday for months.

One afternoon, I was out in the projects, just out there with my crew. I was icy, standing there bossed up, when a car pulled up. A young Black man dressed in XYZ got out and asked me, "Yo, you Fat Joe?"

He didn't know me, but I knew him: It was Chris Lighty. Chris was heavy in the music industry. He got his start working for Red Alert and then went to work for Russell Simmons and Lyor Cohen at Rush Management. He was down with Boogie Down Productions and the Zulu Nation. I had seen him put in work with my own eyes. He was thorough in the streets but he was also the new hot record exec.

Chris told me he had an imprint label with Relativity Records and he wanted to sign me to a record deal.

"A record label?" I asked.

"Yeah," he said. "I have a label and I want to give you a deal. I want to make you a rapper."

He actually brought a contract with him, and I didn't think twice. I put the paper on a car, flattened it out, and signed it on the spot. It was finally my time. The Apollo, *Video Music Box*, Red Alert's show, everything had built up to that moment. A million labels fronted, but all it took was one record company to take a chance on me. I was so excited because I knew this was it. I didn't go see a lawyer or anything. I just signed right there. I didn't know shit about contracts either. I was choosing life.

My celebration was short-lived. I was exultant for maybe an hour, if that. The first person I wanted to tell about my dream coming true was my mother. When I went to see her, she had other news: She had just been diagnosed with cancer.

A few weeks after I signed, I got a $50,000 advance from Relativity. I couldn't believe it. I was running around the projects showing everybody the check I got. Even though we had money, it was like *This is a legit check. I just made* a legit *fifty grand, from my talent.*

It was proof to myself that I could make big money honestly, without doing crime or risking my life. It was also vindication after all those labels turned me down. It showed me that my way was the right way. I could make my art without compromise. I could be unapologetically Joe on the mic and make an impact.

I STARTED RECORDING my first album in 1992 and it came out on July 27, 1993. I released *Represent* under the moniker "Fat Joe da Gangsta." We did the cover shoot for the album packaging right in my neighborhood. You can see the building where I grew up, 1000 Trinity Ave, in the background. Then we had to shoot a video for the lead single, "Flow Joe."

As I've already recounted, a lot of my friends from the street got arrested on drug trafficking and conspiracy charges just a few days before we shot the video; my brother was on the run from the Feds; and when the police busted in my mother's door looking for him they almost arrested me in the confusion—a few hours before we were supposed to start production.

But once the video started, it was all love. I was blown away. The hood came out and my brothers from the music industry showed up for cameos too. That meant a lot for the young Puerto Rican kid coming out for the first time.

Diamond D, who already had a classic album under his belt, is in the video. Lord Finesse, who had a classic album under his belt, is in the video. Grand Puba, one of the biggest rappers in the game after Brand Nubian's album *One for All* and his solo joint *Reel to Reel,* is in the video. Puba was pioneering the hip-hop guest feature at the time—his performance on Mary J. Blige's "What's the 411?" was already iconic. He was the hottest, most sought-after rapper to collaborate when my joint dropped. People wanted Grand Puba on their song the way they want Drake now or wanted Lil Wayne when he was on every hit in the late 2000s.

Greg Nice from Nice & Smooth flew all the way back to New

York from L.A. on an off day of touring just to be in the "Flow Joe" video.

Nice & Smooth were a major group at the time, and two people who paved the way for me. Greg Nice and Smooth B are from the Bronx. I met them through Showbiz and we clicked. Before I blew up, they used to take me to their shows. In '89, they dropped their dope self-titled debut, which included "Funky for You," the party anthem that broke them out. But in 1991, they exploded to the next level with the *Ain't a Damn Thing Changed* album. They had some big, classic songs on there: "How to Flow," "Hip Hop Junkies"—those were monsters.

When you look back at the level of artists making cameos on and co-signing my first video, it's pretty wild. They helped make the single and video a big deal. Not only was the song ill, it was the first time anyone had seen a Latin kid with a half-moon part, iced out, talking that shit.

We brought in the same caliber of collaborators for the album. On *Represent* we built in guest appearances from artists like Puba and Kool G Rap, who was already a legend. The Beatnuts, Chilly Dee, and of course my D.I.T.C. brothers Showbiz, Lord Finesse, and Diamond D all produced.

I had taken Diamond D's advice and transitioned all the way out the game. He and Diggin' in the Crates made sure that everyone knew: It wasn't no more "Fat Joe is coming." It was now "Fat Joe is here." I was proud that I could make Diamond D proud.

"Flow Joe" started ringing off and soon I was booked for my first show ever. The Fever. Before the show, we were hanging out on 166th and Tinton, which was only about a ten-minute drive from the Fever. I was so nervous, I was taking my time.

"You think people are going to show up?" I asked my guys as we stood outside. Everybody was confident the club would be filled out. They assured me I was hot in the streets and would feel the love.

I just didn't know, so I sent a spy over to the club to see what the turnout was looking like. He came back thirty minutes later.

"Yo, nigga, that shit is jam-packed," he told me. "That shit is crowded."

It was like the weight of the world was off my shoulders. I got confirmation that people were really fuckin' with me, to the point they would go somewhere and pay just to see me.

I pulled up to the Fever and discovered it was a sold-out show. The line to get in was still long, wrapped around the block going in two directions like the line for a roller coaster at Six Flags. The people toward the middle of the line and the back, they had no chance of getting in.

I jumped out the car and everybody was like, "Yo Joe, yo Joe!" Every dude I knew from everywhere in the Bronx was there. For all of my usual cockiness, the truth is I was just starting out and feeling vulnerable. But that was one of the most amazing nights of my life.

MY CELEBRITY STARTED to grow little by little after that. People started going crazy for me. But I never thought that the fans I started to gain would cost me the friends I'd known and loved my entire life.

In October, "Flow Joe" went to number one on Billboard's Hot Rap Singles chart. Relativity set up an entire promo tour for the song and my debut album. L.A. was the first date. From there I had an itinerary to travel the country and do interviews at local radio stations.

When I got to L.A., I did radio in the early morning and got a call a couple of hours later from DJ Stretch Armstrong. Stretch and his partner, Bobbito Garcia, hosted a groundbreaking underground radio show that came on late-night on New York radio—it originated at WKCR, a college radio station, then moved to Hot 97. It was raw, you could go up there and freestyle unfiltered without worrying about your curse words getting censored. They played dirty versions of songs on-air too. It was a breeding ground for MCs who were going to be *the shit*, like the D.I.T.C. crew, Wu-Tang Clan, Nas, and later Big Pun.

Stretch was in L.A. DJing at *The Arsenio Hall Show,* and he invited me to come through to attend that day's taping as his guest.

Arsenio Hall had the coolest, most-watched show at the time. His show was the first to consistently spotlight hip-hop on late-night television. Arsenio catered to the young, the fly, the revolutionary. He repped Black culture as a whole, but even Arsenio will tell you, it was hip-hop that blew his show up. He was smart enough to be the first late-night host to feature us, when hip-hop wasn't on the radar of hosts like David Letterman or Johnny Carson.

So me and my guys get tickets to go to the show and sit in the audience. Arsenio comes onstage and does his opening monologue. I'm just chillin' in the crowd as a fan, and all of a sudden Stretch drops the beat for "Flow Joe."

"I see my main man Fat Joe in the house tonight," Arsenio then says.

I'm sitting there like *Whuuuuutttttt! Is this real?*

"Yo, Fat Joe, come through, bust some lyrics. You know you got that number-one song," Arsenio continues.

I don't even remember what I did. It was like an out-of-body experience. I remember coming down from out the crowd and walking onstage. After that, I couldn't tell you what happened.

I was filled with such unbridled joy after performing on *Arsenio,* I cancelled the entire promo tour. I wouldn't advise any artist reading this to follow in my footsteps, but I was so excited. I just wanted to go home and celebrate with my crew.

I left for New York the very next day and got to the city as soon as I could. I was scared to fly back then, so we drove across the country—it took days, but I was hyped the whole time. When we hit the city I rushed back to where I used to hang out, 166th and

Tinton. My friends were out there, Terror Squad guys I'd been tight with since babies. It was love.

I pulled up and jumped out the cab. I walked across the street with my hands in the sky yelling, "Yooooo! Yoooooo!" I was gleeful.

Out of the eight guys, four of them were ecstatic to see me and started jumping up and down. But the other four, they had scrunched up faces. That was the first time in my life I experienced what I later coined "Jealous Ones Envy" syndrome. That moment right there gave me the framework for my second album.

These were people that I had fought with side-by-side in street brawls, people I'd gone to war with, but when I met their eyes I saw resentment. They couldn't even hide it. These were guys I trusted the most, guys I loved the most. I had traveled cross-country in a car because I wanted to celebrate the biggest moment in my career *with them*. But half of them weren't just not happy for me, they actually looked mad. I couldn't believe it, because I loved them and I would have done anything in the world for them. It hurt me to my core. That was a whole new day for me. I realized shit had changed and muthafuckas was hatin'. It was another sobering life lesson. It reminded me that betrayal is always lurking. I really thought that it would be different. I thought that with age and maturity I would have been able to choose better friends who would reciprocate the loyalty I conveyed to them. I was wrong.

CHAPTER 10

D.I.T.C. PART II

"FLOW JOE" went to number one, but if you listen to it now, the truth is I really wasn't that nice. Go ahead, put it on. The raps are very basic: "Bust it, check it. / Watch how I wreck it." It wasn't lyrical. It got over on the fact that people could sense in my voice and delivery that I was a real dude. And I got some credibility because I was affiliated with Diggin' in the Crates. But I knew I had a long way to go before I could sit at the table with my contemporaries as far as the craft and poetry of songwriting goes. And my contemporaries were in the process of revolutionizing the art form.

I remember picking up Showbiz in the Beamer one day, this was early 1994. He got in and excitedly put a disc in the car's cassette player. "Yo, you got to hear this!"

He had gotten his hands on an advance copy of *Illmatic* by Nas. I was transported. It felt like when I first heard Rakim, who had reshaped the art of MCing when he and Eric B. dropped the single "Eric B. Is President" in '86, and the album *Paid in Full* the next year.

Rakim's flow was incredible, slow and methodical. He spit the hardest rhymes ever, but he never cursed. He looked liked a stone-cold gangster, but Ra carried himself in a pristine, divine manner. When people started calling him "The God MC" it made perfect sense. Rakim wore a million heavy gold chains, had on the flyest Gucci. He was a don, but he was about upliftment and knowledge of self and he conveyed his messages with clever language and bone-chilling poise.

In 1994, I knew Nas was about to change how rappers rapped again. Nas's wordplay was on another level from everybody else when he debuted. Nas was saying shit like "Sneak a uzi on the island in my army jacket linin'... / like the Afrocentric Asian, half man, half amazin'."

Illmatic is one of the most incredible albums in the history of rap music. I felt that off rip. The first time I heard it, I knew it was a game-changing classic. But it was scary. It was scary because I was also thinking, "Yo, this nigga just set the bar." He was so nice. I must have listened to that album a million times, and got inspired to step up my game lyrically. Then, I heard Jay-Z, with a song called "In My Lifetime." This was a single he released before his debut album, *Reasonable Doubt*. Jay matched Nas's lyrical skill, but while Nas was rapping like a poet, Jay was talking more like me, about hustlin' in the streets, being a gangsta, gettin' money.

Oh shit! We could do that, I thought.

But to get there, I had to step my lyrics up another level. Anybody who kept rapping like I was on "Flow Joe," they were out the game or headed out. And that's the mind frame I had going into my second album, *Jealous One's Envy*. I worked hard on adding layers to the basic style I'd had on my first album, switching up rhythms and rhyme cadences:

> *Hustlin' is the key to success.*
> *Money is the key to sex.*
> *The life is gettin' cash, drinkin' Mo', gettin' blessed.*
> *The games people play.*
> *The names people slay.*
> *It's just another ordinary day.*

While I was working at Chung King Studios on *Jealous One's Envy* in 1995, the legendary production team of Tone and Poke, the Trackmasters, walked in. Tone and Poke first gained notoriety as producers while working with Chubb Rock in the early '90s. They produced "Ill Street Blues," a classic drug-game joint, for Kool G Rap, too. But they really broke the door down for themselves in '94, producing "Be Happy" for Mary J. Blige, and Soul for Real's "Candy Rain." Poke worked with Puff Daddy on Biggie's *Ready to Die,* getting production credit on the first single, "Juicy." He also co-produced one of my favorite B.I.G. gutter records, "Who Shot Ya."

Ironically, when I saw them in the studio that night, they were working on a track called "I Shot Ya," by LL Cool J. LL had recruited Trackmasters to produce most of the album he was working on at the time, *Mr. Smith.*

"Let us hear some shit," they asked me.

So I played some of the album-in-progress for them and they were like, "Yoooo! Shit, man, you stepped your shit up crazy. Oh my God. We're doing this posse cut with LL, you should get on it." They gave me the beat to "I Shot Ya," right there on the spot. The track was also going to feature Foxy Brown, Keith Murray, and Prodigy from Mobb Deep.

Along with KRS, LL Cool J is my absolute idol as an MC, but while KRS was often the people's favorite, LL was a bona fide superstar. It was a big moment for me and I couldn't wait to do it. But I had to confer with my team first.

Back in them days, crews had to meet with one another before they worked with outside people. So I convened with D.I.T.C. Some of the crew objected, like, "We really don't rock with other rappers."

But there was no way I wasn't going to do that track.

Thank God I did it, because I think that's what got me to the next level. I got busy on that track and it really opened people's eyes about Fat Joe. D.I.T.C. were elite MCs, but we were all underground for the most part, compared to the rappers on that LL cut: Mobb Deep had their music running the streets at the time and they were gold artists. Keith Murray was a gold artist. Foxy Brown was skyrocketing, and of course LL Cool J was a legend. So being a part of that lineup really exposed me to a new audience. *Mr. Smith* went double platinum. After "I Shot Ya," I kept stepping my game up.

STILL, AT THE TIME, I wasn't as good an MC as A.G., I wasn't as good as Finesse, I wasn't as good as Diamond, I wasn't as good as O.C., I wasn't as good as Big L. I was nowhere near as good as any of them. They were more advanced with lyrics and different flows. But I was learning. My whole career was a work in progress. The only difference between me and a bunch of other rappers is that people knew that what I was kicking was real. Whatever I was rapping about, they could tell I'd actually lived it.

I feel like I'm the original Young Jeezy. When Young Jeezy came out, he was kicking that drug dealer shit, but you knew it wasn't just words or acting with him. He was a real one, a young legend in the streets of Atlanta who came up under the organization BMF. You never questioned his certification. It was the same thing with me. I had been co-signed by some of the biggest dons in NYC. My name rang bells.

Showbiz had that same block authenticity. Show was the only other rapper in D.I.T.C. that came from hustlin' in the streets. He was *getting it,* getting it super young. He damn near came out the womb making money. Showbiz is my brother on another level. He's very opinionated and I'm very opinionated, so we butt heads sometimes. But underneath it all, we're family.

Back on the block as kids, Show inspired us. He was fourteen years old, pulling up in crazy whips. Super crispy with the clothes, chains. I never saw him go to school without a fly car and a bad bitch. There's no one like Show.

Show doesn't get the praise he's earned as a figure in the culture. He's a very intelligent guy, he's his own boss, he never told, he never folded on his crew. He's always there for us. There are not too many men on Earth like that—people whose integrity is beyond question.

Me and Show were always close. Hip-hop gelled us together, but it was that street respect that first caused us to gravitate toward each other. Back when we were in the street heavy, he ran with Black crews, I ran with Latin crews. But we became brothers and agreed that we wouldn't let anyone come between us. Boy, did the streets test that pledge.

Some of my real TS day-oners would be like, "Fuck that nigga Show," and I'd be like, "No, fuck *you*." Black guys would come to him and be like, "I'm tired of this nigga Joey Crack." Show would say, "Well, how about this: We're tired of you."

I'm probably *not* dead because of Show. If he got wind of any rumors going around about "somebody is trying to get at Joe," Show would have my back, especially with the Black crews in the Bronx. Show would hear the rumors and come to me like, "You got a problem with so-and-so?"

I would return the favor. Whenever Show had problems with the Puerto Rican crews, that was me. I'd get to it quick. I cut that shit at the quarter. We'd go give it to them together.

There've been times when people have been strongly encouraged not to stand next to me. But Show never ran away from me. And on the flip side, there were times when people wanted to kill Show. *Literally kill.* Like any second, somebody could come around the corner and start shooting. Those were the consequences we accepted as a part of the street life. When you're successful, people want to take what you have or take your position by any means necessary. Rivalries could turn deadly but alliances were cherished, especially by someone like me, who'd seen so much betrayal. Me and Show, we always stood together, no question. I get emotional when I talk about Show because he was with me through the most vulnerable times in my life.

In 1991, Showbiz formed a group with Andre the Giant, A.G. for short. They were introduced to each other by Lord Finesse. Lord Finesse goes all the way back to junior high with Show. Lord admired the way Show DJed and produced, even way back then. So when Lord was making his first album, Show and Diamond D were among the first people he called for tracks. Finesse came across A.G. a little later, in high school. They met battling in cyphers in the schoolyard. A.G. also was dating a girl who lived across the street from Finesse, so they would see each other all the time and eventually formed a friendship around their mutual respect for each other as MCs.

A.G. He's a smooth cat; light skin, curly hair, from the Patterson projects. My good brother in Terror Squad, The Mayor, is from Patterson. I had a cousin who lived in Patterson so I knew some of the history there. The street legend Guy Fisher—who was released in October 2020—lived in Patterson projects. Iran Barkley, the boxer who took championship belts in three separate weight classes, is from there. Former NBA player Rod Strickland was raised in Patterson.

SIDE BAR: Can you believe the Knicks had two hometown superstars-in-the-making, Rod Strickland and Mark Jackson, and traded them *both*? In almost thirty-five years, the Knicks never could find a point guard as good as either one of them. Had to get that off my chest, one of the benefits of writing a book.

Back to Patterson projects: In the '80s and '90s cats used to be out there in the middle of the streets shooting dice for hundreds of thousands of dollars. Not just hustlers—you'd have kingpins running dice games with NBA players and boxing champs. They were out there. And like a lot of places that birthed legendary hustlers and MCs, Patterson also had a huuuge Five-Percent community, who added their own poetic slang to the neighborhood's vocab.

A.G., I don't know his whole life story, but when I met him, he was all about MCing. He got his first buzz from his guest spots on Finesse's *Funky Technician* album. Finesse featured him on a song called "Back to Back Rhyming." A.G. flambéed his bars on there. Whenever I would see A.G. I'd ask him, "Kick that rhyme for me."

"Got a tongue twister to catch a tongue blister," he'd start. Sooooo dope.

He incorporated nursery rhymes into his raps and made it sound like lyrical wizardry. A.G. was special, ahead of his time, one of the most underrated MCs to ever live. In 1992, Showbiz & A.G. dropped a full-length album called *Runaway Slave*. Diamond produced two songs on there and Show produced the rest. Incredible. That was the first time Big L was featured on an official album.

LAMONT COLEMAN, known as Big L, was like my little brother. He was the baby of the D.I.T.C. crew. Finesse discovered him too. In 1992, Finesse was doing an autograph signing and meet-and-greet on 125th in Harlem for his second album, *Return of the Funky Man*. He was at a record store not too far from where L grew up. L approached Finesse at the signing and asked to rhyme for him. Finesse gave him a shot. By the time Big L finished spittin', Finesse asked him for his number.

L's first appearance on a song was Finesse's "Yes You May" remix in 1992, which had everybody asking, "Yo, who the fuck is this kid?" L's superpower was his crazily well-developed vocabulary and his endearing wit; the rhymes could be really humorous and clever, but always with a slew of very serious and biting punch lines. He was cocky, but his loveable arrogance was part of what gave him this captivating presence.

One night around this time I went to a club uptown, near Washington Heights, where Finesse was headlining. That was the night he brought L out for the first time. L was only about eighteen years old, fresh out of high school, but he performed like a seasoned vet. He did his "Yes You May" verse and the crowd went bananas. I knew he was dumb nice. There was no question that he belonged in Diggin' in the Crates.

L was an instant underground star, a wunderkind. This was a guy who went bar for bar with Jay-Z, who a lot of people say is the

GOAT, multiple times. L and Jay-Z first battled in the early '90s right on 139th Street in Harlem. I wasn't there, but as legend has it, they rhymed to a draw. Then on February 23, 1995, L and Jigga rapped a classic, almost ten-minute-long freestyle on *The Stretch Armstrong and Bobbito Show*. Their high respect for each other's skills had been the catalyst for them to forge a friendship as comrades in arms.

About a month later, when L released his debut, Hov was featured on a track called "Da Graveyard."

L was coronated one of the kings of underground rap, and a lot of rappers thought twice before getting on tracks with him. Years down the line, Nas revealed in an interview with Funkmaster Flex that the thought of competing with L "scared me to death." This is Nas—Mount Rushmore of Rap MCs Nas. L, he had the wordplay, the delivery, the flow, the voice, and so much charisma. He had the work ethic. Big L was slaughtering everything.

L came up battling kids in his high school, Julia Richman in Manhattan. Then he took it to the streets, and then to demos and mixtapes. In 1993, while Finesse had him under his wing, L also formed a group of young Harlem rappers called Children of the Corn, with Ma$e, Cam'ron, Herb McGruff, and Bloodshed.

COC would break up but the individual members spread out and left a mark. Ma$e became Puff Daddy's number-one hitmaker after The Notorious B.I.G. passed, selling millions of records. Ironically, Cam was discovered by Biggie, and signed with his business partner Lance "Un" Rivera's label Undeas. Years later Cam would align with Roc-A-Fella Records, go platinum, and launch an all-time great crew called The Diplomats. McGruff caught the attention of Andre Harrell and Heavy D and signed to Uptown Records in 1997. Sadly, Bloodshed died in a car accident that same year.

Big L was the first to pop though. He signed a deal with Columbia. Finesse, Buckwild, and Showbiz produced all but one song on his critically heralded 1995 debut LP, *Lifestylez ov da Poor & Dangerous*. The album didn't do blockbuster numbers in sales, but it really started to cement that L was one of the best on the mic. He had fast-tracked himself to become a star. L was down with Diggin' in the Crates, but he was very ambitious and looking for ways to expand his brand.

A year after his first album dropped, L left Columbia Records over creative differences and later started his own independent label. He called it Flamboyant Entertainment.

Everybody in our crew was so excited for him. This was the young kid we met when he was still a teenager. Now he was not just a celebrated MC, he was making moves with business. In 1998, he dropped a single that was gonna be the one to change *his* life forever. "Ebonics" was clever, animated, and vivid, a hit that everyone loved from the first listen.

L started hanging out with Damon Dash, who's also from Harlem and, along with Biggs Burke and Jay-Z, was one-third of the leadership trio of Roc-A-Fella Records. In early February 1999, Roc-A-Fella was making moves to sign a new crew Big L had put together with Jay-Z, McGruff, and C-Town. After Jay had dropped his third album, *Hard Knock Life*, in '98, he wasn't just the new king of rap, he was running the Billboard charts. L already had a strong core underground fan base. There's no question in my mind that with L having that Roc-A-Fella/Def Jam structure and machine behind him, he would have gone platinum or multiplatinum.

Unfortunately, the world only got a glimpse, an inkling of how great L would have been. He died the day after Valentine's Day in 1999. Big Pun would die the following year, almost to the day. But I'll get to that story later. One tragedy at a time.

L was a casualty of war. The same war we were all living through, as soldiers or civilians. It came for us all, even our genius artists. L was shot nine times in the face and chest during a drive-by in the hood he'd grown up in. He got caught up in some trouble that he didn't start.

L's brother was a super-duper real one on the streets. He was getting money and allegedly putting in that violent work out there.

At the time, he was locked up in the Fed, fighting a murder case, and the rumor is that since the enemies couldn't get to his brother while he was on the inside, they got L as retaliation. There's another rumor that L may have been the victim of mistaken identity because he was wearing his brother's chain.

Either way, L didn't deserve that. He wasn't into the drug-dealing aspect or violence of the streets. I remember L as a nice kid. He had so many jokes; everybody loved being around him. For him to have been murdered in his neighborhood was a tremendous tragedy.

My experience, of course, is that the *most* danger is found where you're from. Look at all the rappers that were killed not too far from where they grew up. Jam Master Jay got murdered in Queens. Nipsey Hussle got murdered in front of his own store in his own neighborhood in L.A. Too many more to name. Aside from my own experiences in the streets, I learned that early on in the industry from watching Bone Thugs-n-Harmony. Me and Bone Thugs were on the same label, Relativity. They're an innovative and charismatic rap group from Cleveland and were selling thirty million records while I was just getting started, but I was lucky enough to open for them on tour. Every arena, city by city, sold out. A hundred cars filled with girls chasing them to the hotel. Real Justin Bieber shit. Bone Thugs weren't regular rappers. Nobody could measure up. *Nothing* was like Bone Thugs. They would rent the whole top floor of hotels and throw the biggest parties. It was crazy.

But even as they got all that love all over the country, they kept telling me how much they were looking forward to performing in their hometown.

"We can't wait to get to Cleveland."

"Five shows till Cleveland."

"Cleveland is tomorrow night."

Finally we got to Cleveland. And that was the first place where I saw hate.

"Fuck them niggas. Them niggas ain't nobody," some people in the front rows heckled when their set started. "This the West Side of Cleveland. Fuck *E. 1999*. These niggas are soft."

Throughout the whole tour, all they wanted to do was go home and say, "We made it." "We" as in the entire city. They had put Cleveland on the map for rap and wanted to celebrate at home. Instead, people gave them their asses to kiss.

Same thing with Big L. If you listen to his verses he goes heavy for his hood: "'Cause one-three-nine and Lenox is the danger zone." They killed him right on that block.

I remember when they called me and told me L had been murdered. I was already in Manhattan at D&D Studios. I drove all the way up to Harlem. I got there fast enough that I actually saw L's body laid out on the pavement. Cam'ron came out too. It's an image that has haunted me. I remember L being in the streets, so happy, so vibrant in his neighborhood. Then there he was, lifeless on the concrete behind a supermarket on 139th.

There were so many rumors about why L was killed, people were scared to go to his funeral. But I went and so did the entire D.I.T.C. crew. We paid our respects to his family, but their suffering wasn't over.

L's brother got a miracle and won the case he was fighting against the Feds. And, man, then he went back to the block and *he* got killed immediately. He didn't even get to retaliate for L first. The man won the case and got killed right on that same Lenox Avenue block he and L grew up on.

In life and in death L pushed me as much as anyone. The best rhyme I've ever written was because of L. I had just gone gold with my third album, *Don Cartagena,* and me and L were in D&D Studios. We were working on his song called "The Enemy," which DJ Premier produced. L was talking so much shit, like little brothers do.

"Yo! I want to look in your eyes and let you know, you went gold but I'm gonna take all your fans," he said. "I'ma gonna take all your fans because I'm underground and I need some fans too!"

We laughed. I think Show was there too. L was saying wiiiiild shit.

"I'm tellin' you, nigga, you better bring your A-game," he carried on. "I'm about to kill you on this." He was hypin' me up. And that's when I came up with the best rhyme I ever wrote. I wrote it right there, looking him dead in his face.

Ay yo, enough's enough.
Federals try to set me up,
Put me in cuffs and crush what I lust into dust.
Plus, they want a nigga's soul, but they know
Big Joey Crack will never rat a cat that he know.
Fo' sho, death before dishonor, I left the streets alone
Since Tone deceased it almost killed his mama.
So I'ma keep doing what I'm doing:
Pursuing my dream till there's enough cream to start my own union
And show these kids how legit it is.
Shit is real, I used to steal but now I own several businesses.

I'm real proud of that song. You know, I make music with all the MCs and it's always a friendly competition. But nobody explicitly threatens you to your face when you collaborate. Big L actually *threatened me*. I had no choice but to stand up. I welcomed the competition.

L was something else, man. We'd always joke and gamble. He'd have beef on his block and he'd call me to come. You know me, I'm ready to come out on the block and hurt everything on some "we don't give a fuck, we ain't even from here."

L would be like, "Nooo. Don't do that, Joey. One-on-one!"

L would start fighting one-on-one in the middle of the street. L wasn't scared of nobody. He'd fight everybody one-on-one and we'd come just to make sure nobody jumped in. If we suggested maybe we could settle things for him with violence he'd be like, "No. No. I can't do it. I grew up with these niggas."

They killed him right on his block. To make matters worse, police suspected it was a guy named Gerard Woodley, who grew up with L. Woodley never went to jail for the murder; prosecutors could never produce enough evidence to convict him. I guess you can call it chickens coming home to roost, or just karma, because years later, Woodley wound up getting shot and killed just a block away from where *someone* shot L to death.

MY MAN OMAR "O.C." CREDLE joined D.I.T.C. after L, but he actually dropped his first album in 1994, *Word . . . Life*, before L came out.

O.C. debuted in 1991. He came out the gate like a rocket ship. He rapped with Nas on a remix of MC Serch's banger "Back to the Grill." Then he unleashed his solo missile "Time's Up" in 1994. That shit had the streets on fire, and it was produced by another D.I.T.C. member, Buckwild.

O.C. is somebody I really respect as an artist. Diggin' in the Crates is so old-school, where we actually have in-person meetings before we add someone to the team. One of the meetings was to discuss bringing O into the fold. He was already a hot young rapper but we knew we could take him to the next level.

"We want to put O.C. down with the crew, what you think?" Finesse asked.

I was like, "Fuuck yeah." It didn't matter to me that O.C. was from Brooklyn and most of our crew were from the Bronx.

So O.C. came to one of my parties at the Fever and we let him know, "We want you down with the crew." He became immediate family.

O.C. is the glue guy. If there's ever any type of disagreement between two people in the crew, O.C. is the one bringing everybody together. That's his nature.

It's so fucked up because in hip-hop it's hard for people to get along and you always hear about groups breaking up. Not this crew. We're so proud of one another. It's so rare to be free of envy.

For instance, when we go do a D.I.T.C. record, Finesse is like our Method Man. The centerpiece of the group. He's *the one* and we fall back. He's the leader. Me, I've got hit songs under my belt: "Lean Back." "Make It Rain." I have a great track record of making hit choruses. So I'm like the hook man for D.I.T.C., the Nate Dogg of the group.

Buckwild started off as a DJ making mixtapes and everybody loved him. But I was there when Showbiz showed Buckwild how to make beats. Showbiz was like, "These are the drums. This is the volume . . ." Buck went on to produce classics: "I Got a Story to Tell" by Biggie. "Whoa!" for Black Rob. He produced "My Lifestyle" for me. But when Buck blew up he didn't use that as an excuse to be an asshole. He stayed a supportive member of the crew—and still one of my best friends.

I'm with D.I.T.C. all the way. It's my dream to become financially stable enough to get some type of situation for all my brothers. And they're not doing bad. Don't take this as a charity. But it's been a goal of mine to make $100 million and situate my guys on another level.

"What you wanna do? What *you* wanna do? You want a McDonald's? Let's rock. You want to do movies? Cool!"

I haven't been able to do it yet. My whole life, yeah, I've been successful, but there've been ups and downs—a roller coaster. When the day comes that I'm financially secure at the right level and I can say to myself, "Yo, Joe, *you good*!," it's my dream to make a U-turn, go back to them, and be like, "Yo, let's do whatever you want to do. Let's rock."

CHAPTER 11

BIG PUN PART I

CHRISTOPHER RIOS was a godsend to me. It didn't even take him two full years to have an unprecedented impact on hip-hop and the world. His greatness was too much for us though. As much as we loved him as a person and revered him as a larger-than-life icon, people still didn't all the way understand what a gem he was. One of one.

I still listen to things he said almost twenty-five years ago and catch something new. And I've heard everything he said a million times over. I quote him with the biggest grin on my face. I laugh out loud, thinking how wicked and witty he was.

You ain't promised mañana in the rotten manzana . . . / Sometimes rhymin', I blow my own mind like nirvana.

If Christopher Rios was a literal godsend, I thank God for sending him to me first, so I could introduce him to the world.

Our divine convergence happened right where I grew up. I didn't have to go far.

As I've mentioned, I used to hang out on 166th and Tinton Ave, that's Forest projects, my stomping grounds. I'd always go to this bodega there and get me a little Diet Pepsi or a Diet Coke and some chips. One day I pulled up. It was a rare time when I was by myself. I was in my white LS 400 Lexus with the beige interior, the big boy.

I was doin' aight at the time. My first album, *Represent,* had just run its cycle. I was in between albums, but I was still making like $2,500 a show and I'd do at least three shows every Saturday. Even though my first single, "Flow Joe," went number one on the rap charts, I was still hanging out in the hood. Nobody gave me the memo: "Yo, you ain't supposed to be in the projects no more."

I walked into the bodega, bought a soda. As I come out, there's four Latin guys freestyling. That was just weird to me because I usually didn't see *Spanish* MCs rappin' in the hood. One of the guys I knew, my man Toom, he was down with Terror Squad. When I think about it, Toom must have brought the other Latin kids there. Anyway, in the middle of the cypher was this big guy, heavier than me—he stood out from the crew. He had on a white tank top and these Rosary beads tied around his head.

"Chill, chill, y'all. Chill! Chill!" he told his group of guys, stopping their cypher.

I was walking to my car when he said he wanted to rhyme for me.

I'm like *What the fuck does this Spanish nigga who's fatter than me have to say?*

Remember, at that time, there were hardly any other Latinos ringing off. Reggaeton wasn't even out there. It was Fat Joe from the Bronx, the homies from Queens The Beatnuts, then on the West Coast you had my brothers Cypress Hill. Cypress have always been solid and I looked up to them. They were the first Latino hip-hop act to go platinum and double platinum.

Any negative preconceived thoughts I had about hearing the really big guy rap were silenced when he started. The rhythm of his bars was impeccable: *daddda, daddda, daddda, daddda, daddda, daddda,* in the pocket, with uncanny breath control. I got caught up in it, and then he just stopped! Imagine if a Bugatti were going 270 miles per hour and just stopped on a dime. He dropped the line "Snatch the moon out the sky," and then came silence. In the pause his hand reached up and snatched air, like he really was grabbing the moon. Then he stretched his arm out and spoke again, "Blow the sun away." He blew at his hand like he was blowing out a candle. Then another long pause. And then:

"Me and my brothers play it hardcore. / Strictly hardcore lyrics till I'm finished breaking God's law," he rifled off as he recommenced the rhyme.

Oh my God! I lost it!

The guy was under six feet, about 5'7", 5'8". He was easily 400 pounds, maybe even 450. His humongous stature separated him visually from his friends, but his words distinguished him from anybody on the planet. I'd never heard anybody in my life like him. I'd been around all of the great MCs: Biggie, Big L, Nas, Rakim, my idol, KRS-One. But when this big Puerto Rican kid kicked his verse, it gave me a bone chill unlike anything I'd ever felt before.

I love hip-hop and there's a certain feeling you get when you hear a song that's absolutely monumental. It's euphoria—you get goosebumps, you feel a little like you're going insane. A mini-hysteria. I remember feeling like that when I first heard Run-DMC's "Sucker M.C.'s." I was in junior high at a talent show. Everybody in the school was in the auditorium. At that time, the popular sound in hip-hop was Grandmaster Flash and the Furious Five, The Fearless Four, Kool Moe Dee and the Treacherous Three. It was old-school but we didn't know it because it was still poppin'.

These three girls came out to dance and the DJ played "Sucker M.C.'s." I saw a thousand kids all stop what they were doing and look around like *Holy shit! What is this?* when the beat dropped. Nobody had heard the song before and instantly everyone knew the sound of rap had changed. Run-DMC sonically transformed the rap game. They changed everything we knew and brought in a new era. In that one moment in junior high school, my sense of what rap was and what it could be shifted.

This heavyset Latin guy, the way he conveyed his thoughts through his words, made me feel like I had in that moment with Run-DMC, but at an even higher level. It was like he had on Thanos's Infinity Gauntlet and could make the rhymes do anything he wanted. He could bend his words into patterns, change his delivery speed, and deliver punch lines with brute, blinding force.

I opened up the passenger side door and said, "Please, get in."

He sat in the car and I looked over at all his friends. Their faces dropped into sad expressions because they weren't going too. He was leaving with me and they deflated.

"Yo dog, yo Pun," all his friends started screaming.

They used to call him "Moon Dog Punisher." A short while later, he changed his name to "Big Dog Punisher" and obviously that evolved into "Big Punisher" and "Big Pun."

He told all his friends he would be all right, and we pulled off. We started talking. Pun was the Lauryn Hill of his group, the breakout star. No disrespect to them. They weren't as nice as Pun but I don't think anybody is. Pun really is the nicest ever. I knew he was going to be a great from the start. I told Pun honestly his group wasn't as good as he was, but not to worry. Once he blew, we would put his team on. I kept my word years later. Pun's guys made records with us and a lot of money with me.

Me and Pun didn't even make it a block before he started telling me his life story. Within twenty minutes I knew all about him. I knew who he loved, who fucked him over, what his dreams were. The minute he sat in the car our bond was automatic. I've met all kinds of characters in my adventures, but I had never met a man who opened up so transparently. I never met a man before or since who was just so vulnerable and honest. I related to him.

I'm the baby of my family. I never had a little brother. Pun never had a big brother. I grew up in Forest projects; Pun grew up in Soundview projects. I moved out of my family's house when I was fourteen; Pun moved out of his when he was fifteen.

Pun told me a story about an uncle of his that was rich. The uncle owned a factory where they made pockets for jeans. Pun went through being homeless when he left to be on his own. He asked his uncle for a job, he asked his uncle for money for food, and his uncle told him, "Yo, why don't you eat rocks!" Then the uncle gave him pebbles. Literally handed him small rocks to eat.

"I want to show my uncle that I could get mines," he dreamed aloud to me. "I want to show him that I'm going to be big, that I'm going to be somebody."

Then Pun told me about his wife, how they'd been together since they were kids and how much he loved her. After that, he told me stories about the rest of his family. These were deep conversations.

Growing up, Pun's mom was heavily on drugs like heroin and meth, his stepfather was abusive. He would wake Pun up in the middle of the night and make him do push-ups and smack him in the back of the head. This was when he was a little boy.

I didn't know why this man was telling me all this the first time I met him. Some people you intersect with, and from the initial meeting, you know you are going to be connected with them for the rest of your life.

When I met my wife, Lorena, I was hoping she was *the one*. I made an agreement with her. "Listen," I began to tell her. "No matter what money we have, no matter what we go through, no matter anything in the world . . . No matter what, we're going to stay together. We're going to work through it." Same thing with my brother DJ Khaled when he met his wife. The next day he told me, "Yo, she's gonna be my wife." Sometimes you just know.

Khaled and Pun hit it off immediately, too. They treated each other like brothers right off the bat. There's a spark that touches something in your brain and heart when you make a commitment, a voice that says, *This is what I want forever*. With Pun talking to me so freely, I almost felt like he said, *I'm rocking with you till the wheels fall off*.

"*You're* my big brother," he told me. "You're The Don."

I knew instinctively I had to bring him under the wing not just as my artist, but as family. When I introduced him to the rest of The Terror Squad, who are some real respected generals all over the hood, they embraced one another. That was his crew when he was dead broke, his crew when he blew up and was successful, and his crew even after his death. Pun is forever TS and we all will always love and honor him.

I wanted to take Pun directly to the studio, but he had me stop and meet his wife, Liza. He rushed me to their crib. He brought me over there to prove to her we were in business.

"Look! I'm with Fat Joe! Fat Joe brought me here," he said to her when we walked into their apartment.

Pun and Liza met and fell in love when they were very young teenagers and got married a few years later at City Hall. Pun was around eighteen and Liza was seventeen. Her father had to literally sign off on her getting married because she was a minor. That was the year Pun went from couch-surfing at friends' and family's houses to affording his own apartment. The money came to him like a bolt of lightning.

When Pun turned eighteen, his family lawyer got ahold of him and informed him he'd won a $500,000 lawsuit. That lawsuit stemmed from when he was about four or five years old and fell at a city playground. He broke his ankle. The courts deemed the city negligent. The money was a mixed blessing though. It changed him in ways that weren't all for the better.

The world, including me, got to know him as this very obese guy, but at eighteen, he was only 180 pounds and could actually have been a *GQ* model. Pun had a great physique back then. He described himself as a guy who loved to play sports, and he had the exuberant appetite of an athlete. He was able to stay lean because he was always active. When you can't afford a car or even to take public transportation, you walk.

While the money vastly improved his living circumstanc also led to him gradually gaining a lot of weight. Liza will this herself, but the first year they were married, they wou at restaurants three meals a day, maybe more, every sin wasn't the conservative type with his cash, as I wor But the point is: He was way less active and ate a '

I was ready to put him to work though. I just kept thinking about the possibilities with Pun. I knew we could make music history. Puff Daddy had Biggie, and now I had my guy. I didn't want to waste a second.

Later that night, I brought him to the studio. I was wrapping up my second album, *Jealous One's Envy,* and I put him on two songs: one track called "Say Word," and then a joint with me and Armageddon, called "Watch Out." He killed that shit. On "Watch Out," I had him incorporate those same lyrics he spit for me at the bodega. He slaughtered that shit. We were off and running.

AFTER THAT ALBUM DROPPED in October, we had a

strong buzz and we wanted to introduce Pun to the streets. We put him on a record called "Firewater," produced by Showbiz from D.I.T.C. Pun loved Show from the first time they met.

I called Raekwon The Chef to come to the studio. It was 1995 going into 1996, and Rae was the fastest rising, hottest MC in the game. Although everyone knew him from Wu-Tang Clan, whose album *Enter the Wu-Tang (36 Chambers)* came out in 1993, The Chef turned into a hip-hop MVP with his classic solo album *Only Built 4 Cuban Linx . . . Linx* dropped in '95 and is one of the greatest hip-hop creations ever; it also set up Rae's frequent collaborator Ghostface Killah as an acclaimed star in his own right. That tandem of the Wu's Rae and Ghost on that album—*and* Cappadonna on a few of the tracks—scared a lot of MCs. Too much fire. *Cuban Linx* runs neck and neck with the first Wu-Tang group album as as impact and quality.

Me and Rae had a long-standing friendship, and when he got studio, he thought he was doing a song with me.

h, this is for my artist Pun," I clarified.

et Pun and Pun started spittin' some real crazy lyrics.

fout!" Chef said with his eyes wide open in surprise. "You *gga!*"

I was also grooming Armageddon, so we put him in the lineup for good measure. "Firewater" was on the B side to my single "Envy" in 1996. The song earthquaked the underground and warned everyone that Pun was about to have the game trembling.

Then I took Pun up to the legendary *Stretch Armstrong and Bobbito Show* and he freestyled up there. It was Pun's first time on the radio and another flawless victory.

Pun's most pivotal early freestyle though was for Funkmaster Flex's project *The Mixtape, Volume 1 (60 Minutes of Funk)* in '95. Flex had the juice. If Flex loved your record, he had the power to make that shit a hit. He could get the whole of NYC behind it. Flex had so much influence, when he decided he wanted to put out his first album, all the most poppin' artists on the East Coast contributed.

He had everybody from Run-DMC, Eric B. & Rakim, Puff Daddy, and Fugees, to LL Cool J and Mobb Deep. When I got the call to get on the project, I wanted my man to get on too. It took some major convincing, but Flex agreed and Pun recorded a hot freestyle with me for the album. That would become another important step in our strategy to keep Pun's rep growing.

Pun was picking up steam and garnering a rep as rhyme virtuoso—with every release he became a more dominant force in the underground circuit.

Not only was his name ringing in the gutter, but the bigwigs in the boardrooms were paying attention too. A friend of mine, Mickey Benzo, helped me set up a meeting with Loud Records founder and CEO Steve Rifkind. Loud was up there as one of the most successful labels in rap, home to Mobb Deep, Wu-Tang, Xzibit, and Tha Alkaholiks; later they had M.O.P., Three 6 Mafia, and so many others.

At our meeting, we didn't have a demo tape, a song—no music period. Steve pulled me outside the conference room to have a sidebar.

"I want you to know ten people called me from the industry

and they were telling me don't meet with you," he divulged. "They said you're an extortionist, you're a gangster, you're a killer, a robber."

I was so pissed off that not only was dirt being thrown on my name behind my back, but this deal could be in major jeopardy. All I could say was "Word?"

"I guess people are scared of you going to the next level," he continued.

"That's crazy, man, 'cause everything I got in the business, I earned."

Steve gave me a reassuring smile and told me, "I'm a gangster, my father's a gangster, I come from a gangster family. So, actually, that shit turns me on."

We went back into the conference room and the meeting carried on. We were meeting with all the company's major A&Rs: Scott Free, Mattie C, and Sean C. They were all there to see Pun. Steve told me that no other artist had ever created that type of excitement in the office. And my brother delivered. Pun hit a grand slam with an a cappella freestyle for them. That sealed it. Before we left, we agreed on a deal.

People don't believe me, but I probably never got no real money with Big Pun directly. Indirectly, because of my success with Big Pun as an artist, I was later able to go to Atlantic Records and get a multimillion dollar deal for Terror Squad Records. But from Pun personally, he refused to let me make a dollar.

Loud gave me a $100,000 check for Pun when we finalized the deal weeks later. He was signed to me as a recording artist and I even started managing him after a while. As we were leaving the office, Pun jumped into the car with his huge, mischievous smile. By this time, we were calling each other "Twin," that's how close we were.

"Yo, Twin? You love me? You love me?" he kept asking.

"Yeah, I love you, man," I told him.

"You sure? You love me?"

"Yeah," I said again. I was so happy.

Pun made me take him to Fordham Road and the Grand Concourse to a jewelry store called Gallery 2000. He looked at the display and said, "Yo, Twin, I've been looking at this watch."

That fucka was smothered in baguettes. It had an invisible setting. All ice.

"Yo, Twin, you love me, man?" he asked again. "Show me you love me. Buy me that shit."

I wound up spending $105,000 on this watch for Pun as a gift. The extra $5,000 had to come out my pocket. Pun was a trip, man.

Pun would drive me crazy one minute and have me dying laughing the next. We used our nickname for each other to introduce him on a broader scale.

IN 1998, we engineered another major breakthrough for Pun, when we sampled Dr. Dre and Snoop's "Deep Cover" for our own song "Twinz (Deep Cover 98)." What can you say about the 1992 original that hasn't already been said? It's one of the greatest songs in hip-hop ever, with Dre and Snoop trading rhymes over Dre's propulsive production. It was Snoop's debut, and one of the greatest debuts in rap history—no exaggeration.

I wanted Pun to have that type of impact as we ushered him to greet the masses. Up to that point, everything he'd been on was East Coast–centric. We had established him in our home base, but I wanted his reach to expand, which is why we chose an iconic beat from the West Coast.

Pun said his most iconic lines ever on that record too: "Dead in the middle of Little Italy little did we know / That we riddled two middlemen who didn't do diddily."

It was a big fight convincing Pun to put those bars in his verse. See, Pun was such a jovial dude, he would say these tongue twisters all day long and laugh. He would just out of the blue say, "Dead in the middle of Little Italy," all the time.

"Pun, put that shit in your rhyme man. That shit is hard," I insisted.

"You're gonna have niggas laughing at me," he resisted.

"Twinz" was an impeccable follow-up to "Off the Books," which dropped in late June 1997. "Off the Books" was a Beatnuts single that started off underground, then charted on Billboard and blew up to be a major club banger. Pun batted leadoff and absolutely obliterated the song's signature beat with its infectious flute trill. That was only the second time he was featured on an album, and it was the first radio hit Pun rapped on.

Like me and Big L, Pun relished posse records. He loved to get on songs with the best and try to outshine them. On records like N.O.R.E.'s "Banned from T.V." or my joint "John Blaze," Pun was rapping with everyone from Nas to Jadakiss and just stealing the show. It was friendly competition, but on the low Pun was trying to decapitate *everyone*.

But out of everyone, Pun had most wanted to collaborate with The Notorious B.I.G. Can you imagine what that record would have sounded like? Those two were so versatile, they could have spun out some hilarious, action-packed narrative, or just gone the lyrical onslaught route and killed the track going bar for bar. It would have been huge.

Pun was a huge fan of Biggie, and the admiration was mutual. Right when Big had finished his double LP, *Life After Death,* in 1997, he called me. I was traveling to a show, driving from NY to VA on I-95, and Biggie was in L.A. doing promo for the project. *Life After* was dropping in less than three weeks, on March 25, 1997, and would go on to sell more than eleven million copies. Big told me that he'd heard some of Pun's work and loved him as an MC. He wanted to collab with him when he got back from the West Coast. We were working on Pun's debut, and of course having a Biggie cameo meant the world to us.

Biggie was a great friend. I met him when I was doing my show-promoter hustle, like '93. Yeah, I was a rapper getting booked for shows, but to make more money, I would actually book other rappers to perform at clubs sometimes. I remember this mad skinny kid named Puffy Combs as a rising star on the music scene. He wasn't just the man behind the game-changing music of artists like Jodeci and Mary J. Blige, he also carefully cultivated their images, in the style of the old Motown system. Puff ran up on me one night, he had a chain on that was so thin it looked see-through. Puff wanted me to book Biggie for a show and I did. It was Big's first show ever, and my payment to him was $1,000 and a bottle of Moët. We were tight from then on.

I could have called Big to get on Pun's album and he would have shown that love, but I didn't want to bother him. He was recording that magnum opus, and of course he had been dealing with all those well-publicized problems with Tupac. Believe it or not, before he got into the depths of *Life After Death,* me and Big had started recording a duo album where we were going back at Pac, lyrically. I'll tell you that story at another time, but you'll never hear those songs. RIP Pac.

But back to Biggie. It was incredible that he reached out for Pun. We were excited about what their pairing would mean to the culture. But that phone call was the last time me and Big ever spoke. He was murdered two days later, on March 9, 1997.

WE HAD STARTED RECORDING Pun's debut album, *Capital Punishment,* a month or two earlier in '97. By then I'd been around enough to know when I was witnessing magic in the studio. From the very first session we knew Pun was about to go on a very special run.

Sometimes Pun would fall asleep in the studio when the producer was working on the beat or the engineer was fixing something. When everyone was ready to record again, we'd wake him up and he'd pop right up and tell the engineer to throw up a new beat. Then he'd go into the booth and record an entire new song. He would have the verses fully composed in his head. It was like he was writing rhymes in his sleep. New songs would come out of nowhere.

The whole Terror Squad was in the studio every day supporting Pun. We were so proud of him: We viewed him as being *the one*. Every new track was better than the last.

When *Capital Punishment* was almost done, I started calling on friends for features. It wasn't hard. I played Busta Rhymes a bunch of songs we had completed and he was like, "Oh, I gotta be on there."

It was like that with everyone we asked for verses. We caught up with Wyclef Jean at a time when he was putting up them Michael Jackson numbers. This was right before he produced and appeared on Destiny's Child's first-ever smash, "No, No, No (Part 2)," and right after he sold close to six million units of *The Score* with Fugees. Clef was enjoying worldwide solo superstardom, trotting the globe and touring off his own multiplatinum, critically acclaimed opus, *Wyclef Jean Presents: The Carnival.*

Clef admired Pun's mic game so much, he used a rare off day to come work with us. The two of them had their own relationship, and Pun just put in a call to get the collaboration. At the time, Clef was on the radio all day, selling unfathomable amounts of records, but Pun brilliantly tapped into Clef's spitter mentality and gave the audience something different. They did a hardcore track instead of going commercial, which Clef reveled in. It was one of the album's big "oh shit!" moments when it came out.

Besides our crew, some other guests who came through on the album were the singer Joe, Black Thought from The Roots, Prodigy from Mobb Deep, Dead Prez, Inspectah Deck from Wu-Tang, and N.O.R.E.

Nore is my adopted little brother, but he was Pun's fuckup partner. They were best friends and they would get in trouble *every day*. Nore would call me "The Fun Killer" because I would come mess everything up. They'd be like, "Here comes The Fun Killer. Party's over."

The party was just starting though. *Capital Punishment* was released on April 28, 1998, and quickly found a spot in the top five on the Billboard album charts. Pun became the first ever Latino solo MC to go platinum. Just like that, Pun was a superstar. The people loved the music and gravitated toward his personality.

Pun loooooved every minute of it. Back then record store promotions were a big part of any new album's marketing campaign. For big stars, there would be people waiting in lines down the block to get into these stores so they could meet their favorite rapper, who would autograph their CDs, cassettes, and other merch. Pun would go to his friends' record store events, like DMX's album signings, and pull up in front of the store in a limo.

He would jump out and throw thousands of dollars' worth of hundred-dollar bills everywhere just to cause chaos. He got a kick out of it. He wanted people to go home and tell all their friends, "Big Pun pulled up."

He would pull up anywhere. My brother was so skilled and hungry as an MC, we'd be in the limo to go and do radio interviews or to go to MTV and Pun would see neighborhood kids outside battling on the corner. Pun, he's already platinum, but would jump out on the corner and battle everybody.

Pun didn't care if you were platinum like him or straight out the sewer, he lived for competition. Whatever if the local MC didn't have two quarters in their pockets—if they thought they were nice, they had a problem when big boy got out to destroy the rap cypher. He didn't care that it would be a blemish on his career if God forbid he got crushed battling these unknown kids and word started circulating. He was with whatever against whoever when it came to rap. He never thought he would lose and he never did.

I'm the same way as Pun. So is Remy Ma. Back in 2004, Me and Rem laid down one of our signature collaborations, "Lean

Back," which went gold. But that same year, Remy found time to battle one of the hottest underground female MCs at the time, Lady Luck. She didn't care that losing that battle could potentially damage her credibility. Remy crushed her though. Pun would have been proud.

PUN WAS ALWAYS COMFORTABLE around the people, that's how he first met Remy. He refused to move out the Bronx. He grew up in the Bronx, he stayed in the Bronx. He bought a house in the Bronx, right around the corner from one of the gulliest projects, Castle Hill. That's where Remy is from. Pun would have ten motorcycles, which he couldn't drive, outside his house. He bought them because he could, and of course he'd let all his friends use them. Pun had a limousine service twenty-four hours a day. There was a driver posted outside his house. If he didn't go anywhere after a certain amount of hours, that driver would get relieved by another driver and paid regardless. Pun always had a hundred guys in this house. I never saw him there alone with just his wife and his kids. He had exotic blue dogs from Europe that I'd never seen before in my life. He kept an arsenal of guns too.

The thing with Pun is that he liked to blow the bag. He was worse than me, and I'm a guy who can spend $50,000 a month on clothes. Pun would spin that paper like nothin'. If he went on tour, before he even got back home, he would buy some new watch, a new chain, new clothes, new accessories. Pun never saved for a rainy day. He wasn't thinking about the future. He was like, "Fuck that, I'm ballin' *now*!" The money was coming in heavy and fast for him though; he had become a star.

For me to go on tour, even today, I've got to sit down with my team, plan, and then three months later I go out. With Pun, he was such a phenomenon, he could sit down on a Monday and be like, "I want to go on tour Friday." Before you knew it, the fuckin' tour would be sold out for two months straight. He would go on the road Friday and come back Monday with duffel bags of money.

"Yo, Twin!!!" he'd say through a grin whenever he saw me. That smile really said it all. He was proud of himself and of what we were accomplishing together.

Latinos can be very tribal. Puerto Ricans say, "I'm Puerto Rican! I'm not Dominican!" Dominicans are like, "I'm not Puerto Rican!" Cubans say, "I'm Cubano, don't confuse me with those Dominicans and Puerto Ricans!" Mexicans don't want to be mistaken for Ecuadorians.

All these guys are Latino. We have that in common, but we're all from different places and cultures. So it's very complex the way Latinos get down.

With me, all the Latinos love me, but the Puerto Ricans claim me as one of their own. With Pun, *everybody* wanted to claim him.

The Mexicans would lie to themselves and say Pun was Mexican. The Peruvians would fake it and say Pun was Peruvian. The Cubans would say he's Cuban.

Pun was proud of his heritage, proud to be the first Latino solo MC to go platinum. But Pun wanted to be universal. He would always say in interviews he was the best rapper—period—and also *happened* to be Latino. The important thing to him was that you understood the first part of that equation clearly: He was the best.

WE FAST-TRACKED PUN to superstardom with the video for "I'm Not a Player." This came out prior to *Capital Punishment* and started to set the table for him. We sampled The O'Jays on the song and got them to appear. We reenacted *Scarface* for the video and had the actor Ángel Salazar, who played Don Chi Chi in the movie, co-star. Raekwon made a cameo; he was there with me. I had on a sky-blue suit—that's my favorite color. We had so much fun on set that day—the whole set was energized by the feeling that our dream was coming true.

Next we came up with the remix: "Still Not a Player." It came about because me and Kedar Massenburg were very, very tight friends. Kedar was the president of Motown Records from 1997 to 2004. However, he's most known and most loved for discovering legends D'Angelo and Erykah Badu. In fact, Erykah's classic first album, *Baduizm,* came out on his label, Kedar Entertainment. His vision and ear helped usher in the whole Neo-Soul movement.

Kedar was managing D'Angelo and a singer named Joe at the time, and we worked it out so Joe sang parts of his gold single "Don't Wanna Be a Player" on Pun's "Still Not a Player." Joe was a big R&B act who had a bunch of hits on the radio, and he was a force on the SoundScan charts.

Getting Joe into the studio with Pun was the favor I pulled. But the actual creation of "Still Not a Player" was all Pun's vision.

I left the studio for like two to three hours while Joe and Pun were recording. When I got back, I heard the song and we all started jumping up and down. One play was all it took for me to realize that the record would change our lives. One play was all it took for *the world* to recognize Pun as a superstar too.

"Still Not a Player" was released on March 28, 1998, exactly a month before Pun's debut album, *Capital Punishment.* We premiered the single on Ed Lover and Dr. Dre's morning show on Hot 97. We did the interview and they played "Still Not a Player" *one time.* The whole city shook. Pun became a hip-hop idol off of that one spin. By the time I went down to the lobby, Lyor Cohen, who ran Def Jam, was down there. Craig Kallman, of Atlantic Records, was down there. It felt like every head executive of every major label was down in the lobby waiting on me.

Ah shit! I'm about to get paid, I started thinking as everybody approached me. I was stepping into the middle of a full-fledged bidding war. My contract with Relativity Records was done. I'd fulfilled my two-album deal and I was a free agent. I'm always loyal, so I gave Steve Rifkind the first chance to lock something in place.

Steve, he wanted to sign Terror Squad Records, the label I was forming, but didn't want to give up that big, big, big guap. I was looking for my payday—I wanted to become a multimillionaire. So I wound up doing a deal at Atlantic Records for my solo projects and to put out other artists under my umbrella. I dropped *Don Cartagena* on September 1, 1998, and went gold. We followed up a little more than a year later with the Terror Squad compilation *The Album* on September 21, 1999.

This was our happiest point. I was selling, Pun was outta here on another planet. His group that was rapping with him when we met, we folded them into Terror Squad along with my little bro Armageddon. Our young artists were growing. When Pun discovered Remy Ma, we knew she was the truth from day one. We had *another* star-in-the-making in our camp. Everything was panning out. It felt like we were catapulting ourselves into a serious empire.

CHAPTER 12

BIG PUN PART II

ALL I HEARD WAS "That's right! Yo Pun, yo Joe, let's fuck these niggas up!"

Iron Mike Tyson was—in that moment, at least—another godsend. As if sent down from heaven itself, Mike Tyson swooped in to save us.

Me and Pun were about to get beat down. There was no way around it. There were twelve brolic security guards lined up against just the two of us. Imagine having to fight a dozen guys who were all the size of a WWE wrestler like The Undertaker. As someone who used to get ganged up on every day by the kids in junior high, I know all too well about the odds being against you.

A peaceful stillness settles into your mind when you know you're about to get your ass kicked. You're still all in. You're still ready to fight until the ship goes down, you're still ready to prove that you're not going to back down, but you also have a realistic conversation with yourself. You know you're going down.

But when Mike Tyson has your back, even if it looks like you're outnumbered, you actually have the equivalent of an army. Back in 1998, Mike was the most feared man on the planet. He's still up there. I don't know anybody who wants to fight fifty-six-year-old Mike right now.

Me and Pun had just done a show in Jersey at this club called Foxes. After Foxes, Pun tells me to ride with him, and he drives us to the Tunnel. The Tunnel was a world-famous night club, where artists and DJs used the crowd as a litmus test to see if a record was hot. Back then, the streets dictated what ruled rap, not streaming playlists. If you didn't have a "Tunnel banger," a song that moved the crowd in that club, you weren't moving as an artist. The Tunnel was also as hood as it could possibly be; some people would get robbed, beat up, or worse in the co-ed bathrooms.

But it was the place *you had* to be every Sunday night. The energy, the people, the music, the stars, everyone wanted to be a part of that. Tupac, Biggie, Dr. Dre and Snoop, Jermaine Dupri and Da Brat, Eminem, Jay-Z, Nas are just a short list of icons who performed and partied there. DMX filmed his concert performance scenes for the "Get at Me Dog" video there. Me and Pun had ripped it down there, too. Funkmaster Flex and Big Kap were the DJs on Sunday.

On this night, for some reason, Pun wanted to go to the Tunnel, even though none of our crew were with us. We'd usually travel at least fifty deep, knowing anything could break out at the spot. So when Pun and I get to the Tunnel at like 2:00 A.M., I tell Pun we shouldn't be going in there two deep. He's tries to reassure me that we're fine with the cargo we're traveling with; he has an arsenal of guns in his gray Mercedes-Benz.

But we had to park way down the block from the Tunnel and, of course, we couldn't bring guns into the club. They check you at the door. Which is how the bouncer beef took shape. A hallmark of the Tunnel was that they used to make everybody take their shoes off while being searched. People used to sneak in guns, razors, all types of contraband in their shoes. So the security started going to extreme measures.

They told Pun to take off his Timbs and he flipped out. He was over 500 pounds at this point and there was no way he could even bend over to take his boots off in the first place. Pun also felt like he was such a huge celebrity that he should be granted liberties the general public were not afforded. He was platinum, his "Still Not a Player" was a certified Tunnel banger that was big on the Billboard charts too.

While he's arguing with security, Flex is all the way inside and you could hear him starting to play "Still Not a Player." This gets Pun even more incensed. I try to calm the situation, but it escalates. Next thing you know, I'm joining Pun in flinging out every curse word known to mankind at the security. I had to rep with my brother.

The bouncers started stretching, strapping up their gloves extra tight. They were getting ready for a brawl. Just as they started to swarm in on us, my good friend Iron Mike Tyson pulls up. He had on his kufi, dress slacks, and Gucci loafers.

"That's right, Joe, that's right, Pun. Fuck these niggas! Let's fuck them up! I got your back!" he said in his signature light voice.

All hell broke loose. Mike had already taken off his shoes so he was barefoot. He then started to chase the head bouncer, who had to be all of seven feet. The bouncer ran into the street around a parked car twenty times to evade getting knocked out. The guy was so scared, he forgot the fact that he had just been dissing us and turned to me and Pun and asked for help.

"Yo Joe, yo Pun, can you tell Mike to stop please?" he yelled.

Things eventually calmed down and me, Pun, and Mike went into the club. We had some drinks and a great laugh about the melee.

Even with gold and platinum plaques on the walls, me and Pun definitely got into our fair share of street altercations. I had embraced violence early on in my life. As I got into the music industry, I didn't go looking for trouble, but I would still hold it down for myself if I was ever confronted. I wanted alllll the smoke. What I eventually realized was that people would bait me into fighting them so they could sue me and get money. I paid out hundreds of thousands of dollars in assault suits.

Same year, '98, the Puerto Rican Day Parade on June 14: This was our moment. Millions of people were out there to celebrate our heritage, and me and Pun were two of the biggest ambassadors of the Puerto Rican people in pop culture at that time. Big Pun, he was like the samurai of the Puerto Ricans. He was the dude. "Still Not a Player" was an anthem that transcended Latino culture. It brought Black and Brown together. Pun specifically wrote the "Boricua, morena" line—*Puerto Rican, Black*—in part to celebrate and unify Latinos and Blacks.

Me and Pun together at the Puerto Rican Day Parade got The Beatles treatment. Everybody showed us love. After the parade though, this guy walks up to me and says to my face, "My uncle told me you were pussy!" Mind you, I'm with the *entire* Terror Squad. I tried to defuse the situation, but he continued with the disrespect and my guys chased him.

I was rich, the kid just wanted to get me caught up in a lawsuit. My guys caught the kid on the 138th Street bridge, which connects Harlem to the Bronx. I never touched the guy. TS pounded him out and *threatened* to throw him off the bridge. Pun got in his gray Benz and zoomed up there. When he pulled up, I started yelling, "Noooo!" because I knew he was going to jump in it too. I started running up the bridge to stop him, then I dove on top of the kid to stop the TS guys from continuing to beat him up.

"Enough, enough," I told my crew.

A few weeks later, the kid said *I* beat him up and robbed him. I got arrested at one of my autograph signings in New York City. I was in the cell chillin' and suddenly I hear the whole precinct starting to go crazy. I hear people cheering and banging on the wall. Pun walks in with a smile. He's wearing all black, a leather suit, and has a bottle of champagne in his hand. He got arrested too.

"We made the papers, Twin!" he said smiling, taking sips of the bubbly. Who have you ever known to get arrested and drink champagne in jail? They really let Pun keep his bottle and drink it.

We were transferred to central booking in the Bronx, and I was once again shocked by the amount of love the cops showed us. They gave Pun his own cell and kept the gate *open*. They let him walk in and out and use the phone all night to speak to his wife. We had a friend who had juice up there and he brought lobsters, pork chops, and steaks to the jail. We fed the entire central booking. Pun was a movie! This was special. I'd never seen anything like it. The charges were eventually dismissed.

IT WAS TIME for Pun to work on his second solo project. Back in those days, you put out an album, you do some shows, you do your tour, you chill. You take your time. Rappers were dead-ass taking three, four years for every album. It wasn't like now where content is king and rappers never rest.

And so we took our time following up *Capital Punishment,* which we shouldn't have done. Pun was doing a lot of features instead of working on his album. About two years after we finished recording Capital Punishment, he got serious and went to the studio to start making *Yeeeah Baby*.

Pun started his work on the album by making these underground-style songs. But I wanted some hits on there. After "Still Not a Player," he loved the money and the fame, but if we would have let the true Big Pun go, he would have been so underground. At heart, Pun was what you would call a "horrorcore rapper." So, if he'd had his way initially, he would have crossed Gravediggaz, with the macabre vibes, with the hip-hop purist sensibilities of a Black Thought. He really just wanted simple boombap rhythms and dark, complex rhymes to show everybody he was the most lyrical one.

That's what he started doing on the second album. I went into the studio and I screamed on him; we argued in front of his wife and everybody. I left. When I came back to see how things were going, Pun just smiled and the engineer put on a song. Everybody was looking at me crazy when it came on.

"What I gotta do, let y'all niggas know? I am the nicest. Ever!" he said to start the song. "Hardcore, commercial. What you wanna do? You wanna wild out? You wanna dance? Don't matter to me, I got it all locked down, baby."

He was talking directly to me in the lyric. He just had a big smirk on his face watching me listen to it.

Obviously, Pun came to his senses and put some big hits on *Yeeeah Baby.* "It's So Hard" and "100%" were irrefutable smashes. His second album was dope—it went platinum too. Pun recorded the bulk of the LP in North Carolina, because we sent him down there to a weight-loss clinic. His health was becoming a major issue.

IT WAS A REAL TRYING TIME. Pun wanted to rap, he

wanted to work, but his health was in jeopardy. He was then over 600 pounds.

Some of his friends would ask him to consider weight-loss surgery like a gastric bypass, but he would laugh it off and dismiss it. I did manage to convince him to go to the clinic and he did well at first. He lost 100 pounds. That's why on "It's So Hard" he says, "I just lost a hundred pounds. I'm tryin' to live, I ain't goin' nowhere."

He did though; he got homesick and went back to New York. Pun ballooned to 700 pounds. With Pun, everything became excess. Despite the masterful breath control that was one of his trademarks as an MC, Pun had respiratory problems his entire career. Sometimes during shows, he would have to take breaks while his hypemen kept the crowd engaged. Even at his heaviest though, we never thought Pun would die. He was only twenty-eight, he had so much life left in him.

If I'd had back then all the knowledge about health that I have now, we never would have let him get like that. We would have really fought with him because he was out of control. But I just didn't know. I was over 450 pounds myself; I wasn't healthy either. Pun was just taking it to a different extreme.

February 7, 2000, was one of the darkest days in my life, one of the darkest days in hip-hop. Our godsend went back to heaven.

I had already dealt with death a lot. I thought it was normal.

When I was a kid, I grew up with like forty guys in my circle who were my peers. Thirty-five of them were killed young. They died before they even hit their early twenties. So I knew *the voice* when I heard it.

Real early in the day, I got the phone call. It was Pun's wife, Liza.

"He's gone! He's gone!" she said while crying. I *heard it* in her voice. I knew exactly what she was saying. I recognized that level of frantic.

"Where you at?" I asked her. "Where are you?"

They were in Westchester County. Pun loved to stay at this hotel that had an indoor pool; he loved to swim. I rushed up there from Jersey. It would normally have been an hour drive—we got there in fifteen minutes. It was the most disrespectful drive you've ever seen in your life. When we arrived, the paramedics were still performing CPR, trying to revive him. They really tried. He was already *gone,* but they kept working on him, pumping his chest. But they couldn't resuscitate him.

We all sat around his body. The EMS technicians let us have time alone just to talk to him. I'd never done that before—had a chance to say goodbye. It was overwhelming.

Last thing I ever imagined was that Pun would be taken from us like that. I went into a deep depression.

PUN HAD A BEAUTIFUL FUNERAL. His homegoing

ceremony was on February 11, 2000, at the Ortiz Funeral Home in the BX. We made sure he had a sendoff worthy of such an extraordinary human being. I took care of everything—I was trying to do whatever I could to make sure his family was less stressed. And I had to make sure we represented my brother the right way.

I was standing with the family when some older dude walked in, before they let everybody else in. The family suddenly looked as if a god had entered. I didn't know who he was. The older man walked around the room saying what's up to everybody. I'd seen that type of reaction before, with Uncle Fello and my brother when he had it: people acting deferential to the one in the family who has money.

"Who's this?" the older guy went, pointing at me.

If you knew anything about who Big Pun was, you knew who Fat Joe was.

"He ain't family, what is he doing here?" the man added.

Everybody was looking scared and started saying to him, "Nooooo! Noooo! Pleeeeeease!"

They knew who would fuck him up, especially that day.

The guy was Pun's uncle, the one who had refused to help him when Pun was a little boy.

"I know who you are," I said to him. "You're Pun's uncle, huh? I'm Fat Joe. I paid for all this."

I started to let him have it right in front of his family, Pun lying right there in the coffin.

"Guess what?" I added. "He told me just how big of a piece of shit you were. He told me when he was hungry you gave him rocks to eat. Let me tell you something else, talk to your family, because I'll fuck you up in here, bro. Bad!"

He calmed down.

"I'm sorry," he said to me.

"Yo, my man, get the fuck outta here," I answered.

One of my biggest fears is that I die and my family or my friends let the wrong people come to the funeral. If I don't fuck with you, I don't fuck with you. Don't let nobody that I didn't fuck with come in there and front like they gave a fuck. If you wasn't with us in life through the good and the bad times, don't come in my funeral like you give a fuck about me.

A lot of Pun's real friends from the music industry came to the funeral to tell him goodbye one last time. Diddy, Lil' Kim, and LL

Cool J all attended the funeral and wake. Pun's DJ LV was there crying. I walked up to him and said, "I got you. Don't worry, you're with me now."

LV became my DJ for shows until he blew as a producer with his duo partner Sean C from Loud. The two of them helmed the lion's share of Jay-Z's *American Gangster*, and have done beats for everyone from Nas, Busta Rhymes, and Raekwon to Diddy.

Pun died while his album was getting mixed and mastered, so we had to finish the last touches without him. *Yeeeah Baby* was released on April 4, 2000, and the entire hip-hop world rallied behind us. A lot of times, when you're in hip-hop and blow up, you get your haters, other artists who get jealous of you. But there was nothing but genuine love for Pun. He had a magnetic personality.

When we did the video for "It's So Hard," everybody came out. Puff, Kim and Cease, LL, Donnell Jones (who sings on the hook of the song), Busta and Spliff Star, Xzibit, Tha Liks, Angie Martinez, Mack 10, Big Tigger, Nice & Smooth, Funk Flex, Tony Touch, Mobb Deep, Melle Mel, M.O.P., Raekwon, Jennifer Lopez, Nas, Missy Elliott, Wyclef Jean, of course Nore. There wasn't a person who didn't show support. It was another ill moment in hip-hop history, but bittersweet.

I had a birthday party in 2019. We had Keith Sweat and SWV perform. Ja Rule got on the stage, Fabolous rocked. It was huge. Floyd Mayweather was there; Mary J. Blige, who's best friends with me and my wife, was there; Tiffany Haddish and Spike Lee came through. A reporter from the *New York Post* snuck in.

The reporter wrote about my shindig the next day and marveled at how the DJ kept shouting out Big Pun like he was *at the party*. What the reporter didn't know is that it's natural for us. It's nothing planned or rehearsed. Without us being aware of it, we shout out Pun like he's in the building even though it's been over twenty years since he passed. That's how much love and respect and admiration we have for him. He's still with us every day, our brother forever.

CHAPTER 13

WHAT'S BEEF?

IF FAT JOE IS WITH YOU, Fat Joe is with you. It could be a neighborhood Navy coming up the street with rocket launchers ready to desolate the whole block, but if you're on my team, or if you're somebody I consider family, I'm not abandoning you. Even if it's to my detriment, I'm ridin' till the wheels fall off. The same protocol I honored while holding court on the pavement, I applied in the music industry. It cost me millions and some of my sanity.

I met Irv Gotti at Battery Studios in New York City. Battery was one of the main labs for artists. A Tribe Called Quest recorded most of their albums there. Michael Jackson recorded there. Destiny's Child recorded there. I used to practically *live* in there until Pun and Tony Sunshine got us all banned by pulling out guns. That's a story for another time.

Battery had a real cool vibe and it was convenient to get to, right in the heart of Midtown Manhattan. One night, by mistake, Battery's administration office double-booked sessions for me and Irv in the same studio. This was back in 1999. Irv was the hottest executive in the game. He was the top A&R at Def Jam, responsible for bringing Jay-Z—who signed an imprint deal for Roc-A-Fella—and DMX over to the label. Both went multiplatinum in 1998. X, under the Ruff Ryders umbrella, dropped two albums that year, and Jay-Z ascended to the top of the rap monarchy, selling over three million records, and then headlining the Hard Knock Life Tour in 1999. Redman and Method Man were on that historic outing, as was X.

Def Jam rewarded Gotti by giving him his own subsidiary, Murder Inc. Records. Irv's cornerstone and leadoff artist was Ja Rule. Ja's debut, *Venni Vetti Vecci*, came out in June of 1999 and continued Irv's platinum streak. He could do no wrong.

I had never met Irv before, but I knew about him. He was at Battery working on Ja's follow-up, *Rule 3:36*. There was no tension over the double-booking; we hit it off right away. We just sat and told story after story all night long until about six, seven in the morning. The bond was immediate.

"We're like fucking brothers, we just ain't never know it," Irv said as we were finally leaving. "I can't believe people try to keep us away from each other, man."

That was a cool night. A few months later, Big Pun passed away. After his homegoing ceremony, I was sitting alone in a corner of the funeral home. I had been crying and was just trying to collect myself when I heard someone approach. I look up and it's Ja Rule extending his hand in love.

"Yo, sorry for your loss," he says to me.

Despite me and Gotti being cool, I had never really hung out or kicked it with Ja before that. To me, people paying their respects at funerals is very important. When I saw Ja, I almost felt like it was a sign from God. Here's this guy I barely even know, standing over me at my most vulnerable moment, showing love. I respected that so much.

"Aight, my brother man, thank you," I told him.

I didn't see or speak to Ja and Irv for several months after that. In that interim, I was going through one of the toughest stretches of my life. I was in a depression. Not only was Pun gone, but my sister and grandfather Cowboy had recently passed as well. While I was down, a lot of people acted like I was dead too. I heard people I counted as some of my best friends saying I was "going back to the projects." I was "gonna fall off." I couldn't "do it again." Some fans and music journalists echoed their sentiments. That really, really hurt me. But it also fueled me to work.

During that period on one random night, I got a phone call at four in the morning. This was when we all still had house phones. My phone was loud. It scared the shit out of me when it rang. I was lying next to my wife and still half asleep when I picked up and heard this really excited, roaring voice.

"Yooooooo, Joe!" he yelled.

"Who is this?" I responded, still a little disoriented.

"Irv Gotti!" the voice exclaimed.

"Irv Gotti? Oh shit! What's up?" I said. I didn't know how he got my home phone number.

He told me I had to come to The Hit Factory recording studio in Manhattan right away. He "had something for me."

I had no choice but to get my ass out of bed. Murder Inc. had become a full-fledged powerhouse. Irv was producing major hits for Ja, like "Put It on Me," and for outside artists like Jennifer Lopez. I definitely wanted to get some of that Murder madness. Everything they dropped was going number one for weeks.

So I went down to The Hit Factory with my wife. Irv was in the biggest room. I walked in, and he was there with Ja.

"Joe!!!" Ja yelled.

Irv greeted me with the biggest smile in the world and said, "Yo. We got something for you."

The engineer pressed play and blaring out of the speakers was the beat to what eventually turned into my song "What's Luv?" When the hook came, I heard this beautiful female voice. Irv told me that it belonged to this new girl named Ashanti he was signing to The Inc. Ja was on the second part of the hook.

"Oh! My! God!" I felt like I'd won the NBA championship! It was a *smash hit*. No one had ever given me a *smash hit* record. All I had to do was pen the verses and the bridge. "When I look in your eyes there's no stoppin' me / I want the Don Joey Crack on top of me . . ." The rest is history.

Irv and Ja were envisioning the song with me and J.Lo. They had recently worked with her on the "I'm Real" remix and felt a combo of me and her would draw a huge international audience. They had just got Ashanti to sing on it as a reference. She was new, she didn't have any hits yet, but she was so dope.

"Let's leave that girl on there, man," I insisted.

That's how "What's Luv?" came about. We put it on my album *Jealous Ones Still Envy*, which dropped on December 4, 2001. "What's Luv?" went all the way to number two on the Billboard Hot 100 in 2002. From that point on, I was stuck with Murder Inc. at the hip.

I SPENT NEW YEAR'S EVE 2002 performing on MTV with Ja and Ashanti. Ja had dropped what would turn out to be his biggest album, *Pain Is Love*, just a couple of months before *J.O.S.E.* came out. He introduced Ashanti to the world on his blockbuster "Always on Time." Then everybody heard her again on "What's Luv?" Everything lined up. Instead of being in the projects like my so-called friends had prophesied, I was on TV screens around the globe, wearing my fuckin' burgundy velour tuxedo. A few months later, me and Ashanti did one of my most iconic TV performances, on *MTV Spring Break*. I came out onstage wearing my giant TS medallion and no shirt on. The crowd went crazy. They'd never seen no sexy, topless, fat Bronx motherfucker tear the stage down, moving with ultimate confidence.

But that was who I was. I was back to feeling like *The Don*. My depression was gone. I had the biggest hit of my career and was finally selling records like the big boys. I was able to be me, and my music was crossing over. MTV, BET were loving Fat Joey from Forest projects.

Murder Inc. Records were dominating too. On April 2, 2002, Ashanti released her self-titled debut solo album and the shit went through the roof. She broke the record for biggest first-week sales for a debut female artist. A storm was coming, though.

See, in 2002, while Murder Inc. controlled the charts and radio,

Irv's and Ja's old rival from Queens controlled the streets. 50 Cent and G-Unit were revolutionizing the mixtape game.

Mixtapes were unofficial releases that weren't sanctioned by record labels. Mixtape cassettes—and later CDs—sold in the streets like crack. You could go to your local bootlegger who was posted up in these hood shopping hubs like Fordham Road in the Bronx or Jamaica Ave in Queens and purchase mixtapes for $5. Sometimes three for $10.

Mixtapes featured music by your favorite hip-hop and R&B artists. In the '70s, pioneers like Grandmaster Flash used to record themselves spinning at parties during hip-hop's embryonic stage. In the '80s and '90s, the game evolved, with DJs like Kid Capri making mixes of him playing popular songs and selling the tapes. Later it was DJs like Ron G popularizing the hip-hop blend, where they would take the vocals from an R&B song like New Edition's "Once in a Lifetime Groove" and mix it over the beat of Big Daddy Kane's "Ain't No Half-Steppin'." Then you had DJs like Clue who would feature all your favorite rappers (both established stars and up-and-coming acts who would blossom into stars) freestyling over popular beats, along with "exclusive" songs. By exclusive, I mean tracks that would eventually become singles or album cuts but hadn't even hit the radio yet. Some songs were gladly given to the DJs by artists, but some exclusives came about via leaks.

For artists in New York such as myself, Mary J. Blige, Biggie, Jay-Z, and Nas, mixtapes became a launching ground for new music. If it was hot in the streets, the radio and clubs would flock to it and you had a hit. Mixtapes were a litmus test. Even though we didn't directly make money from our music being on mixtapes, it was among the most successful and proven promotional vehicles in the game.

In the early 2000s, 50 Cent, Tony Yayo, and Lloyd Banks turned the entire mixtape industry upside down by making their own hybrid underground releases. You have to give it to Fif. He was a visionary and he came along and mastered the game. The early

G-Unit tapes were basically like albums, but they had freestyles, original songs, and songs where they would jack other artists' records and make them theirs. For instance, the Unit had a song called "After My Chedda" where they used the beat from LL Cool J's "Luv U Better." They had their own flows and lyrics for the verses, but though they had their own words for the hook, they used the same melody from LL's chorus.

50 had made a lot of noise on the single "How to Rob" back in 1999. The record was comical, but biting at the same time. 50 had the audacity to rap about robbing celebrities from Jay-Z to Bobby Brown, Mariah Carey, Wu-Tang Clan, and even my brother Big Pun, who was still alive at the time. While some of the stars just laughed it off, some like Pun and Jay-Z clapped back in rhymes. "Go against Jigga, yo' ass is dense / I'm about a dollar what the fuck is 50 Cents?" Hov retorted on "It's Hot (Some Like It Hot)." Regardless of how you felt about "How to Rob," everybody—artists, execs, producers, and fans alike—was talking about Fif. His buzz was strong.

Around that time, him and his crew got into some street beef with Ja and his crew. That's the story I was told, I wasn't there. Apparently there was a brawl in the studio one night between both factions and somebody got stabbed.

Soon after, in an unrelated incident that had nothing to do with Murder Inc. at all, 50 got shot nine times in his neighborhood and almost died right before his debut LP, *Power of the Dollar*, was supposed to drop. The story is well documented. He lost his deal with Columbia Records and not only did he have to recuperate from life-threatening wounds, he had to start his career from the bottom again.

While 50 was going through his trials and tribulations, Murder Inc. became one of music's most successful and consistent brands.

Long story short: Bad blood between The Inc. and 50 was still harbored by both sides. When 50 was trying to make his comeback, unbeknownst to me, Irv "blocked him." Gotti used his power and influence in the industry to blackball Fif from getting a new record deal. Irv told multiple labels that if they signed him, those labels couldn't do business with Murder Inc.

Fif came back stronger than ever though, driven in part by a desire for vengeance. He even changed physically: His body went from stocky to G.I.-Joe-action-figure chiseled. And before long, his music would start to captivate an entire generation. 50's energy and work ethic were relentless, plus he was a great songwriter and had a dramatic backstory. There was an undercurrent of perceived danger in his music and at his shows. He'd been shot nine times and survived. Who ever heard of that? He would perform at shows and appear on his mixtape covers wearing a bulletproof vest. Not only was the music great, his story was extraordinary and he was certified by the streets.

Eventually 50 Cent would sign a million-dollar deal as part of a joint venture with Dr. Dre's Aftermath Entertainment, Eminem's Shady Records, and their parent company, Interscope Records. Wasn't nobody selling more records than Dre and Em at the time. Not even Irv and Ja.

50 fit right in with Aftermath. While building his fan base with bonafide classic singles like "Wanksta," "In da Club," and "Many Men (Wish Death)," Fif waged war on Murder Inc. He took no prisoners on dis records like "I Smell Pussy" and "Back Down." It really got ugly.

The closest thing to that *energy* I'd ever seen was Tupac. I'm not comparing 50 Cent to Tupac. I'm just saying that the *energy* was similar. Pac's outspokenness and his many altercations outside of music, like getting into a shoot-out with the police or nearly being murdered in New York, only made people want to listen to his music more. With 50's cinematic backstory and him always being totally transparent in his mixtapes and interviews, it built up a powerful appetite for an official album. And 50 delivered a classic. I'm going to clubs and I'm hearing the "What up, Blood? / What Up, Cuz?" I'm hearing "You say you a gangsta, but you never pop nothin'..." I'm hearing everybody singing his shit. DJs weren't playing Ja's music like that anymore.

The fans and the industry started to turn on Ja.

All my friends told me to back away from Ja Rule and Murder Inc. Pretty much the whole industry was scared because 50 Cent was crashing over everything like a tidal wave. His debut, *Get Rich or Die Tryin'*, sold almost 900,000 units its first week. DJs were playing almost every song off the album on the radio and in the clubs like they were singles. You couldn't escape 50 if you tried. *Get Rich* pushed over six million copies in the U.S. in 2003. He was a juggernaut.

All my closest friends continued pleading with me to "stay way from Ja Rule and Murder Inc."

I went through another round of depression. Murder Inc.—Ja, Irv, Ashanti—had helped transform my career with their support. They had been there for me at a dark time. There was no way I could back away and not stand next to them.

50 Cent had Ja Rule on the ropes. To keep it a buck, even without 50's assault, Ja was facing heavy backlash. No really, he was on his way *out*. Fans, many of whom supported Ja in the past, were saying they were tired of him singing on tracks and his music was soft. So just like when I was down, the Inc. threw me a record, when Ja was down, I threw him a record: "New York."

I felt Ja needed an undeniable hardcore anthem. No margin for error. Cool & Dre produced the song. That was my record, but Ja is my brother, so I gave him the song. Ja originally had two verses on there, but I got Jadakiss on it for him. Ja went first, I had the second verse, and Jada closed it out. "I got a hundred guns, a hundred clips / Nigga, I'm from Newwwwww Yorrrrkkkk!"

A week later, I was in a car with Irv's brother, Chris Gotti. I was even closer with Chris than I was with Irv. Back when Irv was just producing, Chris was Irv's manager and later turned into his business partner as The Inc. was being started. Chris was actually there in the hospital with me when my daughter, Azzy, was born. Me and

Chris were driving from New York up to Boston to see the Celtics in the NBA playoffs.

"I want to play this record for you," he tells me. Then he puts the CD in. Ja is singing on a demo version of the song that turned out to be "Wonderful." He wanted to get my opinion. Was it good enough to be a single?

"If it wasn't for the money, cars, and movie stars and jewels and all these things I've gotttttt!"

The track was good, but I was worried. I told Chris, "You know what? Two years before the 50 beef, if that record would have come out, it would have been legendary with just Ja on it. But niggas is shitting on Ja so much right now, I don't think that's gonna fly."

Then I had an idea.

"You know what? Give me this song, let me see what I can do." I began to strategize. My plan was to fly to Chicago and get R. Kelly on the record. At the time, R. Kelly was the biggest singer in the game and I had a good relationship with him. So I went out to Chicago to convince R. to collaborate with Ja on it.

I presented the song to R. and he liked it, too. "But yo," he told me, "he's got drama." He was referring to all the heat on Ja with the G-Unit beef.

"Who gives a fuck, man," I huffed back. "Let's just do this record. Ja's my brother."

R. Kelly agreed and he did the record. Ja dropped those two songs—"New York" and "Wonderful"—on his 2004 album, *R.U.L.E.*, and, even with all the drama, it went gold. The mutha-fucka was back. "Wonderful" blew up on radio and the streets ate "New York" up. Not only did our city love the new hometown anthem, but fans from outside of NY loved it too.

I guess, I don't know for sure, but I guess 50 Cent saw what was going on, did the math, and thought to himself, *You know what? It's that fat muthafucka! He's the only one still playing Ja close.*

Everybody had turned their backs on Ja Rule and Murder Inc. except me. I was the only one. And that's when my beef started with 50 Cent. You're reading this book, you know the type of guys I had beef with in the streets—scary guys. So I damn sure wasn't gonna back down from a *rapper*.

Me and 50 have so much love for each other today. If we'd grown up together, we probably would have been life-long best friends. But a decade and a half ago, the hatred was real.

Ironically, rumor has it 50 Cent always wanted to sign with the Terror Squad. This was before he signed with Eminem and Dr. Dre and way before we had the beef. He'd always been a big fan of Big Pun, always a fan of Fat Joe.

All those good feelings came to an end after the "New York" single came out around the end of 2004. 50 started coming at me in interviews and on songs. He made an animated video for the song "Piggy Bank" where he threw shots at me, Jada, Shyne, and Nas. He even made a whole mixtape dissing me, called *Elephant in the Sand*. He got a candid picture of me and my wife on the beach in our bathing suits and made that shit the cover artwork. Although I've never had a problem with being seen with no shirt on—women think I'm sexy, that's all that matters—50 was going too far by putting private pictures of me and wife out to the public.

You know there was no way I wasn't going to shoot back. I got on Hot 97 and dissed him in a radio interview with their morning DJ Miss Jones. I also recorded a 50 Cent dis song to retaliate: "My Fofo" off of my *All or Nothing* album. But this shit started to feel like it was beyond rap—it felt personal. Our acrimony built up for months through music and in interviews with us dissing each other, but we had never crossed paths. It would have been crazy if we did. Lines of disrespect had been crossed by both sides. Threats had been sent by both sides and neither side took those lightly. Both sides refused to be punked. At a certain point, there were no more words to be said. Action was the next step. I was ready to bring the violence and I'm sure 50 was too.

IT WAS MTV that brought us into each other's path. During the 2005 Video Music Awards in Miami, at the American Airlines Arena, me and 50 Cent were both scheduled to be part of the show. 50's crew was extra thick that year. He had his regular G-Unit MCs there: Lloyd Banks, Tony Yayo, and Young Buck. He had just signed Mobb Deep, so Havoc and Prodigy were with him, too. Ma$e was also supposed to have joined 50's label and he was runnin' with them. Plus 50 had brought some extra muscle.

But Terror Squad was deep too—the label and the crew. All of my men-at-arms were with me.

I knew it would get ugly with both of our factions sitting in the audience, so I purposely stayed backstage with my guys for most of the show. I wasn't scared for us. I was scared for *them*. My team was ready to *decapitate* someone. The Squad has so much love for me, they would never let anyone disrespect me without serious repercussions. I knew there was a *strong possibility* somebody would get hurt with all of us in the crowd. I didn't want to disrespect MTV, because they always showed me love. I didn't want to disrespect hip-hop.

Halfway through the show, I went out on the stage to give Missy Elliott an award. What the audience at home didn't see was that during the commercial break beforehand, 50 Cent got out of his seat and started walking the house. He went up to the audience in the cheap seats and started waving to me. It was like he was daring me to get off the stage and physically confront him. Then he went down to the floor and started slapping fives with Jay-Z and Diddy.

He was really trying to antagonize me as I was standing there waiting to speak on the mic but I wasn't trying to pay him no mind. Then 50 actually came onstage for a few seconds. He stood several feet away from me.

I was saying to myself, *Okay, we're about to fight. We're about to get it on right here at the VMAs.*

When the show came back on—this is *live* TV, mind you—50

went back to his seat. The G-Unit started yelling at me while I'm reading off the teleprompter. The Terror Squad, offstage in the wings, started barking back. That's when I dropped my jab: "I feel safe with all the police protection courtesy of G-Unit."

Me and my crew left the building after that. As we were heading out, some G-Unit guys streamed backstage to confront us. The police separated us and we were able to leave without a fight. Later in the show, 50 came out for his performance, a medley of songs featuring G-Unit and Mobb Deep. Tony Yayo's "So Seductive" was the closing performance and when they finished, 50 yells into the mic, "Fat Joe is pussy, man. Pussy boy. Fuck boy." You could hear the curses on TV from what they tell me. You damn sure heard it in the arena. He was going so bad they had to cut his mic.

The funny thing is, right before the show, me and 50 were both saying in our interviews that we were done with the beef and ready to move on. But the VMAs turned Fat Joe vs. 50 Cent on flame broil. It's one thing to beef with each other on albums and mix-tapes, but when you beef live on MTV during the channel's biggest night, things are serious.

I was supposed to be the first artist ever to collaborate with Jordan Brand. I've always rocked the most Jordans, always had the flyest, most exclusive Jordans out of any celeb. No one can compete with my sneaker collection. Me and Michael Jordan are actual friends. I met with him six times going over designs for the Fat Joe Jordan. Some of those meetings were literally just me and him, brainstorming, bouncing ideas off each other. But after the VMAs, Mike deaded the deal.

"You know I love you, Big Joe, but you're too hot right now," he told me on a phone call. "I wanted to do it, but I'm not into all that rap beef. With all this controversy, we can't do the sneaker anymore."

That was it. I lost about $20 million by not getting that deal. I lost out on other endorsements too. Promoters definitely didn't book me and 50 Cent on the same shows. Everybody had to keep us separated. But as fate would have it, after the VMAs, we didn't see each other again in person for almost a decade.

THE VMAS WERE ON August 28, 2005, and on September 5, 2012, half the rap world—including myself and 50 Cent—came out to pay their respects to Chris Lighty at his funeral at the Frank E. Campbell funeral home on Madison Avenue in Manhattan. Chris was just forty-four years old when he was found dead on August 30, from a gunshot wound to the head that police ruled to be self-inflicted.

Chris had a great legacy that spanned thirty-plus years. You already know how he put me on, but after that, he went on to be one of the most successful music executives ever with Violator management. Violator boasted an all-star roster of LL Cool J, Busta Rhymes, A Tribe Called Quest, Missy Elliott, N.O.R.E., Mobb Deep, and even Mariah Carey came under the umbrella, along with many others. Violator helmed the careers of 50 Cent and Ja Rule. Not at the same time, thank God. Ja was at Violator for a cup of coffee. 50, on the other hand, became a cornerstone of the company.

Chris had it all: money, respect, success, and even though it was reported he was going through a divorce at the time of his death, he had beautiful children whom he loved dearly. So when he died and police said it was suicide, it didn't seem real. Mental health wasn't a big topic in the hip-hop community—or Black and immigrant communities, generally—back then and no one could fathom Chris taking his own life. Guys like Chris just didn't die like that.

What hurt the most was that Chris had always been there for everybody, and many of us felt like we had failed him; we should have been there for him. But few people were really aware of how deep his depression had become.

There was a tremendous outpouring of love at his funeral. Busta, Mary J. Blige, LL, Q-Tip, Yo Gotti, even Chi-Ali were there for the funeral. Chi was the first artist Chris signed through his venture at Relativity Records—followed by The Beatnuts and me. Chi became a teenage rap star in the early '90s. In 2000 Chi shot and killed the brother of his daughter's mother and went on the run for over a year. He was featured on *America's Most Wanted* twice. He got caught by the police in '01, was convicted of manslaughter, and served over a decade in prison. He had just gotten out of jail the morning of Chris's memorial and I found myself standing next to him. I felt like it was God's doing, that he could come to Chris's funeral. I also thought about all those lost years—the years Chi lost to a gun he shot at someone else, the years Chris lost to a gun he pointed at himself. So much time lost.

I walked into the funeral home and saw 50 Cent across the room. We immediately lock eyes. He doesn't say nothin', I don't say nothin'. But I know everybody in the whole funeral home was scared that something might pop off—just seeing the two of us in the same place at the same time, after so many years of escalating beef, made people uncomfortable. Rightfully so.

I had a regular button-up shirt on, slacks. I had no crew with me. I went there one deep, no extra people. I didn't want a situation where my guys would see the G-Unit crew and start antagonizing. Both me and Fif had such a reverence for Chris, neither one of us was on no bullshit that day. To be honest, we didn't even have the energy. That was a very painful day for us both.

LATER THAT MONTH, I got a call from Stephen Hill, who was the president of programming for BET. He told me that the BET Hip Hop Awards were coming up in October at the Atlanta Civic Center and he wanted to do a huge tribute performance for Chris. I was with it off rip. I actually had a show to do in Africa on that same date but I canceled it. Fuck it. This was for Chris.

Stephen casually said, "Hey, so for the tribute to Chris it'll be Missy, Busta, Q-Tip, Mobb Deep, 50 Cent, and you." He kind of mumbled "50 Cent" and hoped I wouldn't hear him. I heard him, but I didn't say nothin'. October rolls around and I head down to Atlanta for the taping. I bring a few members of TS: Pistol Pete, Raoul, Rich Player. Those guys are the MVPs of The Terror Squad, the Navy SEALS. For some reason, the organizers put 50's trailer right in front of my trailer. They made no effort to separate us.

The whole industry was in the audience at rehearsal and everybody was stressed the fuck out, wondering if 50 Cent and Fat Joe were gonna go at it. I could see people peeking out from behind a door in the auditorium. It was like high noon in the Wild, Wild West. All the so-called tough guys in the industry, the extorters, they're looking on like *Holy shit! It's about to go down.*

I didn't know, but the security at the door wouldn't let Pistol Pete into the rehearsal. I wasn't at the door when Pete came, but later someone told me that 50 was there at the time. He told the orgnanizers, "I'm not going in if you don't let him in too. Terror Squad and G-Unit, we're together." That's what they told me. I wasn't there for that. I was onstage rehearsing my performance. I did "Lean Back" and then 50 Cent strides on the stage to perform "I Get Money." We were finally onstage together. People were looking at us like we were aliens.

50 had stalked the stage during his song and when he got to the end, he purposely finished right next to where I was standing. Then he pulled out his hand for me to shake.

"Peace," he said with his hand extended. "Chris Lighty wanted peace."

In that moment, our entire feud played out in my mind. Memories unscroll: I see him talking about my wife. I'm looking at him dissing me onstage and on the radio. The mixtapes. The videos. It all flashes in my head.

50 left his hand out for peace damn near a minute without me grabbing it. I just looked at him.

Is he for real? I thought. I had all this anger built up. We'd been beefing for eight years and the only outcome I'd ever seen to this kind of beef was violence. So when he said, "Peace," I couldn't believe it.

"Peace?" I asked him reluctantly.

"Yeah, peace for Chris Lighty," Fif repeated. "He wanted peace." I shook his hand.

You remember *The Wizard of Oz* when they were like, "Ding-dong, the witch is dead . . . / the wicked witch is dead"? That's how people were *merrily* shouting about me and 50's beef ending. People ran onstage in that moment, hugging us. Not just rappers—regular industry insiders were coming up there, hugging us, faces beaming with joy. They were like, "Oh my God. It's peace! Thank God!" It was an incredible moment.

The actual show went flawlessly too. The Violator set was the highlight of the night. A Tribe Called Quest came out first and set it off with "Award Tour." Then Busta Rhymes came out with more thunder with "Put Your Hands Where My Eyes Could See." Then it was my turn with "Lean Back." We kept hitting them with a flurry of classics. Missy came out next with "Get Your Freak On," and 50 batted clean-up with "I Get Money." The whole crowd stayed on their feet. I know Chris would've been proud to see that. Not only was the beef over, but we were actually all rockin' together.

I met up with 50 in a hotel room in L.A. like a week later. We chopped it up, just me and him. I gotta mention too that back in the day, I discovered the director Eif Rivera. He went on to do so many of the classic 50 Cent videos and even directed episodes of *Power* for him. Eif would always be trying to get me and 50 together. "Yo, stop beefing," Eif would say. "Y'all would be the coolest niggas. Y'all would love each other. You don't understand."

Eif set up that initial meeting in L.A. We just chopped it up like, "Yo, you know all these years we've been beefing with each other over nothin'. We never really even had beef." Before long we were in that hotel room just cracking jokes.

For both of us I guess, we'd been living with that feeling you have when you're in a serious beef. Nobody wants to wake up and walk out the house every morning, thinking, *Is this the day we're gonna lock up and really hurt each other?* For eight years it was like, "Yo, we see him anywhere, it's on." We had the same mentality. You know how they say, "kick the can down the road"? We had pushed it to where there was no outcome but violence. *Now let's see who gonna back that shit up.*

I didn't think 50 was a coward at all. I know I wasn't. It was gonna go down, major violence, sooner or later, wherever we finally met.

And just like that, it was over. We shook hands; it was peace.

"Chris Lighty had been telling me for years to squash that shit," 50 divulged to me in that hotel room.

We squashed it. After that, 50 came down to Miami and hung out with me two or three days in a row. I even threw him a small birthday party on a big-ass yacht. Could you believe that? Me and him, *on his birthday,* we're cuttin' the cake on the yacht. We were on the biiiiiig shit! Not no regular yacht. Shit was as big as a building, four stories tall. Me and my wife, 50 and his girl. We were celebrating life instead of wanting to kill each other. That was a really surreal moment.

We work hard. We come from the streets. But you know, if you're reading this book, that we both made a conscious decision to move away from that life. We were entertainers and artists now, working to better our lives and make sure things went better for the next generation, for our families and communities. And to think that over some dumb shit, we would have ended it all. We would have destroyed all we'd built and got some innocent people hurt in the mix: If we'd seen each other in Starbucks, people would have got hurt in Starbucks. It was a relief to squash it. I believe he would tell you the same.

AFTER ME AND 50 squashed everything at the rehearsal for the BET Hip Hop Awards, I immediately went to the artists' trailer outside the Atlanta Civic Center where Rick Ross and DJ

Khaled were. I told them, "50 Cent made peace with me. I shook his hand for Chris Lighty." Ross was and is a close friend and Khaled is my brother. I was excited to tell them what had transpired and I wanted their conflicts with 50 to end as well.

Now, to rewind a little bit: 50 and Ross were also beefing at the time, a conflict that loosely stemmed from my trouble with 50. Back in 2008, during an interview, 50 warned Ross not to stand "too close" to me, just like people had been warned not to stand too close to Ja and Murder Inc. way back when. Ross didn't take too kindly to 50 sending him orders and dropped a track months later called "Mafia Music" where Ross played into a nasty public feud between 50 and the mother of his oldest son.

It had been on between them two since.

50 also levied disses at Khaled throughout the year because he knew Khaled was close to me and Ross.

When I dropped news of the reconciliation, at first Khaled and Ross were taken aback. Khaled was a little more upset than Ross. They both had every right to be pissed. 50 didn't just come at me or at Ross. He played dirty, man. He played with family. So they really were upset with him.

But Ross slowly warmed up to the idea of ending his feud with 50 Cent, too.

But then right after that—and I mean less than thirty minutes later—some of 50's guys beat up Gunplay, one of Ross's Maybach Music Group artists and a close friend, in the trailer parking area.

When I heard the news I thought, *They ain't squashing their beef now.* And I was right: Their conflict kept going.

AFTER MY BEEF ENDED, I affirmed to the Gottis and Ja Rule that I was still loyal to them. I'll always love them. They saved my life. But I realized that fall—with the death of Chris and the feeling that all this beef was taking me back to a life I thought I'd left—that I need to be about peace. I tried to bring both 50 and Ja out at Summer Jam one year, but Ja wasn't with it.

As for me and Fif, I'm proud to say that we developed a real bond. We've actually been close friends for more years now than we had beef. One of the oldest rules in the hood is that you don't get points for picking on somebody who can't defend themselves. Your respect is measured by who you go to war with. 50 will tell you when it comes to his rap beefs, it's mostly just that: rap. But with us, it ran deeper; with G-Unit and Terror Squad, it was going down.

You learn to respect each other from beefin'. 50 once told me, "I get along with you more than niggas I've known for years. More than niggas I grew up with." We have a brotherhood built on mutual respect. I don't think he ever wants to lose that and neither do I.

PART IV
SQUAD STORIES

CHAPTER 14

THE TERROR SQUAD PART I

BY THIS POINT IN THE BOOK, you've read a lot about Terror Squad, or TS, but what exactly *is* The Terror Squad?

It's complicated but let me walk you through it.

The mid-1980s to the early 1990s was definitely the most terrifying era of The Terror Squad. I had a slew of lawless lieutenants linking up with me and rampaging through the streets. Each member had hard-earned carte blanche to bring turbulence on their own, but when we formed like Voltron, we were similar to the nWo wrestling faction, if you follow the WWE. There were insurmountable odds you'd have to overcome to go against us. We had the strength in numbers and the will and skills to push things past the limit in any situation.

But that's not where Terror Squad began. Innocently enough, Terror Squad started out as a graffiti crew when I was just a kid. Gismo and Cosmo started it, rest in peace to both of them, but they eventually started to feel like they were getting too old for graffiti. Cosmo went on to robbing banks and Gismo was doing his own thing. But they were done with Terror Squad, our little graffiti clique. We were in the back of my apartment building when they told me they were handing over the reins to our franchise.

"Yo, we're going to make you president of Terror Squad," they told me. The first thing I did was hold a meeting with all the young guys and girls.

"We're Terror Squad. We're going to take this to the next level," I decreed. "This is going to be the biggest."

What did it mean to go to the next level? Well, we were a graffiti squad, but we were also young punks. So we went through our next phase, which was beating everybody up and robbing people. Then it evolved into being a syndicate running the streets. Then we more or less left the streets alone and went into music with me, Pun, Khaled, Remy, Armageddon, Tony Sunshine, and eventually Cool & Dre being the core of Terror Squad, the label.

As my vision for Terror Squad grew, I wanted the brand to be worldwide, larger than life, not just music. It was meant to express an idea: Being in TS meant being part of a team of people who came from the bottom but were committed to help one another in the ruthless pursuit of our collective goals, which evolved as we expanded. Now we've got guys in Terror Squad who used to be NBA players, like Stephon Marbury and Mike Bibby. We've got guys that are doctors in Terror Squad. Dawn Florio, she's a lawyer and she's Terror Squad.

The squad includes some of my oldest and most devoted friends, like my brother E Philly out in Philadelphia, aka "Crazy Eddie"— truly a brother on another level even though I didn't grow up with him—and my friend Drop, who has been incredibly devoted to TS. He's a producer and engineer and he'll do anything for his friends. He's almost loyal to a fault, because some people take advantage of that. But loyalty is at the core of TS.

People have wondered how I got all these characters to gel into one unit. I think the key is that I treat every individual as special, but our shared dream was always about unity, all for one and one for all. That's what it is. Terror Squad, as it's constituted today, is one large family. Everyone plays a part based on their own passions and expertise, but we share a collective goal: to elevate our community.

TS is in the sneaker business. My brother, and one of me and my wife's best friends, Terrell Jones, is integral in helping me be the flyest with my wardrobe and amass my world-famous sneaker col-

Joe Brady, the missing kid from *The Brady Bunch*

Was this guy laughing or what? I'm still on the couch like this today.

He's a big shot! Me during my run of wins on Amateur Night at the Apollo in the late '80s.

Me and Lord Finesse were so young in this photo. Vintage '90s. This was at one of his shows. He always inspired me.

Don't nothin' move but the money. I was fourteen, right before I moved out on my own, at the bodega in Harlem, 132nd and Park Avenue. Somebody needs to bring that soccer sweatshirt back!

Easter drip! Me and my brother, Angel, looking fly, in the middle of the projects on Easter Sunday.

Yo, that's fresh! Me and my crew.

Harlem on the rise! Uptown with Tony Montana (right) and in the middle is my guy Pie-Eating Jose. This was right on 125th Street. Me and Tone were so close, we wore matching outfits on some EPMD-type vibe all the time.

D.I.T.C. and extended family, including Finesse, Diamond D, and Big L

Wildin'! Me, Full Flex, and the crew. That looks like the Tunnel. The guy with the X hat is my guy Rhino. He was strong enough to literally pick up cars.

A lifetime of brotherhood. Full Flex forever.

"Could you put me on?" Me and the visionary Red Alert. He saw it first.

Drip too hard!/'88. In the middle of the projects with that custom-made Dapper Dan trench. You see the hat to match? The Bronco was known as "The Fat Gangstamobile." I was selling drugs for sure. I had not made the pivot to music.

GTS! The Girl Terror Squad. My sister Lisa and her crew. Look at the building. This was theeee Bronx.

The Originators: Gizmo and Power

TS Royalty. Tone Montana, Full Flex, and DJ Serge

Tone Montana, 88 vibes

Mr. Ness and The Money Man

Trust the process—my crew supporting me at Amateur Night at the Apollo

Get at me, dog! When the King of Yonkers and TS connect. We love and miss you, DMX.

Latino X-cellence

What's love? Twenty-plus years of friendship between me and Ashanti.

The King

Mommy and Daddy 2.0

My heart, baby Joey

The love of my life

Mommy and Daddy

Unconditional love

Politics as usual. At Sylvia's Restaurant with New York City mayor Eric Adams; former Bronx borough president Rubén Díaz Jr.; and member of the House of Representatives in Belize, my brother Shyne.

This is what it's all about. Teaching the youth at a MasterClass at UP NYC on Third Avenue in the South Bronx.

Michael Jordan called me out of nowhere. "I heard it's your birthday. Let's have some dinner at TAO." I was so fucked up at that time; don't let the jewelry fool you. That was when I was really trying to make a comeback—not in music, just from having to pay millions of dollars in back taxes.

School daze! On the set with Kevin Hart. We always have legendary laughs. Me and Kev go all the way back to when he appeared in the "Lean Back" video.

Some friendships last forever. Me and the great Jennifer Lopez in her dressing room during her residency in Las Vegas.

Joey topless.

One of my close friends, LL Cool J, came down to the video for "Success." I was Coogie down to the socks!

Sunday service with the hip-hop congregation.

Crack, RiRi, and Khaled. I see you, Uncle Dan, in the back.

The Architects: Scott Storch, Joe Crack, and Dr. Dre

Time is Illmatic

The Queen and The Don

Verzuz at Barclays with two teachas: KRS-One and Big Daddy Kane

An unbreakable bond. What can I say about this guy? The most humble, the most loyal, Weezy's the best.

Bro and sis spoiled rotten. Me and Remy did a show in Atlantic City; the chinchilla was down to my ankles.

Twinz 2023. Me and Khaled used to be so afraid to fly; now we take jets everywhere together.

Home of the Wave. Our 158th and Broadway location.

The Number One Stunnas.

BX, we made it! All the way to the White House.

lection. The natural progression was to open a sneaker store. So I partnered with my man Slow, who's been with me for almost thirty years, and JB, who's one of the most loyal ever in Terror Squad. They run my UP NYC stores. It's an honor for us to provide jobs for our people.

Like sneakers, jewelry is another passion of mine, and sure enough, the squad has it covered. Pristine Jewelers, they're the biggest jewelers in the game and they're TS. Also, major, major love to my sister Natina. She's a big executive at Def Jam. I met her years ago at the premiere of one of the seasons of *Power* at the London Hotel in LA. She was sitting right next to 50. We connected and she has been a major asset in my life ever since.

We have barbers in Terror Squad. Rich the Barber, he's my brother, there for me when I need him. People make rappers and other celebrities out to be superheroes. But we are human beings—and some of us are dealing with years of accumulated stress and trauma on top of whatever any given day presents. Whenever I have a tough time, my brother Rich comes and sits on the couch with me. We eat a pint of ice cream together and get into it. We talk things through.

The TS family also includes actual family: Uncle Dan, who books a lot of my shows, is my mother's brother. Dan is five years older than me, my birthday is August 19, his is August 20. We used to be so poor, our family would split one birthday cake for me and Danny. They'd sing, "Happy birthday, Joe-eeeyyy," and then right after sing, "Happy birthday, Dann-nyyyy."

I've always looked up to him. Years ago when I used to get in trouble, he'd be the guy who came to get me out of jail—Danny would pay for a lawyer for me. If the cops were looking for me, he would hide me in his crib. If I didn't have clothes, he'd lend me his clothes. He's got a soft spot in my heart because he was there for me before anybody could have imagined I would be "Fat Joe." He was always there for Joey, his nephew.

Some people just feel like family: Percy, I've known him almost as long as I've known Dan. Me and Percy met first day of school in kindergarten. He was getting jumped by two Puerto Rican brothers who were ganging up on him. They were twins named David and Noel and they were bad as hell. I intervened to defend Percy, and the rest of our elementary years, me and him would get into trouble. Percy would be in the principal's office and I'd be right there with him getting punishments.

These days, sometimes Percy gets carried away, because we've been that tight practically all of our lives. He acts like he's got privileges that nobody else's got. He acts like he can say shit to me nobody else can say. But I know I can depend on him if shit ever hits the fan.

Out of all my friends, the most loyal is Raul. We met the first day of Morris High, like I told y'all. We beat up the leader of the kids who used to bully me in junior high. He became TS on the spot. One of my best moves ever was to let him be down. Raul has been with me ever since. He's my brother, and it's funny because he looks just like me, only slimmer. People think we are actual blood brothers. Raul walks around with the biggest TS piece on his chain.

The Mayor went to high school with me. First day of high school, after I had a brawl down the block from my school, I went straight to class. In my homeroom, I met The Mayor, Billy Blanco, and Surge. We had the crew! Mayor, I look to him for advice because he's very intelligent and knows about the world. He brings a lot of wisdom to the table. Billy from Courtlandt Ave, aka Billy Blanco, is a good brother. Then there's Surge.

Surge is so much TS, there were times we had beef with guys he grew up with on his own block and he had to take our side. He never flinched when reppin' us. Surge is a guy who never looked for trouble, never bothered anybody, but unfortunately he had to do two five-year bids in prison. He was at the wrong place, wrong time, and then he was doing what he had to do. It wasn't like he was out there selling drugs or robbing or killing people, he just always had that bad luck. He's one of the greatest people in the world though.

Pistol Pete, we got together in the '80s too. We came together when I used to be hustling in the street. I've never hustled with Pistol, but we knew each other. Our reputations preceded us. He was always that guy walking around in the streets, putting pressure on everybody. Even though he was cock diesel and could beat anybody up, he chose to go another route when getting his point across. Let's just say his name is self-explanatory. Pete's been a project of mine. God bless him, he's not supposed to be in civilization. Guys like Pistol, with that type of reputation, are usually in jail forever or they're dead. These guys cease to exist in the streets.

Rich Player is the opposite. He's the nicest, most lovable guy in the world. My daughter calls him her "favorite uncle." He's probably the only OG Terror Squad member with a college degree. He's always in peak physical condition, working on his physique, inspiring others to be fit and healthy. Athletics changed his life.

Rich was in the streets with us, and he used to get busy. But he was the first to change his life in a positive way. He moved down to Miami and became a youth football coach. He coached the Pembroke Pines Bengals and later became the president of the Carol City Chiefs, which is part of Flo Rida's kid's league. In Miami, he's loved in the streets like Robin Hood. The kids cherish him, their parents adore him. He's a winner. His teams have fourteen championships. He's coached kids who went to the NFL, like former NFL Pro Bowl linebacker Jon Beason. Rich is one of my managers today.

NOW, FULL FLEX, another manager, was definitely not as diplomatic as Rich. Flex is a great example of what TS aimed to do: We took in people who'd been trained since they were kids, since before their brains had even properly developed, to navigate the streets. To survive. Kill or be killed, predator or prey. But they were humans just like anyone else. Like anyone else, they developed the skills they'd need to survive, but didn't have anywhere healthy to put it. They were smart and cunning, they had heart and loyalty, they were determined and bold risk-takers. They cared about what they did and the people they did it with. They were just people, and just like me, they needed to take what they'd learned in the crazy cauldron of the streets and use it to help rather than harm themselves and their communities. That's what TS—as it evolved—was all about. And Full Flex was TS through and through. For better and for worse.

Full Flex used to hang out with my brother Angel. They're the same age. He really ain't have no reason to be hanging out with kids like me and Tone and my crew. He's like six years older. So while we were fourteen, tearing shit up, he was like twenty. But he was *with us*. Flex saw the potential in me before anybody. I remember sitting in front of his building and him giving me the illest speech.

"Yo, nigga, you're just a kid," he said. "You're only fourteen years old. You barely even had any pussy. I'm twenty years old. I'm a grown man. I'm up under you because I know you're a leader and I know you're special. You're gonna get us up out this shit. You're gonna get us this money."

He saw that shit before I even knew what he was talking about. Flex was my guardian angel in the flesh. He got it on legendary. Flex would eventually become my manager for twenty years.

Flex had a real mean temper. We'd always refer to him as "If Mr. Know-It-All Was a Real Person." If the cops were harassing us, he'd be the one telling them he knew his rights. And he did! He would argue with them until they got tired of beefing with him and would just beat him up. One day, the cops whupped on him bad and threw him headfirst into a garbage can. All you could see were his feet swinging. Boooy. That's how much he frustrated the cops.

The boys in blue used to violate us on another level. Nobody got their ass whupped by cops more than me. Flex was a close second though. It was incredible. Police probably used to wake up and be like, "We're gonna fuck these niggas up."

They knew we were never going to tell. They knew we would never make a formal complaint. Tellin' has never been in our DNA. Even today, if you look around my house, you don't see security cameras and all that. Because even if I caught somebody on tape trying to rob me, I ain't tellin'. That's the code.

Me and Flex lived by the same morals. He was one of my closest friends. I'm the godfather of his kids. He's the godfather of my eldest son. When Tony died, Flex became my right-hand man. I lived up to his prophecy and got us out the hood alive. He was managing my rap career and helping me get my bags. Flex was excellent in one aspect of management: He would book me for shows and he was great at dealing with these janky promoters.

When you're rappin' and performing, they have these guys who book you for shows but try to rob you. They don't want to pay you your money that's owed. They'll give you every sob story in the book about not having your bread. If they tried that bullshit with Flex, he'd threaten to send different gangs to your doorstep, depending on where you were. If you were in Chicago, he'd be like, "I'm sending thirty Latin Kings to your house."

Needless to say, no matter what, we always got paid. He got us our money. I'm the only person he managed. When I'd call him a manager, he would always tell me, "No. I'm in the *Fat Joe* business."

As great as Flex was dealing with these guys who book shows, I knew he would be that bad dealing with executives at record labels. He was too hood for the boardroom. He'd always ask to get more involved with my record label stuff, and I'd deny him. He'd ask for a chance, I'd tell him no.

When I did my independent deal with Capitol Records, I set up a meeting between Flex and the vice president of Urban Promo, this woman named Juliette Jones. Me and Juliette were incredibly cool back then and today she's one of my best friends. She goes on vacations with me and my family. She's like a sister to me.

Flex gassed me up.

"Yo, I changed. I changed. Let me go to a meeting with the record label," he pleaded with me.

In twenty years, I'd never let him meet with nobody in the record labels because I knew this guy was crazy.

"Yo, Joe, please. I've changed," he kept appealing.

"All right cool," I finally gave in.

I set up a meeting for him and Juliette to go over some particulars for my album *The Darkside Vol. 1*. It was scheduled for a Wednesday at 3:00 P.M. By 3:12, my cellphone was ringing.

It was a beautiful day. My man Von Zip used to take me to this car wash in Harlem. All the fly cats used to sit out there and get their cars washed and detailed. I had the Phantom Rolls-Royce. I'm out there kicking it. Juliette calls my phone.

"Let me tell you something, nigga!!!" she yells at me before even saying hello.

"Juliette?" I asked in shock, double-checking to make sure it was her who was shouting at me. Our relationship was so amazing. I had never heard her raise her voice before. Let alone at me.

"Let me tell you something, nigga," she fumed. "If it ain't you, I don't ever want to talk to a nigga from Terror Squad again in my life. This nigga called me a bitch!"

"Sorry, Juliette," I said, embarrassed.

"Nah, y'all be trying me. Yo, Joe! This is some bullshit!"

I get off with Juliette and immediately call Flex. The phone rings, he don't pick up. I call again, phone rings, he don't pick up. Call again, no answer. I call a fourth time, he finally picks up.

"I knowwww. I knowwwwww, I knowwwww," Flex said right off the bat. He knew I'd be furious and that he let me down. "I know, but she's a fuckin' bitch!"

I didn't even know where to start. "Flex, do not talk to nobody at the label no more," I instructed him.

"I know. I know," he replied. "But she's a bitch!"

I just hung up the phone. This is the type of shit I had to

deal with. Flex was crazy. He got it honestly though. It was in his genes.

Full Flex, his father, his mother, his brother . . .

Let's just say their street cred was on 10,000. They didn't have a problem with violence.

Flex's lunatic brother is named Mugsi. He never liked me, I never liked him. I don't like him to this day. He was a bully, always picking on people. He was a malcontent, a grinch. I've never seen him have a friend. I've never even seen him smile. He was quick to stab people too. So if you had an argument with him, he wouldn't fight you. He'd just stab you. He once stabbed Flex, his own brother, in the ass.

Flex was looney tunes, but believe it or not, he was *the nicer* of the two brothers. That's how much of a problem Mugsi was. Flex's whole family was insane, man. There were times I'd be hangin' out with Flex at his house and his entire family would pull guns out on one another. The shit would look like *Reservoir Dogs*. This happened multiple times.

One time, the mother, the father, Flex, and Mugsi pointed pistols at one another and I was in the middle of all four. One thing about their house, they always had like nine locks on the door. It was almost impossible to get out of there. Running for the door was futile, so I would try to calm it down. They looked at me as a kid, they didn't want me to get hurt in the middle of their hurricane, so I could coax them to talk it out.

Flex's pop was into getting money, his mother was a real gangster. His mom would come outside and she'd have on a Bata. In English that would be regular grandmother clothes. If she heard Flex outside arguing with guys from the block, she'd put the hammer in her garter belt and come outside. She'd come sit by us and stash the gun so Flex could come over and get it if he needed it. They were just bugged out.

The most ironic thing about Flex is how he died. He survived growing up in that wild household, he survived the barbarism with me in the hood, he survived the trappings of the music industry. He survived it all only to die of a heart attack at fifty years old. No one could believe it, he had been in such good shape.

To this day, we take care of his family's bills. Alpo was Flex's right-hand man, he's still running with us and he's picking up some of the responsibilities Flex left behind. Flex lived like a loyal one; he died a loyal one. For those who stay loyal, Terror Squad is for life—and even after.

CHAPTER 15

THE TERROR SQUAD PART II

WHEN ME AND MY PRODUCER Scott Storch were at our peak we poured out a string of hits—we had a majestic chemistry, like Dr. Dre and Snoop Dogg. We met in '03 through my former A&R and friend for life Rob "Reef" Tewlow. The next year, "Lean Back," our first collaboration, became one of the biggest records of the year in any genre—I found a new level of crossover superstardom and Scottie became a household name and the hottest producer in music. We kept coming back every year with smashes, "Get It Poppin'" in '05, "Make It Rain" in '06, but then everything crashed. Scottie was squandering millions on drugs and then he was just off the map. My greatest collaborator couldn't make music anymore.

My primary concern was for his well-being of course. I stayed with Scott every day for a month, at his mansion in Miami, but he just wouldn't shake the drugs. It was a nightmare. I'd seen that movie before, with my brother Angel. Scott was my friend, but I couldn't babysit him forever. I had to continue with my life.

Cool & Dre saved my career. They filled Scott's shoes and produced all my monsters in the past several years, including "All the Way Up." Besides being my little brothers, they've acted as therapists to me.

When I turned forty years old, I wasn't out celebrating, I was in the house, depressed. I was going through a bit of a midlife crisis. I thought I was going to die. Dre came to my house in Miami to uplift my spirits.

"Yo, let's go to the studio," he said.

"Nah, Dre, nobody wants to listen to a forty-year-old rapper," I explained.

"You crazy," he shot back. "Tina Turner dropped her first solo hit at age forty-four, 'What's Love Got to Do with It.' Are you kidding me?"

In 2018, Cool & Dre wound up sampling "What's Love Got to Do with It" for my hit "Attention," featuring Chris Brown.

Dre has been there for me personally a bunch of times. Times when I wasn't feeling as confident as I usually am, Dre's been there to talk me off the ledge. Professionally, I've been trying to get him to push himself out there more. Dre can sing and rap, he has as many hits as Drake in his catalog, he just has to get himself out there more so people can understand how truly talented he is. He has a new solo album coming that's going to be a classic. I'm hoping it will open a lot of people's eyes.

Me and Dre made a collaborative album called *Family Ties*. Cool & Dre produced the whole thing, we had Remy on there, Eminem, Mary J. Blige. It dropped the Christmas season of 2019. The reviews on it were stupendous, but when the pandemic came a few months later, it killed a lot of our plans for the project. It should have been way bigger.

After *Family Ties*, I *really* retired. Nobody believed me, but I said to myself I wasn't going to make music anymore, I was going to spend the time I'd normally spend in the studio with my loved ones. For months, I really wasn't working. I was home with my wife and daughter.

Then Dre calls me one day in 2021, just at the turn of the year.

"I got one," he said on the phone—a new track that he knew I'd sound great on. We made "Sunshine (The Light)" and the song rampaged the radio. Dre was right. He's really been a lifesaver. Same thing with Cool.

I admire that Cool & Dre have been together for thirty years and they won't bend. They do business together. They protect each other. They love each other. I admire their relationship and their loyalty. They've been like Starsky and Hutch from our initial meeting.

I met them when they were still in high school. A good friend of mine named Robin Fernandez—"Robbie Rob"—he gave me a CD with Cool & Dre's beats on there. It was about thirty beats and the one I picked was for a record called "King of N.Y.," which I put on the *Jealous Ones Still Envy* album. The song featured Buju Banton. Cool & Dre have been my little brothers and, I would guess, at least 80 percent of my production ever since. They are TS for life.

I CREDIT BIG PUN for bringing Remy into the TS fold, but she wasn't the only one he recruited—he did the same thing with Tony Sunshine. I have literally known Tone since he was a baby. He grew up in Forest projects. He should have always been Terror Squad because he was talented and from around the way, but it took Pun to see his talent and bring him to us.

When it was time to put Tony out, the tools that are available to us now, where you can go independent as an artist, shoot your own videos and all that, we didn't know that system. We always relied on a major record label to save us. That's not the case now. Artists would rather be independent than be on a major label. One of my biggest regrets in my career as a mogul, as an executive, is not being able to get Tony to blow. I always felt he was so talented, he deserved to be a superstar.

Armageddon, he was just a kid when I met him. He's been there since day one though. Remember, he was at Jazzy Jay's studio when I was recording "Flow Joe." Armageddon has always been down, never crossed me. We're not as tight as we used to be, I don't know why. But I'll always love him and have a special place in my heart for him.

Before Covid struck the world and we were doing concerts, you saw Pretty Lou do a lot of shows with me. His inspirational fight with cancer has been well documented through the years. He's a warrior. Me and Lou were close before he got sick, but when I found out he was fighting cancer and saw how strong he is, I was impressed with his resilience. I also love how hard he rides for the culture of hip-hop.

Pretty Lou brings me back to the essence of the culture. He's one of the best Masters of Ceremonies no matter where you go. He doesn't rap but he hypes the crowd. The only other person I've seen in my whole life with that type of energy is DJ Khaled. The second Lou grabs a mic, wherever he is, he turns it up. That's how Khaled used to be before he became superfamous.

CHAPTER 16

LISA

FOR MOST OF MY TEENAGE YEARS, I pretty much was known as a villain throughout my neighborhood in the Bronx. Rightfully so, in a lot of instances. But as a shorty, when it came to my sister, Lisa, I always saw myself as a hero. I was protective of Lisa like a big brother even though she was a year older than me. I never let anyone mess with her.

There was one time I let my sister down.

Lisa was being bullied by an older kid. This was when she was maybe like ten, I was around nine. The bully was definitely fifteen or sixteen.

"Joey, this guy keeps bothering me," she told me.

So next time I saw him, I ran up to the dude, just rushed him, but he tripped me. I fell down, then I rushed him again. That time he body-slammed me. I got up and rushed him again, and he body-slammed me again. I might have rushed him about six, seven times with the same result: I got body-slammed. I was a little kid; he fucked me up. Several body slams later, I looked at my sister and the sad expression on my face was a wordless confession: *Lisa, I can't beat him.*

Something you may have learned about me is that I never get *that face.* I never give up, never feel like I can't win. But I gave Lisa that face because the kid was just way bigger than me. I will never forget that.

Me and my sister were always tight through the years, but I know at points she hated me. Or, I should say, hated my actions. I never liked her choice of boyfriends. It was tough for her because her *little* brother was growing up to be this crazy tough guy. And for guys to get with her, I would put them through a lot. If a guy wanted to talk to Lisa, they knew they were talking to "Angel's and Joe's sister." And they knew "her two brothers are crazy," especially me.

My aggression was different. I put a different type of pressure on her boyfriends because I wanted to be her safeguard. When a guy came to visit my sister, I'd literally be sitting right next to them with a bat in my hand. My mom would be like, "Yo, Joey, could you let him talk to Lisa?" I'd be like, "Fuck that." I made it uncomfortable. For real, I was unfair to Lisa. She never liked that about me. But I loved my sister so much, I just never wanted the guys to mistreat her.

LISA WAS A GREAT WOMAN and as an adult, she always lived a modest, simple life. One day, my sister announced that she was pregnant with her second child. She already had one son— Little John John is what we call him. The pregnancy was months along, everything was going well.

I was out of town, on tour, when I got a phone call that things had gone bad with the pregnancy. When Lisa went into labor, the doctors made a grave mistake administering the epidural. Unfortunately for me and my family, because the doctors were careless, the results were tragic. Lisa lost the baby and fell into a coma.

For eight months my sister was essentially brain-dead. My mother, my father, they put her in an extended care facility in Jersey and they would go see her every day. Every single day. My mom, man, was unbelievable. The strength she had, having her only daughter in a coma; she dealt with that. I would go visit, too, but I'd hate seeing Lisa like that because it felt like there was no way she was coming back. It was painful to see her suffer. It was painful to see my mom suffer so much tending to her in there.

Even though my family was in crisis, I still had a career to deal with and I would do shows. The bill didn't stop. I was in Chicago for a show at House of Blues when I got the phone call.

"Your sis passed away," they told me.

I loved Lisa so much and I knew I would miss her like a part of my own body, but I was grateful she was not suffering any longer. Of course I was sad, but in the weirdest way, it was almost a relief. She was tormented in the rehab center. The only things keeping her alive were the machines—ventilators and the like. She couldn't talk, she couldn't breathe on her own, she couldn't do nothing. She was like a vegetable.

I've dealt with death from a young age. When my best friend Tone got murdered it was hard on me. But when Lisa passed, it was part of a thunderstorm of death like you wouldn't believe. My grandfather passed away, Big Pun died, and I lost my sister all in a short period of time. All people who I loved so much, who were such important parts of my life, gone in a matter of weeks. I grew despondent and spiraled into gloom. I dealt with depression for two years straight.

I would come out the house and a bright, sunny day would look dark and cloudy to me. I would spend nights in the bathtub. No water running, just sitting there looking up at the ceiling. I had to go to a therapist for help.

I try to compartmentalize death in order to cope with it. With all my friends and family members that I've lost, I try to not think about them in great detail and instead focus on the fact that life goes on.

It hurts me when I look at my nephew John John because moving on is something he still can't do. It's been more than twenty years since we lost Lisa and John John is still traumatized.

THE REST OF THE FAMILY—my mother, my father, me—we raised him after his mother passed. We paid for his Catholic school, paid all his bills, and he lived with my mother, but John is a bit of a sad story. My sister died giving birth to his little brother who died too, and he has never been able to get over it. I can't talk in this book like I know *everything* about death, but my experience is: You honor your loved ones, you keep their legacy, but you gotta move on.

My mother died, my brother died, John John is stuck on that.

The hospital where my sister went to deliver the baby was negligent in her death. We sued and we won a multimillion dollar lawsuit. In the court transcripts, it actually says, "The doctor killed Lisa Marie Cartagena."

"Killed!" I couldn't believe it when I was reading the paperwork. But that happens all the time to Black and Brown women giving birth in these hospitals in their *own* neighborhoods. There are uncaring medical professionals there—sometimes inexperienced, sometimes just incompetent—who treat these women almost like guinea pigs.

If a Black or Brown girl dies, who gives a fuck, right?

With the settlement for my sister, we were awarded $2 million, tax free. John John was about ten years old back then, and my parents and I decided he should get all the money. We wanted him to live as great a life as possible to try to soothe the anguish of losing his mother and sibling. I put the money in annuities for him. Nobody touched it. When my nephew turned eighteen, it was time for him to get his money. The lawyer handling John John's case was in disbelief that my parents and I had not withdrawn so much as a penny from the fund.

"Never in my history of working with any kid from the hood who won a lawsuit, has his family not taken at least *some* of the money," he explained to us. "Usually they tap it up," he continued. "It's 'I need a Ferrari to a drive my kid to school.' They find some way to tap it."

The way we set it up originally was that John John would get the funds in pieces. He'd get some at eighteen, some at twenty-one, and so on. But he was impatient. He worked around us.

You know how you see those commercials during *Jerry Springer* or anything Black and Latin people watch on daytime TV? The commercials where they go, "It's myyyyy money and I want it nowww!"

Whether they're Black, Latino from the hood, or poor and white, these companies, those predators, are targeting young, stupid kids.

People get a settlement—$1, $2 million—and their families set it up for the money to be disbursed over like a ten-year period. These companies saying, "It's your money and you want it now?" They prey on these kids, wind up giving them $500,000 or some figure way less than what the settlement actually was. Meanwhile, the kid has $2 million that was already in annuities and would have appreciated into $10 million.

They're robbin' us.

They gave John John his "money now" and the kid went crazy. He spent all that money. Immediately he started hanging out with people he'd never hung out with before. Now on top of his mother being dead—he still wakes up every day with that—he's haunted by all his money being gone.

He was living in the Trump Towers in Miami. He was driving all types of new cars. He had all kinds of cats in the strip club with him. I tried to tell him to be conservative with his money. "Save! Don't be spending all your money on all these leeches around you."

I should have pushed the issue harder. One thing I didn't want was for people in my family to say, "Joe stole the money from John John."

So I fucked up there. If I had been smarter, I would have managed that money, "Yo, give me that money. I'll give you a little bit at a time." I didn't do it. I wasn't as hands-on as I should have been for my nephew.

I didn't need any of his money. There's no way in the world I would have taken a dime from John John, but I was lost in worrying about what my family would think. I didn't want anyone saying

I mismanaged his money. I didn't want everybody in the family saying, "Joe robbed him."

But I love my nephew. I encourage John John and I pray for him. He's still a young man, only in his early thirties, and he still has time to get focused and make even more money than he had before. Hopefully he's learned like I learned. Death always has a lesson for us.

I've been surrounded by death my entire life and it's not accidental. I grew up in a racist, predatory system. And that system will feast on you. The system took my sister, the system stole my nephew's money, the system has pirated multiple members of my family and my friends. The vultures will leave you alone and broke or dead. You can never stop fighting, and you have to keep your guard up at all times.

CHAPTER 17

MY TWO SONS

MY SON JOEY is joy walking in the flesh. He's the oldest of my three kids and he has a pure soul. Me and his mother grew up together in Forest projects. We got together before I started rappin' and she already had two kids. In my hood, she was the top prospect. Everybody was trying to go at her, but I had the (unfortunate) luck of baggin' her.

I'll never forget the day after I fucked her for the first time. Me and Tone Montana were in the crib, baggin' up drugs, and she came over, making a movie.

"You ain't call me today! You ain't just gonna be fuckin' me!" she fumed.

We had the biggest argument. If I'd been smart, I would have walked away from her after that first confrontation. It was an omen of how our relationship would be. She was just a problem, she brought constant drama. I don't even want to say her name in this book.

During the growth of our relationship, I'd stopped hustlin'. I got out the game. All my friends went to jail and I knew I had to change my lifestyle before I ended up like them. She knew I was trying to stay away from crime. But if we needed money, this girl would encourage me to go stick up a supermarket or rob somebody. She was about gassin' me to do everything wrong. She was selfish, manipulative, and negative.

I went out with her for a while. I guess you could say I was blindly in love with her. But it got to a point where not only did it not work out between us, I actually grew to hate her. Love turned to loathing. It's true, you can actually be with somebody you hate.

We had a crib together. Even though I wasn't the richest, I would do whatever I could to make sure she and I and her two kids had everything. I would buy all types of toys; I furnished the apartment, made it fly. The crib was all leather couches, big-screen TVs—it was comfortable. I always went all out, so, at least *hoodwise*, the crib was fly.

Nothing was ever enough for her though. Her attitude was so contemptuous, it felt like her soul was laced with larceny. We broke up.

And that worked for a while. We were apart. She was doing her, I was doing me. And what I learned is that when you have negative people in your life, they weigh you down, keep you from moving toward what you want. When we broke up, I was free and starting to thrive . . . for six months. I went back to the block and I ran into her. Me just being a horny young guy, I started talking to her again. We had sex one more time and she got pregnant with Joey.

I will admit, having a baby with her was the last thing in the world I wanted to do. I was young; I couldn't even understand the concept of being a father.

But, she stood firm and I knew I had to be there for the baby no matter how much disdain I had for his mother.

I was eighteen when little Joey was born at Lebanon Hospital on the Grand Concourse in the Bronx. Ironically, that was the same hospital where my sister lost and suffered all those tragic complications due to the hospital's negligence in treating her.

The day Joey was born, I was excited. Over the course of the pregnancy, not only did I feel more confident about being a father, love grew in my heart for the baby. Regardless of who his mother was and how she acted, I loved my boy before he was even born. I was at the hospital with my parents and his mother. She was going through severe labor pains and I was trying to calm her down.

"Relax, I'm with you," I said consolingly.

Joey came out, he was beautiful. My first child, I was moonwalking on cloud nine. Everything was perfect for a few minutes, then the doctor addressed us in an unsettling tone. With a look of extreme urgency, he pulled me to the side.

"Can I talk to you and his mother?" he asked me.

Me, my mom, Joey's mom, and my dad huddled up with the physician.

"I have bad news for you," he said.

"What do you mean?" I asked, as my heart dropped.

He picked the baby up and showed me that Joey's fingers and toes were webbed, almost like a duck. He then opened his own hand and started explaining. Most of us have lines on the palms of our hands. Joey didn't have any.

"He has Down syndrome," the doctor said.

I could not believe this was happening. I was a young kid and it just hurt me so bad. I was scared for my baby. Joey's mom, on the other hand, didn't show our boy not one ounce of compassion.

"I can't raise no retarded kid. I can't raise no slow kid," she barked maliciously at everybody in the room. "We're gonna have to give him up for adoption."

"Bitch, are you fuckin' crazy?" my mom jumped in before I could respond. "This is *our* kid. We ain't giving up our kid for nothing. Fuck that. Hell no!"

That's the type of person my mother is. My mom had four kids and she would work two and three jobs. She ain't give a fuck, she would do whatever for the family. If we wanted a V-bomber, a sheepskin coat, it might come two years later, but she'd get one for each of us.

My mother, right now, at seventysomething years old, she would climb a mountain for her kids. She would do anything in the world for us. My mother would bend over backward to get us whatever we needed or wanted, even if she didn't have the means.

From the first moment, she loved my son like he was her son too.

I don't know why Joey was born the way he was. Later, they found out he has autism as well. I don't understand it, but I also feel like God's doing is God's doing. I loved my son when he was born and I will always love my son. We kept Joey, and between me and my parents, we raised him.

Joey's mother, without exaggeration, has seen him maybe three times in life, including the day he was born. No Thanksgivings, no Christmases, not even just a regular day. Besides those few times, she's never had contact with Joey. There's no excuse for that. To be totally transparent, writing and explaining this story is very painful. It hurts because fuck me, fuck my family, but how could you as a mother turn your back on your own kid? I could never understand that.

Joey was born right at the beginning of my career. I'm blessed that my mother and father were there to help me. With them pitching in, I had the latitude to go out and make records and perform. He still lives with my parents today and I go see him three, four days out the week.

In life, you gotta deal with whatever is handed to you. It's hard, but you have to do it. I've never allowed myself to say, *Why me? Why Joey? Why this? Why that?*

Every day my father says, "All I want is for Joey to talk. Why don't he talk?"

I feel like, bro, it is what it is. That's what God did. My blessing is that I've been able to handle shit and roll with it. And I owe a large part of that to my parents always showing unconditional love to me and my siblings. Throughout all of the chaos I've caused in my life, my parents always loved me, even when I disappointed them. And the love we have for one another has manifested itself in the abundance of love we've given Joey, despite the challenges my son was born with.

I know in my heart that little Joey, he's a happy kid, man. Joey has never spent a day of his life without somebody watching him and making sure he good.

WHEN MY SECOND SON, Ryan, was born, fortunately for him, I had just become successful. I always say, give all the artists coming into the game a grace period to really wild out and enjoy the *perks* that come with being a popular rapper. You have to give them some time to adjust to stardom and not get caught up. When Ryan was born, I was with his mom, but I was really out there with girls. Remember, before Big Pun, before reggaeton, before all that, there was *just one* solo Latino rapper poppin'. Me.

Think about it. Now you've got Bad Bunny, Daddy Yankee, Pitbull, and all these great guys. But when I came out, I was the only one. I was driving girls crazy out in the Bronx and throughout New York.

That was back when you would take girls' numbers and write them on pieces of paper. Me being reckless, I would forget and leave the papers in my jeans. Ryan's mom would go through my pockets and find a hundred numbers.

She was hearing rumors that I was messin' with her cousins, which I never was. But I *was* out there fuckin' other girls. It got bad to the point where we had to separate.

I regretted it because I hate when people don't give the relationship a chance for the kid. But I guess I pushed her over the edge with my antics and she couldn't take it.

I've always been there in Ryan's life. I made sure he lived in a nice house with his mom. Me and her are nothing like me and Joey's mother. Ryan's mom has been active in his life, and me and her remain cool. I always did my best to take care of them.

When Ryan was around ten years old, I moved him down to Miami with me and my wife, Lorena. We've raised him since then—and that's not to take anything from his mom. I put Ryan in private schools, then an expensive college. He's always been a good kid. I'm proud of him.

Where we clash is that Ryan wants to rap. He's pretty good, but I don't think he's really right for showbiz. He can't handle the cameras in his face and all that. Fame ain't for everybody. In 2019, he did one of these reality shows, *Growing Up Hip Hop: New York*. It's a show that focuses on the children of famous hip-hop stars. They had Ja Rule's and Irv Gotti's kids. Kid Capri's daughter, Flavor Flav's kids, Charli Baltimore's daughter, ODB's son, and Ryan.

The kids were on there with their parents. He begged me to come on the show; I ain't really want to do it. I didn't want *him to do it*. I feel like he didn't really represent himself right on the show. All he had to do was be himself. We were fighting when he did that show. Not in a major way, but I was like, "Come on, bro."

Sometimes we get caught up trying to fit in. All you gotta do is be yourself.

Now we're in a better space. He's my son. I'll always have his back. I love him to death. When I think about it though, I may have asked too much from Ryan. I hold down this entire family. I hold down my mother, my father, little Joey, everybody in this family.

If my father gets sick, I'm the only one who's in the hospital—and he's got twelve sons and daughters. If he's there for three days, I'm there for three days. If my mother gets sick, I'm the only one to hold her down. My brother Angel's blind, and we don't know where her other son is. My sister is dead. So for this entire immediate family *and* friends *and extended* family, it ain't on nobody else's shoulders. The buck stops here. With Ryan growing up, I was trying to prepare him for that.

"Yo, you're going to take over," I foretold.

I've told him real shit since he was a kid. "If somebody does this or that to you, you gotta move this way."

I don't know if his mind was just too fragile and I was overwhelming him with too much real shit. I don't know if I went about it the right way. Parenting is custom-made. There is no one-size-fits-all. Every child has a different DNA.

I may have put too much pressure on Ryan. I wasn't supposed to tell him those things. I would do things like sit him down and tell him, "Your brother's autistic. If I die tomorrow, it's on you. I'm gonna leave you money, you have to make sure that kid never goes to a home. He could never be with other people. He has to be happy and cared for his entire life by his family."

That's a big responsibility.

But Ryan's a very smart kid. He graduated from Full Sail University, a four-year college, in two years. You know how some kids go crazy and have to study all night? It's a joke to him. He can prepare for a test last-minute and go in and get 100% or an A+. He's outta control with school. His intelligence is so high, it doesn't make sense.

He wants to do music though. I just want him to be a regular guy. If he was just a regular guy, I'd be straight. We'll help him get a nice job, he can figure out my empire, so he can run it. He doesn't have to prove to me that he's the next Fat Joe. He doesn't have to fill his father's shoes as an entertainer.

Being a second-generation entertainer is hard. You try to do something and they immediately compare you to your father or your mother. But your story is so different.

Even with this book, you can read it and root for me even when I was doing bad shit, because you know I have a good heart. I just came from a rough place.

That's not the case with the children of successful artists who come out the hood. It's been my experience that people are like, "Yeah, he ain't even live in the projects like his father. He didn't go through this or that."

There's so much stigma on them. People give these kids a hard time. You got Busta's son rappin', Eazy-E's son rappin', Ice Cube's son used to rap until he flipped it into acting. Reverend Run's sons rap. It's a hard thing to do. Is it impossible to succeed? No. But it's hard. Me, I'd rather them look at my son as a businessman. A smart guy who graduated college.

Whatever he chooses—music, business, whatever—I just want him to forge his own path. Creating your own path in life is the only way to really be happy.

CHAPTER 18

LORENA AND AZZY

MY WIFE AND MY DAUGHTER, they run around my house like Cagney and Lacey. Sometimes they'll double-team me and tell me I've been in the studio too long, or they'll tell me to hurry up so we won't be late for dinner over at DJ Khaled's house. These are the type of tag team efforts I deal with, but these ladies keep me smiling every single day.

Lorena is my soul mate and the love of my life. I was blessed to find her early in my career. For entertainers, fame is an elephant in the room. When most of us fall in love and think about set-tling down with someone, we may not truly know whether that person is just riding our bandwagon. But Lorena was with me practically from the very beginning. When we met, she was better off financially than me. She proved to me how pure and genuine she was from the start, and we've been together going on thirty years.

In the early '90s, I came down to Miami with my road manager, Steve Lobel, Raul from Terror Squad, and a few others. A bunch of us were in town to promote the single "Flow Joe." The record had just come out, it wasn't really going yet. We had to spread the awareness.

On the second night we were in Miami, Steve tells me, "I've got some friends that moved down here from Queens. They're way too fly. They're way too bad. They're never gonna talk to a fat guy like you."

Now, this was in my "Fat Joe da Gangster" period: Timbs over my ankles, baggy jean shorts, my 10X white T-shirt. I was super hood.

"Yo, bro, you ain't making no real money," he added. "These girls ain't never talkin' to you."

I could have a dollar or a million dollars, but my confidence level is always going to be the same. I never thought I couldn't pull one of the women if I wanted to. The night comes when we were supposed to meet up with Steve's friends. The rendezvous happened at a parking lot at Nikki Beach, which is across the street from Prime 112 on Ocean Drive. Me and my guys were in a big rental van. It looked like a church van.

When we pulled up, this girl steps out of her car and the headlights covered her like she was a star onstage under the spotlight. She had on blue jeans and her ass was sooooo fat. I've never seen no ass this fat in my life. This was before all these women went assshot crazy with the surgeries. Nowadays you got the phenomenon with fake asses, but back in the early '90s, all the women were natural. This one had the fattest ass ever. I was mesmerized instantly.

"Ohhhhh shit. Who the fuck is that?"

She had rips in her jeans and a black tank top on. I felt like jumping out that gotdamn van like Mr. T in *The A-Team*. I played it cool though. I moved casually, but I was already fantasizing about her. I'd never seen anybody that stunning in my life. I was staring at her thinking, *Oh my God! She's so beautiful.* But I couldn't control myself and the words actually came out my mouth. She heard me. Steve introduced her as Lorena.

This was a young Joe Crack, basically a werewolf. I doublebooked that night. We all went back to my hotel to chill and I had *two* other girls meet me in the lobby. On the elevator up to my room, Lorena was looking at me like *Oh, so Joe Crack. He's a ladies man. He's a play-yerrr.*

I was looking at her like *Maaannn. I wish I could trade them for you right now.*

Me and Lorena were feeling each other. I kept talking under

my breath, "Damn! This girl is incredible." Steve arranged for all of us to hang out a couple of times while we were in town. Me and my guys were scheduled to be in Miami for like a week.

Our second time going out, we went to a club that Luke Skyywalker owned. I was blown away by my conversation with Lorena. I guess because it was a love-at-first-sight thing for me, I thought everything coming out of her mouth during our talks was amazing. She was so intelligent, gorgeous, and worldly. Lorena wore these cowboy boots with some tight jeans and she was drinking a Heineken. I wasn't used to girls drinking Heinekens and all that. "This is some different shit," I said to myself.

We had a great time. I asked her out again. I asked if I could take her to the movies.

"I don't fuck with niggas with big mouths," she said coyly.

I was taken aback.

"What makes you think I got a big mouth?" I asked. "I just want to take you to the movies. That's just between me and you."

We went to the movies. That's where I got my first kiss from her. She was telling me the whole time, "Look, I don't like guys with big mouths. If you tell my business, I will never talk to you again."

We ended the night and once I got back around my guys, the first thing I did was tell everybody!

"Yooooo! I went to the movies with the Colombian chick," I bragged. "I slobbed her down."

The next day, I'm calling her, she don't pick up. I saw her a couple of days later at a spot and inquired about the cold shoulder.

"Yo, what's up?" I began to investigate. I was confused as to why she was ignoring me.

"I told you. I don't fuck with niggas with big mouths. You got a big mouth," she answered.

I was about to lie to her and deny saying anything about our date, but I just came clean. One of my guys must have put me on blast.

"You're right. You're right," I started to explain. "You gotta understand, you're so beautiful. I had to brag. I had to tell my friends, but I didn't tell them nothing bad. I just told them we went to the movies."

I convinced Lorena to give me another chance. Looking back on it now, I think she liked me as much as I liked her from jump, but she was playing it cool.

I wound up staying in Miami for two weeks doing promo. It was damn near a vacation. Raul and my crew were running around with a bunch of different chicks. But I was just rappin' to Lorena every day. I nicknamed her "Lori."

"Oh my God! Lori, I need to have you. You gotta be my girl," I proclaimed.

The night before we left Miami, we had plans to go to this club. Me and my guys ate at this Cuban restaurant on Collins Ave first. They mocked me for concentrating on Lorena so much during the trip.

"Yo, you're playing yourself, man," they laughed. "We've been out here wildin' and you're stuck on that one Colombian chick. She ain't gonna give you shit," they told me.

Everybody knew me and Lorena hadn't had sex. I was a little frustrated and I told myself, "If I don't get her tonight, I ain't fuckin' with her no more. She's wastin' my time."

Later that night, we met Lorena and her girls at the Fat Black Pussycat club—that was the hottest club out there. We had a large entourage. Nineteen of our party went in before me and there was no problem. As I'm about to walk in, outta nowhere the fire department comes and says the club is at capacity.

"No one else is getting in," they told the club workers at the front door.

All these people got in on the strength of my presence and I was the one who couldn't get in. When you're standing outside Fat Black Pussycat, you can see a staircase inside through an upper window. I looked up, and looking down at me out the window was

214

The Book of Jose

Lori. Nobody else turned around to find out what happened with me. She's so real, she came back down and outside.

This was our moment. I grabbed her hand, we ran down the block. I'll never forget. She had on these tight leggings. That ass was so fat. I started running with her like ... You ever see *Little House on the Prairie,* when Melissa Gilbert and her sisters on the show were so gleeful running across that big fuckin' field of wild-flowers in the opening credits? It was like that! I was damn near skipping with her.

I took her back to my hotel room and to make a long story short, me and Lorena stayed in there for three straight days. Steve Lobel would be banging on the door like, "We're supposed to go back to New York!"

"Fuuuuuuck that," I would tell him.

We'd order room service. Me and Lorena never came out. We passionately *destroyed* the room. They should have brought yellow tape like a crime scene. It was like a dream come true.

I was siiick like a puppy when I had to go back to New York. I wasn't flying because I was scared to fly. We jumped into that big-ass van to drive back up. I was just staring out the window thinking, *My niggas at home ain't never gonna believe I met the baddest chick in the game, the baddest one in the world. Niggas ain't gonna believe this shit.*

In the Bronx, we never really knew any Colombians. We knew Dominicans, we knew Puerto Ricans, and we knew Black folks. It wasn't no Colombians out there. Colombians were more of a Queens thing.

I got back up top, I started telling all my brothers, "I met the baddest chick!"

They didn't believe me.

"Colombian? Yeah right," they said sarcastically.

"Cuhhh-lumbian! She was incredible," I maintained.

Nobody believed me.

Back in my city, I was back on my grind. I didn't call her for two weeks. Maybe I was feeling myself a little too much. I owned a clothing store on Third Avenue called Fat Joe's Halftime. It was all right, nothing to brag about. No major accounts, but it paid the bills. One day, out of nowhere, the phone rang at the store and I picked up.

"Yo, Joe, you trying to play me?" the voice on the other end said. "This is Lorena. You think you just gonna fuck me and not call me? Are you fucking crazy? You think I'm *that chick*? I'm coming up to New York, you better come get me at the airport."

Lorena told me her flight info. I went with my uncle Dan to LaGuardia Airport to scoop her. I was so scared to fly back then, I used to get nervous just *picking people up* at the airport. She lived maybe two minutes from LGA. Danny was making dumb fun of me.

"Bro, you came all the way from the Bronx to pick her up and drop her off two minutes away? Nigga, you a herb," he laughed.

That night, Lorena came to my crib. Now, you gotta understand: I had had a nasty breakup with my son Ryan's moms and I just told her, "Take everything." So that's what she did. She and her people came and took every piece of furniture. Left me with a mattress. No box spring. Instead of a curtain, I had a 4X bathrobe hanging up over the window, nailed to the top of the wall. I had a couch and a boom box.

Lorena couldn't fathom my conditions when she came over.

"You're livin' like this?" she asked in a tone of borderline disgust.

"Yeah, I'm fucked up," I told her. "I ain't really got it."

That was the early fork in the road of our relationship, but she really loved me. She went above and beyond the call of duty to show it.

MY WIFE HAS AN INFAMOUS "Joey Crack" tattoo on her breast. She got that when I was losing those closest to me left and right. A bunch of my friends went to prison, including my best

friend, who has a life sentence. I started rappin' and I changed my life completely but my crew all wound up getting sixty-five, seventy-five years in jail. When they got locked up, I had just met my Lorena.

Six months later, me and Lorena were madly in love and my people in prison started sending me messages. "Yo, Gordo, sorry, but we're hearing you're gonna get locked up too."

The way the Feds do it, they get people on conspiracy—RICO. They come in and take sixty people. They come in and take everybody: the kingpin, the mechanic, the girl who took the fur coats. I'd already stopped selling drugs a couple of years prior. I wouldn't get involved anymore. So if you looked at the transcripts in the indictments, you would see people calling "Gordo," but Gordo would be saying, "I don't know what you're talking about," on the phone.

The Feds like to get you by using an informant who sees you in person while wearing a wire. Or they try to get you talking reckless on a phone tap. But I had really changed my life.

While all the indictments and jail time were being handed out to my family from the streets, I went to Lorena's house for the first time. I go in, and there's twenty women cutting up dope on the tables in the living room and kitchen. The shit looked like that scene in *New Jack City* at the Carter crack den.

"Come to my room," Lorena told me.

"What the fuck is that?" I asked when we got to her bedroom.

"What do you mean?" she asked casually.

"You sleep here? You live here?" I asked. She had been dumbfounded by my living conditions, but to say I was staggered by the shit I saw at her crib would be an understatement.

Her father was a big-time drug dealer from Colombia. She'd been around drugs so long that the makeshift coke factory out front was normal for her. It was an everyday thing that they were cutting up drugs in the house. I was even more terrified because I had come to tell her that I was about to get bagged by the Feds and go to jail.

I started giving her a similar talk to the one that Diamond D had given me. I begged her to get out the game.

"You're too beautiful," I started to plead with her. "I would hate for you to be in jail. But it's going to happen. You're gonna go to jail. Your father is gonna get locked up."

Then I told her we shouldn't be together. The real hood way of thinking is you can't have a real beautiful wife when you go to jail because she's gonna fuck behind your back anyway. Or she's gonna leave you. You don't want be stressed out thinking about her.

So, with tears in my eyes, I told her, "I love you. I just can't be with you."

"I'm never gonna leave you," she yelled back at me.

She was committed to me and wanted to prove it. That same day, Lorena went and got a "Joey Crack" tattoo on her tit.

Lorena is the realest in the game. What could I do? The Feds never came to get me, but she had me. I talked her into moving in with me a couple of months later. It was me and her on just the mattress.

Even though we didn't have much, life with Lorena was beautiful. There was only one thing that was impeding our bliss. She couldn't cook for nothing. She tried and tried but the meals never came out right.

"The food just ain't no good / I mean the macaroni's soggy, the peas are mushed, / And the chicken tastes like wooooodddddd."

I remember telling her after dinner one night, "Yo, this is wack." I was still foul. I wasn't sensitive. I was on my bullshit and the food *was* horrible. And I told her.

Lorena knew she had to get it right. It took her a little minute, but she freaked the game after that. She would go to a magnificent restaurant called Cuchifrito on Third Avenue in the Bronx. It was one of my favorites. She would buy food from there, bring it home, and front like she cooked it.

"Daaaammmn!" I'd say, digging in. "You steppin' your game up, Ma. This chicken gooood! This steak gooood!"

But one night, Lorena got sloppy. I caught her because she left the food wrappers from the restaurant in the garbage.

"I knew it!" I told her. "This shit taste too good."

"I really gotta learn now," she promised me. God bless her. She was only nineteen. With her cover blown, Lorena didn't give up though. She decided to go to the real Jedi temple of cooking: my grandmother's house.

My grandmother Tati was a phenomenal cook. She would cook for the entire family. We'd have a hundred people in our family eating over at her house. Grandma Tati had nine children and they each had like four, five, or six kids. Back in her heyday, they weren't thinking about condoms or no shit like that.

My grandmother taught Lorena how to cook. She taught her how to season the food—sazón, sofrito.

Today, my wife is phenomenal in the kitchen. She's a real chef. All my friends love to come over and eat her food.

Less than a year after me and Lori moved in together, one of my worst fears came true: Her father got knocked. I told Papi to get out the game. He looked out for us when we didn't have no money. He'd throw her a couple of dollars for us to buy groceries. He'd take us to dinner. We love him.

I'd tell him, "Papi, it ain't the same. These guys are gonna tell on you." Snitchin' was running really rampant back then.

"Nah, Joe, I've been doing this shit forever," he insisted.

They eventually caught him and he wound up doing a decade behind bars. Then the government revoked his citizenship and sent him back to Colombia. It was so tough on my wife to be away from her dad. Thank God I didn't have to go to jail and I could be with her when she needed me the most. She's been there for me when I needed *her* the most.

When I see couples today getting divorced after six months, I realize it really is a rarity that me and Lori have been a couple for twenty-nine years and counting. People always ask how me and my wife have such longevity in our relationship. I tell them, "It's so simple: We vowed early on that this was the last stop on the train. We promised to never leave each other no matter what."

THE GREATEST FRUIT of our labors—literal labor—is our daughter, Azzy. In some ways Azzy reminds me of my mother, Ruby. She's actually my mom's twin. She looks just like my mother. She's nosy like my mother. She hears everything; she's watching everything, this girl. But in so many ways, Azzy *is* Fat Joe. Today I looked at her Instagram, @azzymilano. When I went on the page it said, "Azzy the Don." If we were doing the movie of my life and Azzy were a boy, she would be playing Fat Joe.

She's got a beautiful heart. That's how I started, too, being as nice as her. It was my neighborhood and my circumstances that made me turn ruthless. At fifteen I was a juvenile delinquent, living out on my own, fighting every day, eyes-deep in a life of crime. My daughter's sixteen now and she's an A student who loves music and dancing. She's been dancing her whole life in organized programs and with dance troupes like Alvin Ailey. She gets busy!

Azaryah Milan Cartagena was born May 4, 2006. I can't even begin to express how much I love her. How I remember it, she came out and stared at me. This tiny face looking at me eye to eye. I couldn't sleep that night. Every time I closed my eyes, I would see her face staring at me. I got up and just walked around Manhattan for hours. People who saw me probably thought, *Fat Joe's gone crazy.* Even though it was spring, it was chilly outside. I was cold, but I couldn't go back in the house. The love I have for her is unimaginable. I never thought I could love somebody like that.

I knew who Azzy was before she was born. When she was in her mother's womb, I could already see visions of Azzy on the beach with me and Lorena. I envisioned her blond hair and all that. Azzy is a beautiful friend and beautiful daughter. We are inseparable. She's the best part of me.

Part of the reason my family moved from Miami back to New York is so she can learn where she's really from. We want her to get more real culture as she gets older. I love Miami, but it's like a fantasyland. Azzy grew up with these rich kids, palm trees, nice shit, and all that. We're just trying to give her some real culture. Let her experience diversity, the good and the bad.

Azzy came by surprise. She's a Jamaica baby. I'll never forget: Me and Lorena were in Jamaica and we had unprotected sex. We were in the outdoor shower, living it up, and Azzy was conceived. To this day, she loves reggae music.

When my wife told me she was pregnant, I was nervous. I hadn't had a kid in years. When you look at a lot of these rappers—no offense—they all got like eight kids. They've got ten kids. God forbid you're a sex symbol, you've got like fifteen kids. Me, I was very careful. I think Joey being born with Down syndrome had something to do with it. Joey was a blessing for sure, and I wasn't scared that any of my other kids would be similarly challenged, but I did learn in that experience just how *real* parenting was. So I was very selective. It's nothing you should play with. If you bring kids into this world, you want them to live their best lives.

Azzy's school costs $60,000 a year to attend and some of the parents be droppin' off *five* kids. I'm like *What the fuck? How do they afford this shit? $300,000 a year for school?*

But you want your family to live the best. I didn't want to have a bunch of kids who couldn't live the best. I believe that's almost like the Muslim rule about having wives. You can have four wives, but they all gotta live the same. You have kids, they have to live the same. Ryan went to private school, *Azzy's* gotta go to private school. Ryan had what he wanted, Azzy's gotta have whatever she wants. She's my heart. I just want her to be happy and achieve everything she dreams of in life.

I know one day she's going to fall in love. Hopefully she'll have a man who will respect her on the level that I respect her. I'm gonna be honest with you, when it comes time for Azzy to date, I don't know if I'm gonna be as overprotective with her as I was with Lisa. I don't know. I don't think I'll be bringing out the baseball bat, but I don't trust men. At the same time, Azzy's gotta live for herself. I don't think I'm gonna be on no Sgt. Slaughter shit. I'm not gonna threaten these guys coming to my house, but they gotta respect my daughter. As long as they respect my daughter, we'll be fine.

I believe every girl, not just my daughter, should level up. When you look at the intricacies of my relationship with Lorena, she took a real gamble with me. I was a fat nigga, no money, living in a crib with just a mattress as furniture. Her father used to give us money to eat. Lorena believed in me and we've been living a great life ever since. But I don't want my daughter to go through that.

I want Azzy to be with somebody who's got more money *than me*. Somebody who's got a better family, who has morals, who's got respect. That's what you wish for, but you can't tell your kids who to love. One thing is for sure: No matter what, I'll always be there for her.

For a year and a half during the pandemic, we were together just about every day. Azzy wants to keep it that way. Azzy tells me to retire; she wants a normal dad who's going to take her to school and be there when she comes home. Azzy and all my kids want to spend more time with their dad. My wife wants to spend time with her husband.

I love to spend as much time with my wife and kids as I can, but I'm never gonna just stay at home and be a house dad. I'd go crazy. I'm going to keep touring for now and I'm going to break into Hollywood on the executive side with this movie I just sold to Warner Bros. TV is next. I've done some television and films, and definitely have more acting roles in me. As far as Azzy, I'm meeting her in the middle. I put her as an executive producer of my and Dre's album *Family Ties*, and she is also the EP of my *Big Big Show* on Instagram, where I've interviewed all the biggest celebs from Lil Uzi Vert to Iron Mike Tyson to my idols KRS-One and LL Cool J.

I really can't stop working. Even though I'm providing for the whole family, I know part of it is selfish, too. I'm following my dream. I thank my family—my parents, my wife, all my kids—for allowing me to do it, to live my dream, because without that support system, that cocoon of love, I would be nothing.

PART V

OLD CYCLES,
NEW BEGINNINGS

CHAPTER 19

DEBTS TO PAY

RIGHT BEFORE ONE of the biggest shows of my career, my brother Angel refused my offer to move him out of the New York City rat race and down to live with my parents in Miami. To top it off, he had just gone blind. As mortified as I was leaving the hospital after visiting him, I really didn't have time to dwell on it because of the show I had later that day at Crotona Park. After decades of trying, the City of New York had finally granted me permission to perform in the Bronx, in my hood.

I had rocked every major venue in the tri-state area, including Madison Square Garden and MetLife Stadium in New Jersey. Crotona Park though was extra special because it was a full-circle journey for me. Crotona Park is by my grandmother's house, where I spent every summer. We would stay over there and go to the pool. My father would be out there selling Icees, bacalaitos, and alcapurrias, which are like Puerto Rican beef patties.

For years I've been one of the biggest entertainers to come out the Bronx and I was finally getting my chance to shine at home. It was a free show, and it made me think of the park jams my brother Angel told me that DJ Kool Herc and Grandmaster Flash and Afrika Bambaataa used to throw.

I thought it would be five hundred people coming to my show; possibly a thousand would show up. When I got there, there were over 20,000 people in the park. I know the hood ain't never seen no shit like that. I always say to let your darkest moments bring you the greatest clarity. I had been so dejected before I got to the park, just finding out my brother went blind. But God showed me: It could be your worst day, and it could turn around and be your best day. I felt so appreciated when I looked out at the crowd.

There were definitely times in my career when I've felt unappreciated. I've consistently come with hits for decades, but I've gotten overlooked when it came to critics' lists of Best of the Year; I never won a Grammy Award; hell, a lot of times my album sales weren't as big I thought they should have been. But I've been one of the most consistent ever.

Going to Crotona Park that afternoon, it touched my heart. It felt like the people were giving Fat Joe his due. I saw so many people I grew up with. I saw every babysitter I ever knew, every crossing guard I ever knew, every school teacher, every thug. *Everybody* I ever knew from the Bronx was there to celebrate the show. I've never experienced anything like that before and I doubt I ever will again. It was my grand homecoming, in more ways than one.

It was the summer of 2016 and I was in the middle of a monumental comeback that actually propelled me to the heights I'm at today. In March of that year I released the single "All the Way Up" with Remy Ma, featuring French Montana, and it caused immediate chaos. Radio, clubs, everybody picked it up and it gave me my first megahit in years. "Crills Mania" (that's my version of "Hulka-mania," an affectionate term I use for driving my fans into a frenzy) returned better than ever! Some people had counted me out, and yeah, I'll admit "All the Way Up" served as vindication.

I'd last put some hardware on the board in 2011 with "Another Round," featuring Chris Brown. It was a smash and went gold independently, without the backing of a major label. Although I hadn't dropped an album, the show bookings from all over the world were coming in. My catalog was and is still sweet. If I never made another record, I'd still get booked for shows for the rest of my life. But as an MC, I'm competitive. And while I love the accolades from my treasure trove of hits, there's still nothing that compares to dropping a brand-new record, having it steaming up the radio, smashing the charts, and the sales of the single going through the roof.

"All the Way Up" was such a defining moment of my career, because I had to come from all the way down.

LET'S REWIND: In 2013, I hit rock bottom. My career and life derailed. I found out I had been robbed of millions and I went to jail. It was the Feds who jammed me up. For years I'd watched them arrest friends and family for drug trafficking, murder, all types of serious crimes. I'd had nightmares about them coming to get me as well. But I'd been legit for so long, the looming threats of getting knocked by the Feds had been in my rearview mirror for decades. Ironically, I got put behind bars while I was operating totally above board.

My accountant had worked with me for many, many years. He did great business and I trusted him. But then one day his son got into a car accident and became quadriplegic. Having to attend to his family meant putting his practice on the back burner; I needed to find a new person to help me take care of my money. My attorney introduced me to a new accountant.

For two years, I proceeded with business as usual, wiring my new accountant money every thirty days to pay my taxes and other monthly bills. I didn't really give it a second thought. One day I walked into a car dealership to buy a car and discovered my credit was out-of-this-world low. The car dealer told me he had some bad news for me. I thought he was playing.

"Mr. Cartagena, you should sit down," he advised before giving me the news that turned my world upside down. He had just gone over all of my financials.

"None of your mortgages, none of your cars, nothing has been paid for," he revealed to me.

"Impossible," I told him.

I called my accountant up, I was furious and confused.

"You ain't paid none of my mortgages?" I asked. "You ain't pay none of my bills?"

"Hey, buddy, don't kill me, buddy," he said, flustered. Then he started pleading to me, "Don't hurt me."

"I never said I was going to hurt you," I insisted, my tone lowering and my demeanor calming. I didn't know if he was trying to set me up or anything, plus I needed answers. If I had scared him too much, it might have hindered him giving me the info I needed.

"I send you money every month, and you ain't been paying my bills?" I asked again.

Truth was, he was robbing me.

So I got a brand-new accountant. We contacted the IRS and told them what was going on, that my former accountant had been robbing me and didn't pay two years of taxes. We even showed them wire transfers. The government didn't care. They told me *I* was responsible for who I hire. Even though they knew the guy robbed me, they locked *me* up. Can you believe that shit?

I had paid the tax money once to my crooked accountant, and I wound up having to pay it again, with interest, to the IRS. *Plus,* they gave me four months in jail. That whole case cost me like $5 million. I never thought I would even be able to pay it all back. I paid whatever the nut was, like a million and change, before I got sentenced. When I came back to court to get sentenced, even though I had no prior criminal history *on record,* they locked me up.

I felt like the judge was under a lot of pressure to put me in jail. Either because I'm a big-name rapper or because my past came back to haunt me—I suspected people in law enforcement were calling the judge like, "Yo, you've got to jam this guy up. He's a baaaaaad guy."

There were other people who owed way more back taxes and had way worse delinquency than me. They didn't pay their taxes back and they got probation. But they gave me four months for tax evasion, August 2013 till November 2013. Booooyyyy, did I experience some shit in there.

"HOW IN THE FUCK did I get *here*?" It literally seemed like yesterday I was in Dubai performing in front of a sold-out crowd of 100,000 people with my brother Ja Rule. But today, I'm in a federal penitentiary. Tonight, "The Don" is actually going to be told when to go to bed. I can't hug my daughter, I can't kiss my wife. It was like a nightmare.

On my first day locked down, I had to come to grips with my situation real quick, because it felt like at every turn, I might have to fuck somebody up.

I was in my cell, lying on my bunk, and two Puerto Rican dudes walked in. One was a super cock diesel Latino Brock Lesnar–looking cat. I wound up naming him "Super Boricua." The other one wasn't as big, but clearly a *bad* guy.

I was still lying in my bed, but on alert in case some bullshit started. What was crazy—for some reason the Puerto Ricans in jail couldn't say "Fat" as in "Fat Joe." They kept saying, "Fawwwhhht! Fawwwhhht!"

So the one guy, Super Boricua, started telling me in Spanish, "Oh yeah, Fawwhhht. We love what you did with Big Pun. We love that you represent the Puerto Ricans, but here in this jail, Puerto Ricans stay with the Puerto Ricans. Blacks stay with the Blacks. Whites stay with the whites. You can't be cool with the Black dudes like that. I see that the Black dudes are cool with you.

"All the Spanish people in here, they're my sons," he added. "I got to protect them. I got cousins in New York, they've got nothing but love and respect for you," he added.

When he stopped, I sat up in my bunk so I could check his ass.

"Listen, my brother, you finished yet?" I asked him rhetorically in Spanish. It was crazy-funny because I speak broken Spanish.

"My man, first thing you got to do is call your cousins in New York so they can tell you, *I'm not a rapper.* Number two, I'm only in here for four months. Imagine if I came here for only four months and let you run *me.* I would have to give you a Grammy or an Oscar, some type of fuckin' statue when you get out of here, for you to be able to say that you actually 'ran Fat Joe,'" I continued tempestuously. "I've been running niggas so long, you gotta to be out your fuckin' miiiind if you think you could run me in this muthafucka."

He started laughing because he must have realized, *Yo, this guy is crazy.*

I told him I respect everybody. I don't care if they're Asian, white, Black, whatever it is. If you respect me and you show me love, I got the same love for you.

"Well, you know the Puerto Ricans ain't gonna hold you down," he warned me.

"I didn't come in here thinking the Puerto Ricans were gonna hold me down," I snarled back. "I came in here to do four months and go home."

IT'S ONE THING to get locked up, it's another thing to get locked up and be as famous as I am. I was prepared to go to jail in my home state of New York when I got sentenced. Then at the eleventh hour, the courts threw me a curveball. I guess they felt I had too much influence in New York and they were right. Every Fed jail in the state had three hundred guys waiting for me. The biggest guys in the game, the inmates who run the jail, were literally giving speeches the night before I was supposed to come in.

They were telling everybody in lockdown with them, "When *he* comes through here, y'all better walk with him like he's the fucking president!" These were big dudes handing down the mandates to treat Fat Joe like royalty. They were telling their underbosses, "When he comes through, he represent the Bronx. Y'all better salute this nigga."

Every jail in New York, we had it on smash. Honestly, all jokes aside, I don't think they'd ever seen some shit like what it was about to be with me walking up in a New York jail.

Last-minute, the courts switched it up because my residence was in Miami, and they made me go to FDC Miami. I drove past there two days before I had to go in just to see where I was going. The building looks scary from the outside, rusty and decrepit. When I woke up the morning I had to actually go in, it was a Friday. My wife, Lorena, was on the couch crying hysterically. I'd never seen her like that. My mother-in-law was in there crying. I was just trying to get it together. I had my manager, my brother Rich Player; my brother chef Mark; and my son Ryan with me. They all drove me over to the prison, which is actually only ten minutes away from my house, but it was a world of difference.

I got into the car and took like five grand in cash so I could get whatever I needed in jail. It didn't work out like that.

I pulled up around 7:30 A.M. I had to walk across the street to surrender myself. There's a guard with a rifle on a post above the building. He's ready to shoot in case somebody tries to escape. They got the biggest gate in the world separating the inside of the prison from the free world. The gate, it looked like it extended to the sky. As I was walking across the street, I got a phone call from Lil Wayne.

"Joe, my brother. I know you're turning yourself in in a little bit, man. I wanted to call you before you went in," he told me.

Remember, Weezy got arrested in New York City in 2007 for gun possession. In 2010, he did eight months in Rikers Island. If anybody knew about being a top-tier rapper and then having to go to jail, it was Weezy. So it really touched me that he would take time out to call me. Our brotherhood has been one of my most cherished relationships in and out of the music business for years.

"Wayne, how did you make it in that muthafucka?" I asked him. I was confused. His answer was as simple as could be, but powerful.

"I was just humble," he said. "I was just being humble, man. You be humble. Treat everybody with respect and you'll be good, no question."

It was beautiful. I thanked him.

As I was about to walk in, I looked at Rich. Then I looked at my son; Ryan had hurt in his eyes. He was on his way to start his freshman year at Full Sail University in Orlando the next day. Even though I had tax issues and money issues, I still sent him to college, which was fuckin' $8,000 a month. We didn't have no loan. It's crazy when you go to jail but you still have to worry about tuition. You still have to worry about your people outside, and still have to pay their bills.

That's an ill mindset to have: Keep going at all costs.

It weighs heavily, knowing that responsibility is on you. You still have to provide, *while in jail,* and most of your money was stolen. Then most of what little you had left was paid out to the Feds.

As I walked up, two men approached me. They were all dressed up in suits. I was saying to myself, "Damn, what the fuck is this about?"

The two guys were the warden and a captain. The captain was a white dude; he was slick-talking. The warden was this Black cock diesel dude. He looked like he'd played in the NFL. The warden was really cool, but the captain was talking all this bullshit. "In here, we do this, we do that." All that.

"We've got rapists in here, we got kingpins, we would like for you to be in protective custody," the captain told me.

"I can absolutely not be in protective custody," I told him. "I cannot do that."

"We've never had a rapper, or somebody famous like you, and it's a lot of dangerous guys in here," he tried to rationalize.

"I hear you, but I could never live with the fact that I went to jail and I went into protective custody," I responded, standing my ground. "I'll remain humble. I won't start nothin' with nobody, but I gotta live in regular population."

WHEN YOU WALK INTO THE PRISON, *you're in.*

There's no coming back until you complete your sentence. There's no time-out in jail. I always equate it to being on an airplane. Once the wheels are up and you're in the air, there's nothing you can do. You're on that muthafucka until you land. You gotta make the best of it.

When I walked in there, I talked the warden out of putting me in mandatory protective custody. They rushed me upstairs. They didn't want me in a holding cell. We got on this elevator and went to the sixth floor.

A female correctional officer opened the door and I saw literally 2,000 dudes doing jumping jacks, pull-ups, sit-ups, working out. It's just like you see on TV. Everything was metal. They had an upstairs and downstairs, upper tier and lower tier.

As I'm walking in, all 2,000 of the inmates started screaming at the same time, "Ahhhrrrrrrr!," when they saw me. They started jumping up and down and going crazy. For the first time in probably my whole life, I had to give myself a pep talk. My circumstance was a little daunting.

"Yo, Joe man, you're realer than everybody here, man. Don't fold," I told myself as I was being escorted to my cell. "Do not fold."

It was weird because I'm always so confident in who I am. But at that moment, it felt like one of the dragons from *Game of Thrones* was breathing in my face. That was the most intimidated I'd felt in years. It felt like me against 2,000 people. I didn't grow up in Miami. In New York, I would have walked through the door and people who were my mans for twenty years would have been running up like, "Yo, Crack, what's up!!!"

In FDC Miami, I didn't know anybody. It was legitimately overwhelming to say the least. Before I could even get to my cell, a bunch of guys were running up to me like, "Yo, Joe Crack, Joe

Crack," and trying to rap for me. They thought they were gonna get on.

"I'm not in here for this rap shit," I had to let them know. "Don't ask me no rap questions or nothing like that."

OFF RIP, some people ain't like me, some people did. I told you, I went in there with over five grand, but it means nothing in the Feds. It takes them at least a week or two weeks for them to process you, no matter who you are. Even though I came in with five thousand in my pocket, I didn't have commissary.

Commissary is how an inmate really eats in prison. The most simple thing we take for granted on the outside, like a piece of fruit, is fine cuisine in the pen.

A line started forming at my cell. Somebody brings two bananas, one guy brings a couple of oatmeals. One guy brings a plate, one brings a spoon. This is called "setting you up." The inmates fuck with you, they set you up and look out.

There was this Afro-Latino dude who was really great and helpful. He was dark, really dark, like Akon dark. But he spoke Spanish. He was Puerto Rican and he brought me this thing that looked like a Walkman. I didn't know how important that was. Later I found out you can't watch TV without the Walkman device and headphones. They've got three TVs: One is on the Spanish channel, one is on sports, and the last one is on English-language American TV. The volume doesn't come out of the TV speakers, the only way to hear it is on these Walkmanlike devices that played the audio.

My first time walking out of my cell, I looked down on the tier. There were around a thousand inmates, but only twelve seats in the common area: three tables with four chairs at each table. So if you wanted to watch TV, you had to go find yourself a chair at one of the tables or just stand. I stood next to this dude, I don't know if he was Haitian or African American. He had gold teeth.

"Yo, what's up? Who sits *there*?" I asked him, looking at one of the metal tables. He really didn't say anything, but he gave me a look as if to say, *The real ones sit there.* So I went to the table. There was a dude sitting at it. Mind you, I had been in jail for about fifteen minutes, and I know I had been advised to be humble and that's what I wanted to do. But my survival tactics from years on the front lines in the Bronx kicked in. Just like on the streets, in jail you have to be the predator or be the prey. I went back to my earlier programming.

"Yo, my man, get off the table," I commanded him.

"What? This is our table," he replied.

"YO! My man. You've got to run the table, B," I told him calmly, but with a scowling tone, practically warning him. "It is what it is, B. This *my* table."

Thank God the guy got scared. He punked out. He just walked off and I sat at the table. That let everyone know I wasn't in there on no "Fat Joe the Rapper" shit. It showed everybody that they were gonna respect me as a G. At that point, the entire tier was looking at me from the corner of their eyes like *This nigga here is on some bullshit.*

I was. I had to be. That wouldn't be the last time I would be forced to impose my will. I also sought advice from a few of my friends besides Lil Wayne who had served time in jail. All these guys did at least twenty-plus years. During our phone calls, they told me the blueprint on how to survive in the bing. My guy Opey Megatron was one of the main ones consulting me on how to navigate. I kept their words in my mind and played them over and over like I was reading a pamphlet.

One of the first rules is when you share a cell with somebody, the guy who sleeps on the bottom, he's the toughest one in the cell. The celly who is the softest one, he's gotta be on the top bunk. My cellmate was an Arab dude who was really cool. He did big time, and he was on the bottom bunk. I walked in and approached it the same as I had the table. "Yo, my man. You got to get to the top bunk."

"What do you mean?" he asked, startled. "This is my cell. I've been here for eighteen months."

"I hear you and all, bro, but you gotta hit that top of the bunk," I reiterated. "It is what it is."

He went to the top bunk. Me and him didn't have no problems.

My first night staying in jail was a muthafucka, boy. I finally lay on the bunk and looked up at the frame of the bed above me. It was full of these engravings in the wood, like "Chico 127," "Johnny Was Here," "Elroy Was Here." It finally hit me: *Holy shit! I'm in jail.* That's when it became reality.

TALKING TO MY CELLMATE helped me pass the time during those first days. He was heavy into religion. He said he got locked up because he was racially profiled. He was living in Florida and Feds would be harassing him and his people because they thought they were terrorists. The Feds would run in the mosque and they were running in their cribs and shit. He was telling me the difference between Shiites and Sunnis. He was deeply religious.

About a week later, I blew his mind and showed him an egg. This man had no clue who I was. He just knew me as his fat Spanish bunkie. In the Feds, or at least where I was, for some reason, the only eggs you got to eat were powdered. They didn't give real eggs to the inmates. So I started regulating and going against the system, living by my own rules as much as I could. I was making sure that I was straight. So homeboy in the cell was bugging when I showed him my boiled egg.

"Eighteen months, I've never seen an egg in here," he marveled.

I wound up having like seventy eggs.

My cellmate and I were opposites. I was the center of attention and he was so low-key. There are some guys who go to jail and they do their time under the radar, where no one knows who they are or what they're doing. Some other guys want to be loudmouths and want everybody to know who they are. Me, I was trying to stay low-key for the most part, but celebrity status made it impossible for me not to be in the proverbial fishbowl. This guy never saw nobody move how I was moving. I was giving him eggs, taking care of him. Eventually he inquired about who I was.

"I've been in here eighteen months and nobody talks to me," he noted. "Now everybody talks to me, like they want to be my friend. They asked me questions about you . . . Who are you?"

I broke it down to him. He was cool. Eventually he was released and I got a new bunkmate. A Cuban dude. I used to call him "Tony Montana." He was short with that Napoleon complex. He was a good Spades player and me and him didn't have problems, until I found out there was an Italian chef who was staying in another cell. I heard the guy could really cook. Of course I wanted him to come be my cellmate so he could prepare food for me. I went and met the chef, he was solid. I broke the news to Tony Montana that he had to move out. He was mad as hell.

"Yo, I was in Atlanta with all the Black guys. They couldn't move me out the cell," he started to inform me.

"I hear you, Tony, but you gotta leave, bro. You're gonna leave," I responded casually.

Tony moved out and went with another Cuban dude. The Cuban dudes stayed close in jail.

My new bunkie came in, Chef Junior. The Chef used to make me fresh mozzarella and fresh ice cream, man. We even had linguine and clam sauce in that muthafucka one time. How were we able to eat so well? There's an inmate kitchen, and right next door to it, there's an officers' kitchen. As you can imagine, in the officers' kitchen, they ate different. They had a better quality and selection of food.

Junior used to steal food like clams out the officers' kitchen and bring it to our cell and chef it up. He would even bake cakes! If you know anybody in the Feds, they usually make "cakes" out of cookies. They take a bunch of cookies, smash 'em up, and make the cakes out of cookie crumbles. Not us. We had the real shit: cake mix, eggs, flour, and everything.

Not to glorify sneaking the food, but the man was cooking me everything under the sun. And anytime I ever caught beef, he was one million percent down to go the whole nine yards. I'd never met anybody who, after knowing them for two, three months, became my best friend. But time moves different in prison. Chef Junior definitely is one of the coolest dudes in the world to me. We would call each other and stay in touch from the time I got out of prison to when he recently passed away.

CHAPTER 20

LOCKED UP

IN THE FEDS, you get three visits a week for family and friends but your attorneys are able to visit you whenever they want. There was a visitor's room downstairs and you could sit there for like six hours, eating burgers, talking shit. It was almost like going to Club LIV. So I'd have my lawyers Dawn Florio and John Cain come in from New York and Tampa frequently and visit me. I tried to get a visit every day if I could. That was the best way to pass time and stay out of trouble.

A few weeks into my sentence, the corrections officers had to sit me down. Because somebody ratted me out.

I had gotten a pair of Jordan slides while I was in prison. In jail, where I was at, you have gray sweat suits or you have a beige Dickies-like jumpsuit. You cannot wear Gucci, Louis Vuitton, none of that. Nobody's got that, right. But somebody snuck me in a pair of Jordan slippers during a visit. By the time I came up from the visitor's room, I had them on.

This Latin dude, mad cool, he was the barber. He walked up to me and went: "Maybachs! Maybachs!" I'm looking at him like *What the fuck is he talking about?*

"Maybachs!" he kept yelling, pointing at my feet. So basically, he was saying having those slippers on in jail was the equivalent of having a Rolls-Royce or a Maybach in the streets. The whole prison started zeroing in on my feet. It was a little awkward. I felt like Antonio Fargas in the classic *I'm Gonna Git You Sucka*. Remember the scene when his character gets out of jail and he's wearing the shoes with the fish tank platforms and everybody is staring at him? Everybody was staring at me.

Now, at this point, I gotta front. I gotta walk around in them shits like whatever. The very next day, I get a visit from the Superintendent of Industries (SOI). They're like internal affairs. They investigate not just the inmates for corruption, but the corrections officers too. In the Feds, they feel like the kingpins got money and they gotta watch the corrections officers to make sure they're not taking money. But I'll tell you: I offered money to a lot of COs, not one of them took it. I don't know if it was because I was high-profile, so they didn't want to fuck with me like that, but they wouldn't take my money.

So boom, I'm working out and the SOI comes to talk to me. They take me to my cell and search it while I'm standing outside. They find a whole bunch of eggs, they find a whole bunch of chicken—chicken is worth more than lobster in jail. They find some other contraband. I knew what it was. They were looking for the slides. The whole jail was looking at the SOI searching my cell like *They about to get this nigga for them Jordan slides.*

The SOI finally found the slides, and then they walked me into a room. Sitting there is the assistant warden. She was a chubby white woman whose face looked hardened from years of dealing with inmates. I had always shown her love. I never had a problem with her. I'd see her in the hallway and say, "Hey, how you doing?" She was cool, but tough.

"Fat. Fucking. Joe," she said to me, exasperated.

I was standing there with my innocent face on.

"Do you know who's in this building?" she asked.

"No," I answered.

She named four notorious Pablo Escobar–type cartel heads that I'd never heard of, then asked more questions.

"Do you know, every floor I go to, do you know whose name I hear? Fat. Fucking. Joe."

"I can't do nothing about that," I retorted. "I'm humble. I don't get into no trouble. You ain't see me with no problems. I'm just famous and I guess they're talking about me."

She accused me of paying off a CO to sneak in the Jordan slippers. I told her that wasn't true and made up a bullshit excuse. I told her there was a guy who had been in there for many years and he was about to go home, so he gave me the slides. That way, nobody would get in trouble. She looked at me skeptically, but gave me a chance. She didn't send me to "The Box," solitary confinement.

"You know, the minute you wore those slides, my phone went off around forty times in here?" she informed me. "The people in here, they're telling on you. They don't really like you, Joe. Be careful."

I realized that because I had about three weeks left, I was starting to run around really comfortable, acting like I could do whatever. Maybe wearing the Jordan slides was a little bit too flagrant. But there was certain shit in jail I needed and couldn't go without.

Imagine, with as much as we all like chicken, that you could only eat that shit once a week on Thursday. That was a big problem for me. People would trade different things for an extra piece of chicken. It was a big deal. Me? I ate ten pieces of chicken *a day*. Teriyaki, fried, baked, barbecue chicken, you name it. I had ten to a dozen pieces of chicken coming my way every day.

One time, a corrections officer caught me eating chicken on a Sunday. She was like, "Yo, chicken is on Thursday, man. How do you have chicken today?" And the chick took the fuckin' chicken leg out of my hand.

"Fat Joe, you're really disrespectful out here," she said with a grin. But it is what it is.

I had this dude named "Loco" I used to pay and he would clean my room and then wash and press my clothes every day. Every time I went to see my wife on a visit, my clothes would be pressed. I also used to sneak colognes into the jail. It's a thing with me: Anytime you stand next to Fat Joe, he smells great. So one of my priorities was smuggling in colognes to make sure I smelled good. That was more important than food. In prison, when I walked down the hallway, you could smell me coming through.

One of the older guys in there we called "Old-School." He was almost blind from diabetes, but he was real cool. He'd come up to me anytime of the day and give me a pop quiz: "Yo, Joe, Muhammad Ali or Floyd Mayweather? Chris Brown or Michael Jackson? Bobby Brown or James Brown? Jordan or LeBron?" He's old-school, so the right answer was always the older one.

He never really had much, so I would give him extra food, set him up, just out of love. One day, I was about to go to a visitation to see my lawyer and he approached me with information.

"Joe. I ain't gonna lie to you," he began to reveal. "I seen Trap with my own eyes talking to the police, and he told them about your slides."

Trap was an inmate, maybe like 6'5". He was a chiseled NBA-type. He used to play basketball every day. I was thinking that would be a good fight for Fat Joe one-on-one. It would be competitive. Minutes later, I was walking down the hallway when I saw Trap standing there, talking to this cop named Officer Page. When you go for visits, everybody has to go through a hallway that separates the north and south side. It was mad noisy, about 150 people were going on their visits. I walked up to Trap and the cop.

"Officer Page, let me ask you a question," I said.

"What's up, Crack?" he asked.

"Can an inmate do time in here and come home and get a deputy's badge?" I continued, sarcastically.

Everybody started crying laughing. Even the Spanish guys who don't know English, they knew this was disrespect. To imply another inmate was working with the authorities was to invite violence.

"Yo, Crack. I think you trying to disrespect me," Trap interjected.

"Nooooo. Don't think. *I am* disrespecting you," I confirmed. I was already cocked back, ready to let it go.

Trap just meekly said I was buggin', and walked off.

I went down to my visit with my wife. I was angry, I told her what had transpired. But seeing her made me forget everything. I had a burger, some sugar-free cookies, I was good. I went upstairs four hours later. As I'm walking, the biggest Black dude you ever seen in your life came up to me. He looked about as tall as Shaq. He was cut up too. You could see the *ten-pack*. He said he wanted to talk to me.

"Me and my brothers, we don't like how you talked to Trap earlier," he began to chide.

I didn't know what that guy was there for. I was naive. So I gave him advice.

"Yo, bro, you stay away from that guy," I warned. "He told on my slides. That guy's with the cops all the time, he's a snitch."

I was about to walk away and the guy blocked me.

"No, no, no. Maybe you don't understand. Me and my niggas don't like how you walking around here and we're ready to go to The Box for it," he declared, continuing to try to intimidate me.

What he meant was *We don't give a fuck what you're talking about. We just don't like you. So we're ready to set it on you. And if we got to go to solitary confinement for beating your ass, we ain't got no problem with it.* The worst punishment in prison was to get sent to The Box.

This guy was so fuckin' big. I knew a one-on-one with him was gonna be a task, let alone fighting him *and* his crew. But I couldn't show signs of backing down.

"What?!" I yelled, getting more assertive.

"Yeah, you heard me," he affirmed.

I looked over his shoulder and didn't see no one else.

"Yo, my man. You talkin' violence *to me*?" I yelled. "You need to go get ninety-nine more! You came by yourself. When you step to The Fat Joe on some beef shit, you need to be a hundred deep! Go. Get. *Ninety-nine* more muthafuckas!"

I'm screaming at the top of my lungs, "Are you fucking crazy?! Do you know who the fuck I am?! Who gave you the fuckin' authority to even speak to me?!"

I have all these incredible war stories where I've come out victorious. If I ever got beat up, I wanted to get beat up by John Gotti. I wanted to get beat up by Supreme McGriff. I wanted to get beat up by Boy George from the Bronx. The legends of all legends. Not by some random dude who's just cock diesel. *That* muthafucka's not authorized.

I was screaming on the guy, and then I noticed he was getting smaller and smaller. He wasn't 6'5" no more. His muscles were deflating. I realized he was all show. He may have been locked up but he ain't 'bout that life. I was screaming on him so legendary, he realized *Yo, this is a psycho. Fat Joe is nuts.*

Turned out the big Shaq diesel dude was just talking out his ass. I tried to fight him in front of everybody, but he didn't want it. That was the last of my drama in jail.

MY LAST NIGHT IN THE FEDS, Chef Junior was more excited for me to get out of there than I was. He gave me a lot of encouraging words and cooked for me like I was a king. We had enough food for all of the Knights of the Round Table. He made linguine and clam sauce and we had baked cakes. I made sure the entire jail ate good too. I ordered a hundred pizza pies and spread them out all over. Everybody had a slice of pizza in their hand.

Me buying those pizzas, that was almost like a nod to them saying, *Y'all stay strong. No matter how tough I am, I know y'all let me carry on in here.* I only had four months. A lot of guys in there are doing real time. I could have got cut up or whatever by people who didn't have a reason to live. Being that they showed love and respect, I showed them that respect back and bought the pizzas.

Let me break down how I did it. In FDC Miami, they give you a limit of $200 commissary a month. I would finance five guys who were broke and tell them, "Listen, here's two hundred bucks. Take $50 out the commissary, get whatever you want. But here's a list of stuff you're going to buy with the extra $150 worth of commissary for me."

I'd have them buy bottles of Diet Pepsi. I love them—I drink those all day still. They'd buy me food, whatever I wanted. My cell looked like Walmart.

THE MORNING OF MY RELEASE, they held me three extra hours so the warden could come and personally tell me good-bye.

"Yo, bro, nothing but love," he said when he finally made it down to the area where I was being released.

The guy loved me, man. In every cell, there's a blackboard where you can put some pictures or posters. I had a Big Pun poster hanging up. The warden would come by and go, "Biiig Punnnnnch." He pronounced it "Punch."

"Biiiig Punnnnch. That's my man," he would say every time.

No preferential treatment, no looking out, but he showed love. He came to tell me, "Do your thing, man, change your life. Stay focused, man. You don't belong in no shit like this."

I thanked him and finally got to the other side of that big gate to the sky. I got into the car with my wife. I had bought her a brand-new 560 Mercedes-Benz while I was in jail. She was driving me. I remember we went across the Venetian Causeway and it felt like slow-motion. I could not believe I was on the way home.

I called my favorite aunt, Titi Barbara. She started crying. I called my man Jimmy from Jimmy's Bronx Cafe because he would always check up on me while I was in there. I reached out to LL Cool J. He would always check up on me while I was in there too. LL would hit my family up and check on them as well. He wanted to visit me, but I was like, "I only got four months, man. Don't worry about it. I'm going to be good." He's a real one.

I spoke to Pitbull too. Pit, I knew him before his career got started. I passed his demo to the heads of TVT Records and they signed him to his first record deal. When I was going through all these problems with the IRS, Pit would always be like, "Yo, Joe, come see me." Out of all my friends in the entire industry—I'm talking about *allll* my friends—Pitbull was the only one to ask me, "You need something? You wanna hold something? I'll give you a couple hundred grand."

I told him, "Nah. I'm good." My pride wouldn't allow me to take it. But it felt good to know this man loved me enough to make the offer and give me that. Pit is special when it comes to his wealth. I would visit Pit and he'd be sitting with these old Cuban men and he'd be buying *schools*. Literally buying schools and hospitals for kids.

"How do you do this?" I asked him, about amassing that level of wealth.

"That's easy," he responded with a grin. "I watched every mistake you made and I didn't do that."

Wowwwww! I thought. It was cold-blooded, but it reminded me of how much I learned from watching my family gambling, smoking, and drinking. He learned.

I'M NOT GONNA FRONT THOUGH. I could have used that $200K he offered when I got out of prison. I started working like a dog to earn bread. I was doing shows, I was in the studio, and I got into this work release program right away. The courts were insistent that I get a job. So I got a job with my people at Market America as the president of Urban and Latino Development.

Market America has been around for about thirty years. The people I know there are the owners; they're billionaires. They were there for me when I got locked up. I'm still heartbroken over the recent loss of brother J.R. Ridinger, who started the company with his wife, Loren. The Ridinger family has championed everything Fat Joe since we became close friends and evolved into family. J.R. passed away in August 2022, and he was loved so much that, when they learned of his death, everyone from Serena Williams to Jamie Foxx to David Beckham to my sister Ashanti publicly spoke about how beautiful a person he was.

While he was here, J.R. took me under his wing as a mentor. We talked every day for the past five years. When the Feds jammed me up, the Ridingers offered to give me a million dollars. At my sentencing, for some reason, me and my sister Loren Ridinger locked eyes after the judge handed me my time. She was crying heavily and told me to come see her later that day. When I got to her mansion, she was begging me to take some money to hold me down in my time of need. This is a true a story, she was literally chasing me around her house with a million-dollar check before I went in jail. I love both of them so much. But I wouldn't take it, that's just not me. I was running away from her and her money.

So instead of giving me money, my Market America family were like, "Joe, let us show you how to get this money." And then they taught me.

Their offices are in a 150-million-dollar mansion in Miami with a yacht in the back, a swimming pool, everything. When you go on work release, parole officers check up on you. My job was in the mansion. Every day I'd go to work. I'd be chillin', hangin' out, doing my thing, going to these meetings, drinking these Diet Pepsis.

I told the courts, "I don't know why I'm in here, I own *my own* company."

They finally let me off work release after a few weeks, because they saw how lavish my work environment was. Market America turned out to be a major blessing in disguise. People could look at it like *Yo, that's one of them get-rich pyramid schemes*. I don't know, but I tried to make the most of it.

MY FAVORITE PART of coming out of jail though, was going home the day of my release and surprising my daughter, Azzy. She didn't know I was coming back that day. I hid in the kitchen and waited for her. When she came in, she ran into my arms and started crying. It gets me sentimental to this day to talk about it. That wouldn't be the last time I was almost brought to tears upon my return home. The second time it happened to me, it felt like my heart was being ripped out.

CHAPTER 21

THEY SMILE IN YOUR FACE

I WAS A YOUNG SAVAGE with a loaded firearm in my hand. That really is a combustible combination. I've robbed a lot of people in my day. I've mugged modest, honest, hardworking citizens unfortunately. I've pilfered the pockets of the most nefarious criminals walking the streets. I was literally *a kid* when I became a stickup kid—fourteen years old.

I was initially taught the ways of the gun by an adult who I considered an uncle. We'd hold up numbers spots. Imagine being a little boy and inflicting sheer horror on an adult. When you read the panic on a man's face as he stares down the barrel of a pistol while his well-being is compromised, that's an image you don't forget.

I learned that karma has no expiration date, and maybe it was karma that caught up to me when I had millions taken away by the government. This was *after* my accountant robbed me of millions. And just when I thought I'd lost it all, I found out worse was on the way.

You're born into this world by yourself. With the exception of tight, tight family and friends, the ones you know love you without condition, you can only *hope* your other loved ones love you the same as you love them. But you never know.

My relationship with my best friend Tone Montana was so tight because of that time he jumped in front of a machine gun to save my life. You can't show love better than that. *You're willing to give your life for your homie?* That's when I knew he was my best friend on Earth.

Blood is no guarantee of real love. You don't pick your family, you're born into it. I have family members who used to call BCW—that's the Bureau of Child Welfare—on *their sisters*. That's foul shit to me running both ways. BCW, they could take your kids away and put them in the system. But what are you doing to your kids that your own sister feels like she has to tell? So we've all got those bad apples that just so happen to be our kin.

See, me, I don't know how to fake love. If I don't fuck with somebody, I just can't be fake. It's my DNA. My soul won't allow me. If I love somebody, I make it clear that I love them. As long as they don't try to take advantage of me.

If somebody gets locked up, I'll pay for their lawyer. If somebody's mom dies, I'll pay for the funeral. But you can't come to me every week talking, "Yo, Joe, give me $2,000." I'm not going to let nobody do that—no family, no friends, nobody. That's just the way I get down.

Things get even more confusing when you have money. I look at some of my friends that are really wealthy. They've got every toy you could think of: mansions, an armada of cars, yachts. They throw events, huge lavish parties. All their friends come, fifty, sixty friends. Everyone is eating steaks, lobsters, and everybody *loves* one another *at the party*.

I know I truly love my wealthy friends just like I love my broke friends. I don't need money from them; I don't need nothing from them. But I sit there and ask myself, *Do these other people at these events they're throwing really love them?*

If you're going to a mansion and they've got all the food in the world, and everybody's drinking champagne for free, everybody's on a yacht, how do you confirm that these people really love *you*? Would they love you if you didn't have all of that? Would they love you if you weren't in a position of power?

I HAD A FRIEND, *a best friend,* who we're going to keep nameless. I didn't want to speak on him, but I think we've got to talk about him in this book. This guy was my friend for over twenty years. He was a confidant so close to me, I made the same mistake my brother Angel did decades earlier: I let my friend have access to my finances. That's how much I trusted him. No one ever saw me outside the house without this guy by my side. I was closer with him than even my own brothers, my own blood.

If I had a Ferrari, *he* had a Ferrari. If I had a Lamborghini, *he* had a Lamborghini. His kids were like my kids and vice versa. He was a huge part of my life and I trusted him with everything, including my bank account and my credit cards. Now these were *my* accounts, not *our* accounts. In case of emergency, he could get money to hold me down.

My grandmother, when I walked into her house, she would ask me where homeboy was. The elders in the family accepted him as one of their own, like a grandson.

It was always me and him. What's crazy is that I lost so many relationships, so many friends, because if he was like, "Yo, Joe. I'm not feelin' them. That ain't it," I didn't mess with them.

If *he* wasn't feelin' them, *we* wasn't feelin' them. Even if I didn't totally agree, I followed his counseling. You know when you're walking, and you have a shadow? I thought he was my shadow in the living flesh. I thought he had my best interests in mind at all times. There was no question. I believed in "till the wheels fall off."

Unfortunately, when I had the taxes situation, he was jammed up too. Part of my cop-out with the courts, my plea bargain, was for me to take all the blame so they wouldn't bother him. And *I'm the rapper,* bringing in money for everybody. But it is what it is.

I remember when we were going through it, he looked so stressed out. I guess everybody can be stressed out, but *I* was the one in trouble. I would tap him on the shoulder like, "Yo, bro. I got this. Don't worry about this. We're gonna be aight."

When I went to jail, I had strict instructions for my wife to pay $10,000 a month for this guy's bills. He would come to her and she'd write him a check for the full ten Gs. Even though I was in jail for four months, I couldn't let my best friend look crazy out here. I had to make sure his bills were paid and he still looked good.

The Feds took millions from me. It wasn't just the taxes I had to pay. I had to pay the number-one criminal defense attorney, Jeffrey Lichtman, and the number-one forensic accountant in America for my defense. I had to pay court fees, tax penalties. Part of the war with the Feds is they take your money. It ain't just about locking you up—they want your money. The drug kingpin, they want your money. Bernie Madoff, they wanted his money. They drain you dry *and then* they lock you up. The Feds are like the boogeymen. They took most of my money. I went from being a multimillionaire to having just a couple hundred grand.

I know people who work a nine-to-five every day will be reading this like *Damn nigga. You were still rich.* No. Not when you're used to having millions of dollars and you have a huge overhead. I pay all my family's bills. When I say "my family," I mean twenty members of my family, not just my wife and daughter who live with me. I pay *all* my family's bills; I pay all my employees.

I did my four months in jail. When I got home, my accountant says, "Yo, Joe. Can you come down and see me?"

When my accountants talked with that stern timbre and said, "Come down and see me face-to-face," it just didn't sit right.

"What the fuck I do *now*?" I thought. *The minute* I got home from jail, I was back at work. Literally the next day, I was in the studio with Cool & Dre, recording music. I was booking shows in *Timbuktu,* in every nook and cranny in the world you could think of. I had to work every single day of the month to come back with some money to fund my career and pay my bills. I make and distribute music independently. My daughter goes to private school. My son was at an expensive private college. I was paying for that.

I never complained, I worked hard and made it happen. My

family never, ever felt like there was a recession. They never felt like *Y'all, we fucked up*. I kept it going.

So here I am doing all of that, trying to get back on my feet, not trying to splurge or spend unnecessarily. I know when it's time to close up shop, not spend a bunch of money, and save. I know how to do that scientifically. Like a turtle, I'll go back in the shell. So I was really racking my brain to figure out what my accountant could have been getting at.

I go see the accountant and right off the rip he says, "Yo, Joe, what the fuck is wrong with you?"

Confused, I asked him, "What's up?"

"Bro, you're spending a bunch of money," he stated, chastising me. "You know you've got a tax case. The IRS is all in your new bills. You know they want their money. They want their penalties. They're not going to let you just come out here and run through all your money."

I couldn't understand what he meant because I had just been in jail. All I could spend was $200 a month in commissary.

"What are you talking about?" I questioned.

"Look," he said, pulling out receipts. "You spent $60,000 on this. You spent $50,000 here. You spent $40,000."

I'm thinking it's Lorena buying Gucci, Fendi, or whatever. My accountant went through the entire paper trail with me. He had two years of receipts. The minute we got to the bottom of it, my accountant just sank in his chair and put his head down in his hands. He was in pain on my behalf.

He laid out the documents for me. I started looking at these statements and it all became clear: All of this money was being spent by my best friend. My brother for life, his name kept coming up. He took $5,000, he took $10,000. He paid for this, paid for that. It was all *his* personal shit, like his kids' schools.

When my accountant revealed everything to me, at first I refused to believe it. But the proof was right there in my face. There was a paper trail. There's no way to confuse things, *it happened*.

So now I'd been through a lot. I'd been to jail, my best friend Tone died. Pun died. My sister died. My brother went blind. I dealt with my mother having cancer. I never cried when they sent me to jail. I never cried when my sister died. But I cried that day.

When I got back to my house after seeing my accountant, my wife was cooking. She didn't know what was goin' on. I sat down and looked again at all this paperwork with my friend's name on it. I couldn't go any longer without resolution. I called this man and I casually told him to come by the crib. He was there in less than thirty minutes.

"What's up, God?" he said nonchalantly, walking into my house as he had countless times during the past twenty-plus years.

I got right to it.

"Man, something's wrong," I told him. I still didn't want to believe he was stealing. I was still in denial. "My accountant called me. He backtracked two years," I continued. "All this money is missing from my accounts."

I turned around, and when I looked him in his face, that's when I knew. When you know someone for so long, you can read their face. They don't have to say a word. His face was so . . . so . . . sad. He couldn't hide it. The only way to describe this is another movie reference: It was like the final scene in *The Godfather Part III*. The part where they try to kill Michael Corleone and actually murder *his daughter* instead. Michael holds her in his arms as she lies lifeless, and he screams out with such pain, he's almost on the brink of exhaustion. I felt the same way.

"Whyyyyyyyyyy!? Whyyyyyyy!!!???" I yelled in agony, looking at him. I was so overwhelmed, I couldn't control my body. I started convulsing.

"Whyyyyyy!!!??? Whyyyyyy!!!???" I kept screaming.

That was the straw that broke the fuckin' camel's back. The government had taken my money. I was an over-forty-year-old rapper who didn't know if I could ever come back. And now my best friend had stabbed me in the back? I felt a swell of all these emotions pulsating through me. One of the few people on Earth I completely trusted betrayed me. I just started shaking uncontrollably. Lorena came in like a linebacker, dove on me, and grabbed me.

"Joey stop! Joey stop!" she shouted frantically.

My body was just spasming, affliction coursing through my veins.

"Whyyyyyy!!!? Whyyyyyy!?" I kept yelling. I couldn't even control the pain.

"Please don't kill me. Please! Don't kill me, please," he begged me.

I said, *"Kill you?"* As much agony as I was in because of him, I could never physically harm him. But I had to make a tough decision. Tough, because you can't just erase love.

I couldn't keep this guy in my life. As much as I loved him, if I forgave him, then I ain't true to the code. How could you let your right-hand man steal from you and then keep him around? He probably stole millions from me. Me and my accountant only looked back over two years and found hundreds of thousands missing. If you went back twenty years, imagine how much he stole.

When I let my mind wander, I realized, *Damn man. This muthafucka had more luxury cars than me.*

So with my money depleted and my best friend just stabbing me in the back, I had to walk these streets again by myself. Something I ain't been used to in twenty years. I was with him every fuckin' day, traveling across the world. And now I had to go walk through Harlem, the Bronx, Miami, everywhere by myself. People I knew saw that I was vulnerable.

I really pray to God about this every night. It's about loyalty. It's about respect. I respect the kind of men who, when they pass away, we can walk up to their coffins and look at them and say, "Yo, this nigga did it. He was a real one. He never told. He never fucked his friend's wife. He never abandoned the code." All these old-school morals.

So when I got betrayed, it put into question: Does it really exist anymore? Because here was somebody I gave that benefit of the doubt. Here was somebody that I trusted more than my own blood. And he double-crossed me. Was it greed? Did he have a complete sense of entitlement over my money? Was he harboring resentment and jealously for decades? I'll never know.

I loved this guy so much that even after the fact, I purposely never told anybody what happened. I didn't want anybody trying to impress me by trying to hurt him if they saw him one day.

I only saw homeboy one other time after I confronted him at my house. That's when Full Flex died. Homeboy showed up to the funeral with his wife. We let him in and that was that. He tried to say what's up to me, but I just ignored him and kept it moving.

Sometimes God teaches you hard lessons. So instead of asking, "Why, God?," I try to look for the lesson for myself. I always say let your darkest moments bring you the most clarity. That's what I get from it.

Maybe God knew I was going to make millions again, get back on my feet. Maybe God said, "You know what, Joe? I'm going to save you. This guy is around you, he's been stealing from you for twenty years and you really thought he was good people. Next time, when I give you a lick, I want you to keep your fortune."

CHAPTER 22

REMY MA

IF YOU HAVEN'T GUESSED it by now, I'm a film buff. I love the movies. The only thing I love more than watching a good drama is a good comedy that makes me laugh until I cry. I'm a sucker for a laugh.

When *Eddie Murphy Raw,* came out, a hundred of us, the whole projects, went to the Dover Theatre in the Bronx to see it. Eddie was so funny, I couldn't take it. I was being loud and obnoxious. I was in the middle of the aisles acting a fool. The security came and threw me out the theater because I was being too much.

I always compare scenes in my life to scenes in movies. If the Terror Squad story were a movie it would be *300.* We'd be a crew fighting an army of 10,000 and not relenting. We'd be getting our ears chopped off and getting stabbed, but we'd keep going till the death.

Remy Ma would be one of the main warriors, sword and shield, in the trenches next to me. Rem, that's my sister. She's Terror Squad and together we formed a super group and dropped a classic album. And while I definitely helped to cultivate Remy's career, I can't take the credit for being the one to actually find her. Reminisce Smith was introduced to me by Pun.

She's from the Bronx just like us. She grew up in the Castle Hill projects and lived around the corner from Punisher. Pun is the only guy I knew who went platinum, got nominated for a Grammy, and stayed in the hood around the corner from the PJs.

One of Pun's people lived in Castle Hill by Remy and heard she could rap. The day that friend met Remy, he took her to Pun's house. Rem was so young, she brought her mother with her. She dropped endless bars for Pun and he was totally taken, enamored with her as an MC. The very next day, Pun surprised Remy and pulled up to her projects. He told her he was going to a video shoot and wanted to know if she could braid his hair.

Just so happens, Remy is just as skilled doing hair as she is ma-rauding music. The video was for Jennifer Lopez's "Feelin' So Good" off the *On the 6* album. Me and Pun were featured in the song and video. That's the first time I met Remy.

Pun was my artist and he said to me *he's got an artist* and "she's the nicest."

I wanted to hear her right away. So Pun set it up where Remy came with him to the studio. I think it was Sony Music Studios in Manhattan.

I get there and this young girl comes in. She looked every bit of fifteen, sixteen years old. She was skinny and had a leather vest on, but she didn't carry herself like a teenager. Remy had high confi-dence. She knew she was the shit. Pun told the engineer to throw a beat on and Remy killed it for like ten minutes straight. This is the hungry Remy Ma, from day one, just destroying shit. I fell in love with her as soon as I heard her rhyme. I knew she had the makings of a rap legend.

I was jealous of Big Pun. Because Remy was *his* artist. I'd been looking for a female artist like this. I already had Pun in Terror Squad, but we needed our Foxy Brown, our Lil' Kim, for the team. I was just looking at her rapping and I was so excited and emo-tional on the inside, but I didn't show it. I was stoic. I put the poker face on. Let her tell the story, she'll say, "Yo, I thought Joe hated me. He was looking at me with an ice grill."

But the truth is I loved every second of her spittin' bars. She had lyrics and presence. She was authentic. She believed everything she was saying. Even as a teenager, Remy felt that no one on the planet—male or female—could fuck with her bar for bar. She made *you* feel it.

After she stopped rappin' in the studio, I was walking away and Pun pulled me to the side and asked, "Yo, Twin, how she sound?"

I looked at him; all I could say was "incredible." He tapped me on the stomach and started smiling.

"Don't worry, Twin," Pun started to reassure me. "That's *our* artist. Me and you! Don't worry, Twin. Me and you!"

"She's so dope!" I told him. "We can really blow her up."

Remy and Pun would hang out every day. As I got to know her, I found out she came from hard beginnings: a mom on drugs, a dad she barely knew. Castle Hill projects are where the Bloods in New York City originated—her hood. She was surrounded by all that.

Remy wanted more though. She had dreams like me and Pun. She became our little sister. We took her across the globe in '97. I'm not even sure if this was legal. She was still a kid going on a fuckin' world tour with us. We took care of her though. We watched over her like big brothers. I wouldn't let nooooo guys rap to her. We're such family, to this day, she feels protected by us.

If she wore some shorts that were a little bit too short, I'd be like, "Yo. Take that shit off. Don't play." That's the type of relationship I had with her.

WHEN PUN DIED, me and Rem had to comfort each other. We both had a bit of fear, a bit of depression settling in. But even with Pun gone, I stood with her and told her, "I got your back."

We went on tour again. We got even tighter on our brother/sister vibe. We used to be with each other every day. I was getting her ready to compete at the highest level. She officially debuted on Pun's second album, *Yeeeah Baby*, in 2000, the year he passed away. Remy recorded the song "Ms. Martin" with Pun before his untimely demise.

"Sometimes you gotta send a woman to do a man's job," Pun said on the song, setting up Remy's intro. "In this case, my girl hit like a grown muthafuckin' man."

Pun had Remy rap the same bars she kicked for him the first time they met. He wanted the world to have the same first impression of her he'd had. That was really important to Pun.

"Ms. Martin" was a grand arrival. We were getting calls like, "Who the fuck is the chick? She murdered shit on the album."

Remy was originally "Remy Martin," before we shortened her name to "Remy Ma" for legal reasons.

A few months later, she did a guest verse on M.O.P.'s "Ante Up (Remix)" with Teflon and Busta Rhymes. That was a huge deal. The original "Ante Up" was the number-one street anthem when it came out. It was the hardest shit in the world. M.O.P. were talking about robbing and kidnapping, saying "fuck the judge." But it was pure magic. The energy on the song was so undeniable that the record went from an underground joint to an actual radio hit.

Everybody wanted to get on the "Ante Up" remix, including me! Shit, Jay-Z was supposed to get on the remix at one time, but it didn't manifest. Prodigy from Mobb Deep actually did a verse for the remix but they took him off because he was dissing Jay in his rhymes. They had an open slot on the song.

Me and M.O.P. are family. They had a mutual love with Pun too. They're on *Yeeeah Baby* as well, on a track called "New York Giants." It took them a week to make just that one record because Pun was such a funny guy. They would book sessions and not get any work done. Pun would be joking and everybody would be in the studio laughing all night. Remy was at every session too, so they were familiar with her.

People think I got Remy on the remix, but the truth is Remy *got herself* on the remix. Fame and Billy of M.O.P. asked her to get on the song. It was a huge deal to us.

"Ante Up (Remix)" blew Remy up like The Beatnuts' "Off the Books" blew Pun up. A breakout guest appearance can make all the difference. With me, LL Cool J's "I Shot Ya" took me to another level. It often takes some form of collaboration to validate an up-and-coming talent.

"Ante Up (Remix)" blew even bigger than the original. I may be a little biased, just a little, but strictly from a hip-hop fan perspective, Remy stole the show. When she said, "Wish I could bring Pun back / bitch run that," oh my God! Everybody killed their verses, don't get me wrong. That's what makes it one of the most incredible remixes ever: Everybody was on their A game. But for Rem to be the youngest and the only female on the track and get so much acclaim, I was proud beyond measure.

I remember my wife and Misa Hylton, one of the legendary stylists in the game, dressed Remy for the video. They threw the fur on her. They put a bandanna on her. She was fly, but hood as fuck. We always took care of Remy, spent big money on her outfits, on her glam. We wanted her to win.

REMY'S NEXT BIG MISSILE was "Lean Back." She strong-armed her way onto the song. "Lean Back" was actually supposed to be a solo record, but we did a partnership deal with Steve Rifkind and put "Lean Back" on a Terror Squad compilation album. Usually when you have a crew album, the big boy, the big smash on the LP, would be a solo record. I watched Jay-Z bring his whole crew to the forefront on the album *The Dynasty: Roc La Familia*. But even though his team was featured on most of the album, the big single, "I Just Wanna Love U (Give It 2 Me)," was a solo song.

Originally "Lean Back" just had me on it: I rapped three verses and when I was done, we all thought it was a hit. Remy wasn't at that session, but somehow she heard about the recording. A few days later, she comes to our recording session early, hours before I get there, and threatens the engineer, my man Drop. He's a real one, but Remy threatened him. She's wild!

Remy told Drop to erase my second verse and record her new

verse in its place. I don't even remember what I said on my second verse, but I know it was dope! It was in that "Lean Back" wheel house. I had hit a rare flow.

There's a strategy to Remy too. She's best when she's on a collabo and somebody already started the flow. Remy will pick up your delivery and kill you with your own flow. She's a master at that.

So they erased my verse, Remy did her thing on there: "R to the easy . . ." and left. I came to the studio later that night and everybody looked nervous when I walked into the room. Then they broke down to me what Remy had done.

"What!!!???" I yelled. I was shocked and angry because "Lean Back" is one of those once-in-a-lifetime records. I didn't want anybody to fuck that up. I was siiiick! I was vexed! I calmed down when everybody—Khaled, Cool & Dre—was telling me, "But she killed it though."

When they played the new version of the song, I was like, "This shit is dope! She bodied that shit!"

I went from being distraught to being elated in just a few minutes. It worked out better with her on the song because that way we both blew. I always want my people to win, too. We were building her career. "Lean Back" turned out to be the biggest record for both of us up to that point.

WITH ALL TOP-TIER FREE AGENTS, eventually there comes a bidding war. All the labels wanted her, but we went with Steve Rifkind at SRC/Universal. It hurt us because we took less money to do another deal with him.

Steve is usually generous, but we had to take a pay cut. "Lean Back" was number one, he blew that song out of the water, so we wanted to be with the home team. We gambled, taking a short with the bread, anticipating it would pay off greater in the long term.

Her debut solo album, *There's Something About Remy*, to me is a classic. It came out in 2006 and had hits like "Conceited,"

"Whuteva," and "Feels So Good" with Ne-Yo. But despite what we thought was a timeless project, we couldn't bring in the big numbers. The quality didn't translate to the sales. The LP didn't do as well as we wanted, especially with Remy coming off of the momentum of "Lean Back."

"We got it, we're gonna promote it," is what Steve promised. I started telling Remy what my guy was telling me. When it didn't pop, it hurt my and Rem's relationship because she had worked hard and put everything into that project. She believed me when I told her, "Yo, this album is gonna be big," because I believed what Steve, the guy who had changed my life, was telling me. But I was the executive producer of the project and Remy blamed me for the meager success.

This led to us falling out for almost ten years.

At the time I just didn't understand how we fell out so severely because I love Remy like a sister. It really distressed me. It damaged me to the point that ever since, I've tried not to love an artist I signed like that. I just do business and don't get emotionally wrapped up in it.

Sometimes feelings hurt more than bullets. When your soul is hurt, it hits harder than anything else. Imagine marring your relationship with someone you embraced, someone you told, "You're gonna be my family. You're gonna be my sister. We're gonna ride things out. We're gonna love each other. We're gonna go through the ups and downs. We're gonna emotionally be there for each other. We're gonna be unbreakable."

That was the type of foundation I built with Terror Squad, not just with the artists, but with my guys from day one.

It cut deep when the loyalty I thought me and Remy had established was bruised for a long time.

Years later she explained herself.

"You never lied to me," she told me, trying to articulate her frustration. "Since I was a little girl, whatever you told me came true. Whatever you said *was* gonna happen, *happened*. You told me

I was gonna blow with the album and I didn't. So I blamed you. Now that I'm older and I know the business, I realize there was only so much you could have done."

Before *There's Something About Remy* was released, I was going up to the label every day, arguing with them, trying to see how they were going to support the project. Maybe I could have done more, but I tried. Times like that are what made me want to be an independent artist. I like to take my destiny in my own hands. I want to be in control. If I want to work radio, I put up the budget for radio. If I want my video played all over, I put up the budget and hire my own team to work the video. That way I know for sure everything I want is being worked on.

For so many years we as artists go to these labels and have to ask, "Are you working my record? Are you working my video?" We're depending on them. You don't necessarily know if they're working, not to mention what their math is. They spend a dollar, they charge you $10,000 for that dollar. Their numbers are crazy.

If we had put out *There's Something About Remy* independently, maybe the narrative would have been different.

WHEN ME AND REMY FELL OUT, we fell haaarrrd. She broke my heart. I remember listening to her on the radio one day and she was doing an interview. Here was this woman that I'd worked with from the beginning and she was *dissing me*?

I bought her a pink Mercedes-Benz when she ain't have no money. I always treated her like my sister and she went bad on me on the radio. It was like a lightning bolt struck me in my heart. I couldn't believe it. When I had the beef with 50 Cent, she was like, "Tell Joe to let me sign with 50 Cent. I want to be G-Unit." That was craaayyyzzeee!

Soon after, she caught that case. It was a really ugly situation back in the summer of 2007. Remy turned herself in to the police and was charged with attempted murder. She was accused of shooting one of her best friends in the wake of her friend stealing some money. It was like $3,000. On March 27, 2008, Remy was convicted on a myriad of charges, the most serious being assault and illegal weapon possession. She was sentenced to eight years in prison.

I hated that I couldn't be there to support her because we were fighting. If I had been there in her life, she wouldn't have gotten no eight years. She would have copped out to a one to three.

I would have told her, "Even if the gun went off by accident, you got a girl saying *you* did it. Cop out!" Nobody was smart enough to force her to cop out. She pleaded not guilty—and for the record, Remy maintains her innocence. When she got that time, I felt bad for her. She was in the prime of her career and had to put it on hold for years. Worse, she had a young son and would be missing out on a major chunk of his life. She couldn't be there for him every day like she always was.

Remy stayed locked up for six years, until August 2014. We didn't speak that entire time. Then, a week before she got out of jail, she called me out of the blue.

When somebody calls you from prison, you get a message on the phone saying, "You are receiving a call from an inmate in jail." Then you hear their voice.

The voice on my phone said, "Remy."

"Yo," I said coldly.

"Yo," she responded. Then it was quiet for a minute or two.

I started getting frustrated.

"Yo, Remy, you called me, man. Like what the fuck, man?" I growled. "What you want? You called me."

"I love you. I'm stupid," she said. "I was wildin', I was crazy. You're my brother."

That was it. That's all she had to say. All the feelings for her that I thought had gone away were still there. They came right back.

"I love you too, sis," I told her as my wall of harshness melted. "I'm happy for you."

Then I gave her some words of advice. I told her come out and be humble.

"When you went in there, you were real arrogant and talking to people crazy," I recounted. "When you come out, be humble. Get your life together."

I gave her some pointers and she really listened to them. She still adheres to them. When she came out, we were meeting, having lunches, dinners. People would see us together and be buggin'. She would ask me about life, I would give her advice. She had to get back into society. She didn't have a license, parole was fuckin' with her, she was going through a lot. The biggest change in her life, which meant a slight change in our dynamic, was she had a husband now. She married the rapper Papoose while she was in jail. Reminisce Smith became Reminisce Mackie. Pap stood by her and really showed love and loyalty throughout her entire ordeal.

Sometime after her release Remy and Pap had the full bells-and-whistles ceremony like they deserved. It was televised. Honestly, I felt a little weird when I attended their wedding because for so many years it had always been Joe and Remy at all the big events. I had to fall back and let my sister get married to her husband. It was the first time I didn't stand beside her. I had to let her be a partner to her husband.

And that carried over to when I would give her advice. I'm a husband too, so I wouldn't recommend that any man tell my wife what to do. So in some instances, I would say, "Look, you're married now. I can't answer certain questions like that. You have a husband. He runs the show."

Papoose is one of the best guys in the world. He's one of my closest brothers. I never thought I would love the guy who married my sister like that, but I do. She found a king who really worships her. She needs that in life. She grew up hard and Pap was there for her, stood by her side. Now she and Pap, they have a baby daughter together. Reminisce Mackenzie was born in 2018. I'm the godfather.

I'm at every birthday party for my goddaughter. Remy comes to my kids' birthdays. We go to each other's family events. Both of our families recognize us as each other's siblings. My mother refers to Remy as "your sister." That's a beautiful bond to have.

We vowed to always support each other and to never argue again. And then, of course, there's the success. Me and Remy are still hitting them out the park.

WHEN REM GOT OUT OF JAIL, I had to get her back into the right frame of mind to make music. She wasn't really on her music vibe. She was starring with Papoose on the iconic reality show *Love & Hip Hop*. The Mackies' relationship journey was being documented every week on TV and the two of them were epitomizing the term "Black Love."

Rem was doing little things music related here and there, but she was focused on family. Everything fell into place for us to make the musical reunion when I got a call from BX Hov. BX Hov was sponsoring this event called BX Fight Club. The motto was "Put your guns down and put your gloves up." If you have beef with somebody, y'all can box and nobody has to kill anybody.

BX Hov wanted me to perform for the people. I told Remy. We were already hanging out every day and I told her I had a charitable show. We did it just for the love. I came out and I started rockin' then I brought Remy out as a surprise. When she came out, the reaction was *different*. Our estrangement had played out publicly, it was well-documented, and the people didn't know we'd reconciled. They didn't know we were back to being brother and sister. They thought they would never see Fat Joe and Remy together again.

When they saw we were all good, they lost their miiiiiiinds! We were in the middle of a boxing ring performing "Twinz (Deep Cover 98)." Remy rapped Big Pun's part. "Dead in the middle of Little Italy . . ." The whole time we were performing, Papoose kept yelling to me from the crowd, "This shit is different! This shit is different! They don't act like this when she's alone."

After the show, Remy got into the truck so she and Pap could go home. It was snowing outside. Before the truck pulled off, she lowered the window and gave me the thumbs-up.

I was like, "Wait a minute." I walked closer to the truck and said, "What?"

"Start it up," she said, smiling.

Like I told you, when you're really close to somebody, you don't gotta talk a lot. You know what they mean. You can read them.

"Yeah. Go to Miami, cook it up," she finished.

I asked if she was sure, she said yeah.

THIS WAS 2015. I went down to Miami and started working with Cool & Dre, coming up with concepts, picking beats for what would be my and Remy's group LP, *Plata O Plomo*. Remy couldn't come down to Miami because she was still on parole, but we started it up for her. When I had a batch of records ready, I came back to NY. Me and Remy went to Heatmakerz's studio in Manhattan. Rest in peace to my little brother Fred the Godson, he was there. I loved Fred so much. He was a great friend. It was such a tragedy to lose such a good person to Covid-19 in 2020. I was honored to be a part of his Bronx street-naming ceremony in 2021.

When Remy came in the lab, I gave her words of inspiration while Fred and everybody else hyped her up too.

"People *like* Remy, people *like* Fat Joe," I started to explain. "But people *love* Remy *and* Joe together. It's like sticking a thread through a needle. If we do this right, we have a very big chance of knocking it out the box and smashin' shit."

Remy was in a different place. She wasn't the Remy I met with Pun at Sony Music Studios. She was ready to make music but she wasn't *war ready*.

I had to act like a coach psyching up his team before they leave the locker room on Super Bowl Sunday. I started shouting so loud and hard, I was sweating bullets.

"Fuuuuuck these bitches," I screamed at her to motivate her. "I'm tellin' you, go to waaarrr!"

I was trying to bring *that Remy* out. I carried on; "Fuck that! You're the biggest in the game!"

I was goin' bad. She went in the booth and did her verse for "All the Way Up."

Every line was coming out like razor blades. She was sharp, jagged. She was sounding like the gladiator we loved. And her swag was crazy. She was all the way back. Remy was ferocious on the entire album.

When were shooting the video for "All the Way Up," I dressed her. I took her shopping and told her what to buy.

"Yo, this is a lot of money," she griped.

"Invest in yourself," I retorted. "Invest in yourself. Believe in yourself."

She might have spent about $15,000. And Remy is conservative with her money. She does not believe in ballin' and trickin', none of that stuff.

I asked her to trust me.

Eif Rivera shot the video and the rest is history. "All the Way Up" came out in March 2016 and orbited the planet. That was the biggest redemption ever. We started getting to the bag again, we started taking home all these awards.

We should have won the Grammy in 2017. We were up for two Grammys that year, Best Rap Song and Best Rap Performance.

Chance the Rapper won for Best Rap Performance with his song "No Problem," featuring Lil Wayne and 2 Chainz. No disrespect to Chance, but if the Grammy had any sense of the culture, we would have won. The Grammy committee should have said, "The people love this guy Joe, he just came out of jail. This woman Remy is loved too. She just came out of jail. The song's a smash. Let's award them the Grammy."

But even without the Grammy, we had the time of our lives. So many instances we were performing on TV shows or other award shows and Remy would just squeeze my hand. It was like we were living the dream *again*. She was in jail for six years with murderers, man. They told her every day she wouldn't be shit. Every day they told Papoose not to visit her. It was a serious thing. But she came home and we *did it*.

The biggest performance we did when "All the Way Up" was in rotation was the On the Run II Tour date at the Rose Bowl in L.A. This is a big-ass stadium with over 92,000 people jammed to capacity. "All the Way Up" was number one. Khaled was the opening act for Jay and Bey. Khaled would start off DJing then hand the reins over to DJ Nasty. Khaled would then come from behind the turntables and go to the front of the stage, hyping up the crowd on the mic. As a surprise, whatever top MCs were in town on the show day, they would come out to perform with him.

Nobody would turn down a chance to perform with Khaled period, that's how much love and respect he has. But, to perform with Khaled on a *Jay-Z and Beyoncé* tour, muthafuckas were lining up! They were flying in from all over just to get on that stage.

In L.A., Khaled had a whole roster of people come out and rock. Me and Remy were guests and unleashed "All the Way Up." When she came out, it was like Tupac was alive. That's how crazy they went. Nobody had seen Remy perform in L.A. for years and they just showered her with cheers.

Backstage, Jay-Z was like, "Oh my God! Rem! I ain't know. For real?"

It was a beautiful day. I'm glad after all those years locked away, my sister got to feel the love. It's really one of the most legendary comeback stories ever. Even though me and Remy aren't blood, we share DNA: No matter how many times she's down, she will always bounce back even stronger. I'll always be right there with her too.

CHAPTER 23

DJ KHALED

VIOLENCE WAS MY THERAPY. Hurt people *hurt people*. When I was a young man there were days where I would walk around the street like a one-man gang. Acting as a conduit for chaos weighs heavily on you though. And yeah, having a reputation for being a barbarous brute will make your name respected and feared in the hood. But I've learned that spreading love will make you legendary across the globe.

Part of my inspiration for writing this book was the biggest ambassador of affinity I know, my brother DJ Khaled. Now, if you have a pair of functioning eyes and ears, you pretty much have not been able to escape Khaled, especially not for the past six years.

On December 14, 2015, Khaled famously went on Snapchat and documented himself getting lost in the water while riding his Jet Ski in Miami. This turned Khaled into a social media star and his popularity exploded. He went from a hip-hop superstar to an international icon who gets money with Michael Jordan and Oprah Winfrey. Mind you, Khaled had already put out a litany of platinum and gold records since 2006. He actually has over a dozen albums, more than a lot of your favorite rappers.

Khaled's first project, *Listennn . . . the Album* came out through a joint venture between Terror Squad Records and Koch Records in '06. When Khaled told me he wanted to create an album, I went to Alan Grunblatt, who owned Koch Records. Ironically, Alan was the head at Relativity at the time I signed my first deal over there in the '90s, so me and him have a great history. Alan was hesitant about signing another album by a DJ because he had just put out a project by Funkmaster Flex and, unfortunately, it hadn't met their expectations sales-wise. I convinced Alan to do the project with Khaled: "Khaled is going to be bigger than Fat Joe," I told him. Khaled put a gold plaque on the wall. He's been one of the most successful artists to do it ever since. His latest LP, *God Did*, debuted at number one on the Billboard Top 200 in August 2022, the fourth number-one album of his career.

Khaled's projects are part compilations, part soundtracks, and all all-stars. My brother has been able to parlay his relationships into recruiting everyone from Jay-Z and Beyoncé to myself, Rick Ross, Drake, Busta Rhymes, Chris Brown, Lil Wayne, Nicki Minaj, Justin Bieber, T-Pain, Nas, and Rihanna to record for him. He then weaves it all into a cohesive body of work.

Once he zeros in on a guest to collaborate with, Khaled won't take no for an answer. He has an incredible imagination and he'll convince you to see his vision through his lens, no matter how grandiose. His talk game is so galvanizing, Khaled could inspire a one-legged man to enter an ass-kicking contest.

Not only has the bro churned out heralded opuses, but he's become a certified maestro with a slew of smash singles. You can get all the big names in the world you want, but if you can't properly marry them with the right music and song concept, it could turn into a high-powered mess.

Khaled does like Phil Jackson did when he was coaching the Bulls and Lakers dynasties. Phil had this wide array of talent, but was also able to devise brilliant game plans so his teams could win.

Khaled has so many hits, his catchphrase "Another One" has been embraced and used in pop culture. Ever since Khaled exploded on social media, his fame, money, and work output have expanded exponentially. Besides touring stadiums with Jay-Z and Beyoncé, Khaled has been featured in blockbuster films like *Spider-Man: Homecoming* and *Bad Boys for Life*. We've seen him in national television commercial campaigns for Fortune 500 companies such as WeightWatchers, Geico, and Paramount Pictures. Jordan Brand has partnered up with him on several sneaker releases. Yeah, Khaled has his own line of Jordan sneakers.

Most beautifully though, we've watched his journey of becoming one of the most loving and giving family men with the nurturing of his two young sons, Asahd and Aalam.

I can honestly say I don't know anyone more deserving of the blessings and success that he has. We first met Khaled and his right-hand man, DJ Nasty, at a New Music Seminar. This was like 1993. I remember DJ Clark Kent had a battle that day. When I met Khaled he had the vinyl of my debut album, *Represent,* in hand.

"Yo, Fat Joe, can you sign this?" he asked, walking up to me.

"What the fuck are you doing with the vinyl of my album?" I asked him, surprised. This was several weeks before *Represent* came out. *I* didn't even have a vinyl copy.

He was the same charismatic DJ Khaled as you see today. Energetic and magnetic.

"Nah, I do my thing," he explained. "You know what I'm saying? I'm out the wind. Nobody's gonna stop me from winning. I gotta get my Fat Joe shit early."

I took such a liking to him, I kept in touch with him and we became friends. Khaled is originally from New Orleans. When I met him, he and DJ Nasty were living in Orlando, Florida, but Khaled eventually moved down to Miami.

He told me there was more opportunity for him in Miami and he was gonna set it off. I told him I was gonna support him.

"Yoooo, I wanna rep TS."

"What you talkin' about? *You are* TS, man," I assured him.

You could see the pride in his eyes when I established what it was.

"Aiiiight! I'm gonna rep it like never before," he promised with a cluster of excitement in his tone.

I was still living in New York back then. I came down to Miami to visit like six, seven months later. For a New York artist, getting on the radio was hard because Miami radio was all Uncle Luke, all that booty music. This was when Wu-Tang was out, Mobb Deep was out, Jay-Z had *Reasonable Doubt* ringing off. You had Nas with *Illmatic*. All that shit was heralded everywhere, but in Miami, all you heard on the radio was "Pop that Pussy."

I'm not disrespecting that booty music in no way, but I like to hear variety. When I got to Miami, me and Pun and some of our guys were driving around and stumbled across this underground radio station on the dial.

"What the fuck is this?" I yelled out in the car.

The station was playing Gang Starr, Wu-Tang, Mobb Deep. I couldn't believe it. Then I heard this voice shouting across the airwaves.

"This 'The Don Gon Gon,' 'The Arab Attack!,'" the radio personality howled. "This is Terror Squad! Mix 96 with the one and only Deeeee Jayyyyyyyy Khaled."

I was so happy he was on the radio. I kept listening and he gave the station's phone number out on air. I called him up.

"Yoooo! What's up? This is DJ Khaled," he said answering the phone. "Who am I talking to?"

"Yo, Khaled, it's me. This is Joey Crack," I told him.

"Stop playing. Who's this?" he asked again.

"Khaled, it's me! It's Joe," I maintained. This was live on air.

"Oh! My! God! Stop the music," he cheered when he realized it was me. "They've been telling me I was lying. Can you tell them I'm Terrrrrrrrrrror Squaaaaaad? Can you tell them I'm Terrrrrrror Squad?"

"Khaled, you're *beyond* Terror Squad, you're my brother."

After that, we continued talking on the phone off the air. He gave me the address to the station and me and Pun went up there. We freestyled live for the listeners for like three hours. That shit was legendary. That was the first time Pun met Khaled and they clicked right away.

Pun would go down to Miami without me and get up with Khaled. When it was coming time to drop *Capital Punishment* in '98, Pun drove all the way down to Miami just to play it for Khaled months early. Khaled gave him some great A&R advice. He recommended some things he should change or add to the album.

Having Khaled on my team early on was probably similar to Jay-Z having a Kanye West *and* a Just Blaze in his camp without really recognizing just how great these guys were. They were *in-the-making*. You knew they were dope, but you didn't know *they were* the greats. Kanye West was doing Jay-Z's beats under Jay-Z's wing. It wasn't clear that he was going to be one of the all-time greats.

Just the same, Khaled was there for all our albums, sitting in the back, before he ever made his first album. He would always give us insightful consultation: "No, you gotta flip it like this. Joe you gotta rhyme like Biggie right here." He was always there, but we didn't know he was *Khaled*.

ONE OF THE MAIN REASONS I moved to Miami was because of Khaled. My philosophy has always been: "If any of us wins, we all win." That's been my mantra since I was a kid. That's how I've been moving since the beginning of this book if you're paying attention.

I love it when I go to Khaled's house, Remy and Papoose's house, or I go to Cool's and Dre's houses, or Scott Storch's house, and they are living like emperors. I love it. My crew got mansions with tall-ass ceilings. They got stars in the roofs of their cars.

Khaled forged an incredible legacy that has been built on unity and championing others. When you see me and Khaled in the back of the Rolls-Royce, top down on a sunny day, dancing to my song "Sunshine (The Light)," we aren't just putting it on for "The Gram." We truly enjoy each other's company and have fun.

We talk every day and are neighbors. I'm always over at his house eating lunch, eating dinner. One of my most relaxing activities is to go to Khaled's mansion and watch a great movie in his big-ass home theater. We vacation together with both our families. His wife loves my wife, my kids love his kids and vice versa.

The best way I could express my love for Khaled was by asking him to be the godfather of my daughter, Azzy. He's Muslim, but he stood up in the Catholic church with us when my daughter got baptized. When you pick godparents, you hope if something happens to you, they'll take care of your kids. This was *before* he blew. Before he had a record deal. Before he had anything. Just out of love. I knew his heart was pure.

Just so happens he got filthy rich, which is a plus for my daughter.

The truth is, Khaled does not need anything from me and I don't need nothing from Khaled. I never asked him for nothing—not a beat, not a song, not a dollar. Well, that's a lie. The most I ever ask him for is a good meal at his house; "Yo, let's eat some good shit." Luckily, Khaled recently *healed himself* from being allergic to seafood. We eat the biggest lobsters at his crib. Them lobsters are as big as Moby-Dick.

Khaled is like the kid who grew up in the roughest neighborhood and, out of all his peers, becomes the most likely to go to college or go on to be an NFL player or something like that, so the street cats in his hood protect him. They say, "He ain't gotta join no gang. Let him go, bro. Let him live."

That's how we do with Khaled. He's just such a kind soul, the gangstas love him. The craziest guys in the crew wanna hang out with him all day. We're all like, "Let's let him spread his wings. Let him do Nickelodeon. Let him be in the streets getting 'fan luv' from ten thousand of his admirers. Let him keep brokering all these deals. Let's see how much this seed we helped plant ends up growing."

CHAPTER 24

LIFE BEGINS AT FIFTY

ME AND JAY-Z WERE COOL, stopped speaking for years, then out of nowhere, he literally embraced me. Today we are family. Throughout the years, me and Hov had an up-and-down relationship—I'll take the blame for the downs. You guys all know I can be hot-headed and stubborn at times. Me and Hov even had a little back-and-forth on record about our teams competing in the Rucker Classic, which I famously referenced on "Lean Back."

But to keep it real, it never got to the point where it was a real beef or anything, where we wished each other real harm. We just didn't speak.

Everything changed in 2015. I sat next to one of Hov's closest friends and business partners, OG Juan Perez, at a Miami Heat game. My brother Shawn Pecas, who worked for Roc Nation at the time, had set it up for us to sit next to each other.

It was nothing but great vibes between me and OG Juan. We told stories and laughed the whole game. Two weeks later, I was at a Jordan Brand party during NBA All-Star weekend in New York. I'm walking in there and out of nowhere, Jay-Z appears from behind a wall and grabs me in a friendly hug. That night was the first time we'd talked in years. It broke the ice.

"All the Way Up" came out about a year later, blows up right out the gate. I was thinking about the remix, and most of all, I wanted Jay-Z. As an MC, you always want to rock with the best. Me and Biggie started recording an album around '96, '97, that will never see the light of day. But I got a chance to hear myself with Big. I've made songs with Nas, Raekwon, my whole D.I.T.C. family, obviously Remy and Pun. Jay was the guy on my bucket list who I'd never collaborated with. One of, if not the, greatest of all time.

After the Jordan party, Me and Hov would see each other at events from time to time, but we didn't exchange numbers and hadn't communicated in several months. So I called Nore and asked him to link me with Memphis Bleek to try to make this remix happen. I spoke to Bleek, he said he would relay the message. Ten minutes later Jay-Z called me. We had a great conversation, he said he had the verse ready, and we made history. We showed our city and hip-hop that people who had differences in the past can come back around and unify. Remy was ecstatic too, because Hov is her favorite MC.

I had the opportunity to get another major superstar on the remix as well, Drake. I love Drake, I'm a huge fan of his music, we always have a great time on the few occasions we got to hang out. Drake FaceTimed me so he could get on the remix, but ultimately, I felt with the history me and Jay had, it should just be me, him, and Remy on the record. I still would love to work with Drake. Hopefully soon. I know we could make a legendary smash hit.

At the same time me and Jay are getting cooler than we ever were, I was developing a friendship with OG Juan and his wife, Roc Nation boss Desiree Perez. They were enlightening me on several things when it came to business and it just made perfect sense for me to join Roc Nation as one of the clients they manage.

Hov, Juan, and Desiree have kept their word on everything. They've helped elevate me and I'm happier than ever. I'm blessed to be a part of their family. Hov goes out of his way to really come in and give me his take on my new music and other business. He always has great ideas. Having a team that not only has your back but can add on to what you have going on or open new doors for you is glorious.

———

THE GOAL IS TO GET STRONGER as you get older. I've always loved birthdays. I love to celebrate life. But when the huge milestone birthdays came along, I never commemorated myself like I was supposed to. When I turned twenty, my best friend in life, Tone Montana, had just died. My heart felt like it had been carved out of my chest with a machete. When I turned thirty, even worse. I was seriously in the doldrums after the deaths of my grandfather Cowboy, my sister, Lisa, and another best friend, Big Pun. They all died within weeks of each other. I stayed in a fog of depression for two years. When I turned forty, it wasn't as bad, but I damn sure was in my feelings. Melancholy suppressed me.

We were always taught that turning forty is a death sentence to your career. "Rap is a young man's game." There weren't too many forty-year-old rappers who were successful at that age or into their forties. I felt like I was at a serious professional crossroads. I didn't even want to leave the house.

When I turned fifty, the entire world was in a pandemic. Hundreds of thousands of people died, damn near everything was shut down. The economy plummeted, Trump was running amuck. It was the summer of Black Lives Matter protests in the wake of the brutal police murders of George Floyd, Breonna Taylor, and a slew of other unarmed Black men and women.

Even with so much turmoil and chaos all over the world, I ironically found myself at peace. I counted my blessings. I kept praying extra hard. I was elated to see another year. I had an epiphany: Life starts at fifty. I reflected on my life. I thought about everything that had come my way, everything that made me who I am. I was bullied every day as a kid, the police tried to frame me, my right-hand man robbed me for over twenty years. My accountant robbed me. The IRS took all my money and then put me in jail. I have so many friends who are in jail or dead. Tone died in his early twenties. Pun died in his late twenties. So many people didn't make it to where I'm at. I am ultra grateful for being here and still flourishing because for a hundred reasons, I shouldn't even be here. It was only determination, love, luck, and God that brought me through. When I made it to fifty, I was happy. It felt like I had cheated all the potential traps and downfalls in my life.

I celebrated my life on my fiftieth birthday, August 19, 2020. Khaled took me to the Caribbean. Our families rented the biggest mansion in Turks and Caicos, with the sea as our backyard. The water looked Listerine blue. It was almost surreal. The pictures we took only conveyed half of the beauty of the water. I couldn't stop staring at it. It was unreal, an invitation into the clarity that could define the rest of my life. We swam all day, caught some sun, me and Khaled played one-on-one basketball—sports are the only games I'm playing now.

Something happened when I hit fifty years old, the other games I used to play, I don't want to play no more. It's like a mechanism activates in your brain and things get clearer. Things that you thought were funny, ain't funny no more. You just want to get serious. I got from age fifty to sixty to financially secure my family's wealth. And I mean for fuckin' generations! I also got from fifty to sixty to do what God really wanted me to do: philanthropy. I want to help my community, give back to the youth. I'm still a guy who's an OG and who they respect and who comes from the streets.

One of my callings, I feel, is definitely mentoring young kids who might otherwise want to join gangs or sell drugs or whatever the case may be. When I was their age, adults were putting guns in my hand. They were teaching me how to rob people and sell drugs. I want to be the one telling kids that there's a light at the end of the tunnel. I want to show them that I've made more money and more of an impact on the world as a legitimate citizen than I ever did as a criminal.

THE MINUTE I WOKE UP on my fiftieth, my daughter was there in the bedroom like, "Daaaad! Happy birthday!" It was like a dream. I was on this exotic island, Nore had given me a bath-robe for my birthday. It was this fly Versace robe, baby blue. Blue, the color of the sea and sky, is my favorite color. All my cars are sky blue. I got up and put my robe on. Khaled's son Asahd, who we believe is like a prophet, he's there, too, saying, "Happy birthday, Uncle Joe." It was a beautiful day.

Today, I'm looking at life differently but working with an even fiercer sense of vengeance. I watched Jay-Z become a billionaire. I watched Puff do it, I watched Dre do it. These are all guys my age. They hit it out the park. I've been thinking I can do it, too. If I don't, then I let myself down.

Right now, I just have to stay healthy. I'm working out every day. I'm eating right. If I'm healthy, I'm gonna do it. It's not even a question. I'm lined up. Everybody I've ever come up with is lined up. I tell all these people I helped get rich, "That's Diamond D's legacy." Diamond opened the door for me and I opened the door for them.

Being an author is different from anything I've ever done be-fore, but it has been so therapeutic for me. Before now, I've never elaborated on my life so in-depth. I did it in part for me: I wanted to see my own truth and understand where I came from and how that played into the development of my character.

And I did it for my readers: I wanted you all to see that a person can really change. For thirty years I haven't touched a drug, even if for a long five or six years, selling those drugs defined my life. The moral of the story is you can go through the most traumatizing shit in the world, you can fall as low as you can imagine, and you can still change.

I keep in mind that all my vulnerabilities are still here though. I have the same soul. It's hard to forget who I was. My wife asks me all the time, "When are you gonna dream a good dream? Every night you have nightmares."

I thought that everybody had nightmares *every* night, but I guess that's not the case. I toss and turn every night in bed. I don't get a good night's sleep most nights. I guess that's part of my punishment for all the dirt I did. And I did a lot.

We sold a lot of drugs and made a lot of money, but when my brother Angel went from kingpin back to addict, it was agonizing. We had to endure so much for three decades with him. All the pain we went through with my brother is the type of pain families we were selling the shit to were going through back in the day.

So, the drug game, yeah, it gives people in the hood money and gives you an opportunity, but I also know it causes generational suffering. People are losing their mothers and fathers. When crack was out, I watched the most decent women on Earth sell their jewelry, sell their cars, furniture, sell their own bodies for get-high money. They sold everything, and in the end, they would simply die—of AIDS or addiction.

But today I'm trying to push something else: "The Light." Positivity. I'm stressing to people to stay on a positive path. Stay focused and make your own path in life. That's what I've tried to do for thirty years and counting in this music game. I look back at my legacy in the industry with real pride. There are not a lot of MCs—not a lot of artists period—who can say they've had multiple hits in the 1990s, 2000s, 2010s, and 2020s. That's a lot of work. And I'm only getting better.

IN 2022, I got a call to come speak at the White House. I had previously spent some time with Michelle Obama in Miami when she was spearheading a get-out-the-vote effort at the University of Miami. But in early 2022, I was a featured speaker at the White House.

First off, the White House was actually smaller in size than I thought. But it was amazing to be in the building. I went there with an organization called Power to the Patients. That organization's goal is to bring transparency to the way hospitals and insurance companies bill patients. The only place in the world you don't want to ask for the price of a service is in a hospital. And the only place where people don't tell you how much they're going to charge you is the hospital. So you have people who paid $300 for a CAT scan and then you've got people who paid $4,000 for the same CAT scan at the same hospital. We have to hold the healthcare system more accountable for transparency, fairness, and equity.

We brought that message to the White House, and they accepted us with open arms. It wasn't just the White House officials who welcomed us, of course. All the people who worked in the kitchen, all the people that worked cleaning up the joint, everybody ran out to the hallway when we came through like, "Yo, we got a real one in here, Joe Crack is in the White House!" It felt amazing to receive that kind of love.

Way back when in Forest Projects, if you would have told me how my life would unfold, there's no way on earth that I would have believed that one day I would go to the White House. There's no way I would have believed that I would be able to accomplish any of this stuff that I have: living outside of the hood, owning a home, owning businesses, touching people's lives through music, living out my dream. I never thought this would be possible. I've been through some dark days—if you've read this far, you know just how dark the world outside could be; but also how dark things could get inside of me. But I have seen the light; I try every day to walk in the light and to shine it on others whenever I can. Just watch how I elevate during my next fifty years.

ACKNOWLEDGMENTS

FAT JOE: Thank you to everyone who's ever played a part in my life. Whether your role was good or bad, it's only made me stronger. God is great. God bless my wife and kids, the rest of my family, my friends and my fans. A special thanks to Roc Nation, the Cartagena family, the Delgado family, the Castro and the Rios family. TS4LIFE!

SHAHEEM REID: God is the greatest. Gail and Ari, we did it! Thank you to my family and friends, who always supported me. I would not be here if it weren't for you all. Thank you to everyone who has ever edited my writing; you made me that much sharper with the pen game. Thank you to all the great writers I've had the pleasure of editing and exchanging jewels with. Peace and thanks to all the artists who have sat down with me for interviews. I truly appreciate building with you all. Polaris, Conglomerate, I love y'all. Thank you to all the media outlets who published my writing, and of course, love and gratitude to everyone who has read a Shaheem Reid article and/or watched and listened to my interviews.

Infinite love to Roc Nation; Chris Jackson, the editor of this book; and the entire Terror Squad. My brother Joe, there is nobody realer and more loyal than you in this universe. I am truly honored to make history with you. Thank you for always believing.

FAT JOE, born Joseph Cartagena, is a rapper, actor, and entrepreneur from the birthplace of hip-hop, the Bronx, New York. He began his music career as a member of the hip-hop group Diggin' in the Crates. In 1993, he released his first solo album, *Represent,* and founded the record label Terror Squad, to which he later signed top talent like Big Pun, Remy Ma, Tony Sunshine, DJ Khaled, and featuring producers Cool & Dre. Fat Joe is perhaps best known for his platinum album *Jealous Ones Still Envy (J.O.S.E.)* and hits like "Lean Back" with Terror Squad, "What's Luv?" featuring Ashanti and Ja Rule, "Make It Rain" featuring Lil Wayne, and "All the Way Up" with Remy Ma featuring French Montana and Dre.

Instagram: @fatjoe
Facebook.com/fatjoe
Twitter: @fatjoe

SHAHEEM REID is a journalist and industry mover. His career in hip-hop spans over two decades. Highlights include reporting at MTV, *Vibe,* and *XXL*; serving as the president of Busta Rhymes's Conglomerate record label; and launching Polaris, the first Black-owned, free, ad-supported streaming channel, in 2021.

Instagram: @shaheemreid

ABOUT THE TYPE

This book was set in Caslon, a typeface first designed in 1722 by William Caslon (1692–1766). Its widespread use by most English printers in the early eighteenth century soon supplanted the Dutch typefaces that had formerly prevailed. The roman is considered a "workhorse" typeface due to its pleasant, open appearance, while the italic is exceedingly decorative.